MOM, DAD.

I'M GAY.

OTHER BOOKS BY RITCH C. SAVIN-WILLIAMS

". . . And Then I Became Gay": Young Men's Stories

The Lives of Lesbians, Gays, and Bisexuals: Children to Adults
(With K. M. Cohen)

Beyond Pink and Blue: Exploring our Stereotypes of Sexuality and Gender.
A Program for Ages 13 to 15 (With T. Robinson-Harris)

Gay and Lesbian Youth: Expressions of Identity

Adolescence: An Ethological Perspective

MOM, DAD.
I'M
GAY.

How Families Negotiate Coming Out

by Ritch C. Savin-Williams

American Psychological Association
Washington, DC

First Printing Dec. 2000
Second Printing Nov. 2001

Published by
American Psychological Association
750 First Street, NE
Washington, DC 20002

Copies may be ordered from
APA Order Department
P.O. Box 92984
Washington, DC 20090-2984

In the U.K., Europe, Africa, and the Middle
East, copies may be ordered from
American Psychological Association
3 Henrietta Street
Covent Garden, London
WC2E 8LU England

Typeset in Goudy by World Composition Services, Inc., Sterling, VA

Printer: Sheridan Books, Ann Arbor, MI
Cover designer: NiDesign, Baltimore, MD
Technical/Production Editor: Emily I. Welsh

The opinions and statements published are the responsibility of the authors, and such opinions and statements do not necessarily represent the policies of the APA.

Library of Congress Cataloging-in-Publication Data
Savin-Williams, Ritch C.
  Mom, Dad. I'm gay. How families negotiate coming out / Ritch C. Savin-Williams.— 1st ed.
    p. cm.
  Includes bibliographical references and index.
  ISBN 1-55798-741-6 (alk. paper)
  1. Gay youth—Family relationships. 2. Coming out (Sexual orientation). 3. Parents of gays. I. Title.
  HQ76.24.S39   2000
  306.874—dc21

                                                                    00-056910

British Library Cataloguing-in-Publication Data
A CIP record is available from the British Library.

Printed in the United States of America

CONTENTS

PREFACE

It would be difficult to overdramatize the visibility revolution that has occurred during the 1990s for sexual-minority youths. As someone who lived his Midwest adolescence during the 1960s without so much as a name for his unconventional sexuality, I marvel at the contemporary transformation of what it means to grow up gay. Perhaps if I had possessed current notions of "alternative sexualities" or role models such as Greg Louganis or Ellen DeGeneres in my small Missouri town, I would have labeled my preadult erotic feelings considerably earlier than I did. But my high school had no gay–straight alliance or support group for sexual-minority youths. The monthly *Christian County Ozarker* carried no news features on homosexuality. There were no 1-800 or even 1-900 numbers. No online chat groups or magazines. No gay characters in nightly television programs. No movies featuring positive gay characters or themes. No visibility. Nothing, period, except silence.

In retrospect, I am quite certain that I was not alone in small-town Missouri, and I have my suspicions! I would like to name names and to ask questions about the passionate friendships of several female classmates, the notorious study hall "hand jobs," the late-night drinking, and the suicides. I want to know the true story of our most "homo" ridiculed classmate, Ricky (pseudonym), who never joined the Future Farmers of America, never played sports despite our need to press every male body into athletic teams, and never dated. Ricky wore green on Thursdays, thus cementing his homo-status in high school. He married, had children, and died at a young age of an "unnamed" but remarkably AIDS-like disease in the mid-1980s.

The narratives of contemporary youths often follow a very different story line.[1] Michelle Klucsor, 19, of San Jose, California, accepted her status as lesbian when she was 15. A year later she disclosed to classmates by refusing to hide her sexuality. "Instead of changing pronouns and being vague, I was just myself. That was hard." But few believed her. She was "very femme [and] because I didn't look stereotypical, people would come up to me and say: 'Oh, I heard you're a lesbian, but I know you're not.'" After an all-girl dance, she told her mother about her sexuality, who said, "Oh, why didn't you tell me? If you told me earlier, I would have driven you there." Her father was less accepting, but several months later he attended a P-FLAG (Parents, Families, and Friends of Lesbians and Gays) meeting. He now facilitates their meetings and marches in gay pride parades. Michelle is politically active and educates teachers about how to make schools more accepting of sexual minorities.

Justin Clouse, 19, grew up in Richmond, Kentucky, and describes himself as the average gay-boy next door who wants to fall madly in love with the redheaded man of his dreams. In ninth grade, Justin mustered the nerve to type the word G-A-Y on his computer; he had always known he was "different." He told his best friend and soon everyone in school knew, but "it was never a big deal. . . . I read about all of these things where coming out is some big monumental day, but that never happened. I'd known these kids since I was in kindergarten, they knew me much more as a person." Telling his mother was more difficult; she cried, doubted it, and then said she only wanted to protect him from being hurt by others. His father was accepting, and their relationship remained unchanged. Justin remarked, "It was really cool to have them totally interested, asking, like 'Have you found anybody lately?'" Justin is still looking for the redhead and keeps his diary on the Web for others to learn about the life of a "normal gay guy."

The most striking aspects of Michelle and Justin are an early awareness of their sexual identity, a pride in being sexual-minority teenagers, and a willingness to confront societal attitudes and prejudices while in high school. Furthermore, they disclosed to their parents this sexual identity *while still living at home*! This is light years from my Missouri town where it was understood that everyone was to remain heterosexually intact, and sexuality was non-negotiable.

Despite these stories, researchers, clinicians, educators, and health care professionals frequently highlight the pain of living—and the hardships sexual-minority youths encounter—without saying a word about their resiliency or diversity. For example, it is widely reported that youths who self-identify as gay in high school are disproportionately at risk for having mental and physical health problems, using illegal drugs, having physical fights with injuries, carrying a weapon to school, feeling threatened at school, skipping school, being intimidated at school, and attempting suicide.[2] If true, these would indeed be grave concerns that should be attended to. However, as a class of individuals, gay youths have been almost solely presented as victims who are necessarily harassed at home and in school, as gender benders with multicolored hair and multipierced bodies, and as mutilators of their own lives by placing themselves at risk for HIV and suicide. This portrait restricts and distorts our perception of their lives. As a result, we have committed a great disservice to sexual-minority youths—portraying them as victims, weirdos, or "the other." These children cannot possibly be *our* children. They're sick!

In earlier publications,[3] I criticized this single-minded focus on the problems of sexual-minority youths, the pathology of their lives, which in turn is unthinkingly and incredulously applied to all who are young and gay in contemporary society. Surely they must have all killed themselves by now! Ignored is the rich diversity that characterizes their lives and their uncanny resiliency in overcoming cultural stigmatization—especially youths such as Michelle and Justin who are living the promise of healthy lives as lesbian and gay.

Throughout this book the personal narratives of a diverse group of lesbian, bisexual, gay, transgender, questioning, and unlabeled adolescents and young adults illustrate experiences relating with family members. These sexual-minority youths have many intricate decisions to make that reflect and ultimately shape the relationships they want to have—or can have— with their families. Should they disclose? If so, when? While in high school? In college, when away from home? Once no longer financially dependent on parents? And if so, how? Through a direct telling? By leaving hints around the house? By not appearing to be heterosexual? Who should be told first and for what reason? Following disclosure, how should they relate to family members? These are not questions I could ever have imagined asking myself when I was a youth, but are now common concerns of contemporary adolescents with same-sex attractions, including the ones in this book. Their narratives serve as a striking alternative to my life story.

ENDNOTES

[1] The following two narratives were reported by *Oasis*, an online Web site for sexual-minority youths. The stories were taken from the "Profiles in Courage" section in the December 1995 issue. Jeff Walsh interviewed both Michelle and Justin.

[2] DuRant, R. H., Krowchuk, D. P., & Sinal, S. H. (1998). Victimization, use of violence, and drug use at school among male adolescents who engage in same-sex sexual behavior. *Journal of Pediatrics, 132,* 113–118; Garofalo, R., Wolf, R. C., Kessel, S., Palfrey, J., & DuRant R. H. (1998). The association between health risk behaviors and sexual orientation among a school-based sample of adolescents. *Pediatrics, 101,* 895–902; Goodenow, C., & Hack, T. (1998, August). *Risks facing gay, lesbian, and bisexual high school adolescents: The Massachusetts Youth Risk Behavior Survey.* Paper presented at the Annual Convention of the American Psychological

Association, San Francisco; Hershberger, S. L., & D'Augelli, A. R. (1995). The impact of victimization on the mental health and suicidality of lesbians, gay and bisexual youth. *Developmental Psychology, 31*, 65–74; and Hershberger, S. L., Pilkington, N. W., & D'Augelli, A. R. (1997). Predictors of suicide attempts among gay, lesbian, and bisexual youth. *Journal of Adolescent Research, 12*, 477–497.

[3] See my 1990 book, *Gay and lesbian youth: Expressions of identity* (New York: Hemisphere) (especially chap. 10) and, more recently, my 1998 book " *. . . and then I became gay": Young men's stories* (New York: Routledge).

ACKNOWLEDGMENTS

This project would not have been possible without the inspiring, provocative lives of the 164 youths who form the core of this book. They were always supportive, wanting through their sharing to better the lives of future generations of youths with same-sex attractions. I hope that they can forgive me for the imperfections between their telling and my writing and my inability to fully comprehend the complexity of their lives.

Neither would this book have been possible without the encouragement of my colleague and friend Steve Ceci, who believed that I should and could write this book. If the world of heterosexuals were filled with individuals such as Steve Ceci and his partner and my friend Wendy Williams, much of the trauma faced by sexual-minority youths and their families would disappear. I hope this book encourages the movement of others into their camp of love and support.

From the outset, the staff at APA Books has been incredibly enthusiastic and supportive of my efforts to tell the stories of sexual-minority youths. Julia Frank-McNeil, Director of APA Books, never wavered from encouraging my pursuit of this project. Judy Nemes, who I feel is the best development editor working today, offered many excellent suggestions on the first draft that served to focus and tighten the book's content. Shepherding the project through the technical nuts and bolts, Emily Welsh, Production Editor, has been invaluable with suggestions, directives, and patience. Other APA staff have also made their unique professional contributions that have lightened my load and added to this book's development: Vanessa Downing (Project Editor), Chris Davis (Supervisor, Technical Editing and Design), Elaine Dunn (Copy Editor), and Mary Lynn Skutley (Manager of Development). Working with this staff has made the process of moving from my printed page to theirs truly easy.

My life partner, Ken Cohen, recently crowned Dr. Cohen, provided more than sufficient affection, encouragement, and motivation for the initiation and completion of this project. We eagerly share and compare experiences about our families and marvel at the stories of today's generation of youths. Our lives apart and now together we dedicate to increasing sensitivity, caring, and openness. We simply want all families to love.

MOM, DAD.
I'M
GAY.

1

INTRODUCTION

This book is intended for sexual-minority youths and their families and for those who care for them. It documents variations in the relations sexual-minority youths report that they have with family members before, during, and after disclosure of their sexuality. My two central purposes are

1. to demonstrate the vast diversity in the life experiences that sexual-minority youths have with family members, and
2. to document the inherent resiliency and mental health of sexual-minority youths.

Readers might wonder what makes this book unique from the sizable and burgeoning staple of books on "coming out" written by lesbian, gay, and bisexual authors, their loved ones, and mental health experts. Simply put, I base this book on the *personal odysseys* of 164 young women and men, *my perspectives* as a clinical and developmental psychologist who specializes in sexual minorities, and insights derived from *empirical studies*. This does not mean that the odysseys are representative of all sexual-minority youths, or that my perspective is the correct one, or even that the research base is ideal or comprehensive. In particular, I make numerous references to places in which the research is insufficient to answer questions that intrigue me (e.g., whether the age at which a gay youth comes out is associated with her or his father's reaction).

The voice in this book is given primarily to youths and only secondarily to parents. Given the choice between interviewing a limited number of youths and their parents or a large number of youths or parents, I chose the latter. A comprehensive book would have presented the experiences of a wide range of parents and sexual-minority youths; this book is not that one. Because most families are "in the closet" about their sexual-minority family member, this task may only be possible once cultural acceptance of such households reaches a higher level than is now the case. Until then, popular books are available that recount the experiences of parents.[1] It must be kept in mind, however, that these perspectives are usually derived from parents who attend support groups or have had traumatic experiences with a gay child, altogether poor venues for eliciting diverse opinions given the selective nature of those who join such groups. I nevertheless quote liberally from these texts in chapter 3.

By focusing primarily on youths, I attempt to balance two disparate methodologies: (a) the empiricism of developmental investigators and (b) the life histories approach prevalent in the clinical and popular literatures.[2] Each provides readers with a legitimate, although limited, perspective from which to assess the lives of sexual-minority youths and their families. A life histories approach is often restricted by the kinds of youths who provide their stories (usually White, "out" youths attending support groups), whereas empirical investigators frequently curtail the type and depth of questions they ask their young respondents.

The approach I take here maintains the individuality and uniqueness of particular lives through the narration of life stories. Concurrently, an external voice is present, that of myself as researcher discerning patterns across the experiences of youths. The narratives of adolescents and young adults relate an assortment of "coming out to parent adventures" and illustrate the many different occasions, circumstances, reactions, and consequences of disclosing to family members.[3] As such, they often explode myths—for example, that a parent's reaction to the news of a child's same-sex attractions is ineluctably negative, violent, or retributive. As readers will see, it seldom is. Or that a mother is the best parent to tell. Indeed, in my interview data, a significant number of fathers are more supportive than mothers upon hearing the disclosure.

Before presenting these stories, I describe in chapter 2 a theoretical perspective, a *differential developmental trajectories* approach, that heightens the focus on diversity within sexual-minority populations, recognizes the continuities and discontinuities among sexual minorities in their development, and highlights the turning points in each life that contribute to the unique profile of an individual biography. This approach forms the essential nucleus of the perspective presented in this book. In addition, definitions of several key concepts are provided.

Within most developmental frameworks, disclosure to parents is considered to be a critical milestone. The importance of parents to sexual-minority youths and some of the difficulties and pleasures youths encounter with disclosure are discussed in chapter 3. The reactions of parents to "the news" have been understood by many to follow a grieving–mourning sequence of emotions and behaviors. These are understood in the chapter to represent the diversity of responses parents have on learning of their child's sexual status. Factors that influence the reactions parents have to the disclosure are briefly discussed.

The next four chapters form the core of the book. They present narratives of sexual-minority youths who reflect on the nature of the relationships they have or had with parents before disclosure, whether they come out to parents, reasons youths have for and against coming out, when and how parents are told, the initial reactions parents have to the news, and the relationships youths have with parents after disclosure. Although division of this material could have been apportioned in diverse manners, the one adopted for this book is based on sex of child and parent: the relations daughters have with their mother (chapter 4) and father (chapter 5) and the relations sons have with their mother (chapter 6) and father (chapter 7). Each chapter begins with three narratives that illustrate the diversity of experiences youths have with their parents; relevant empirical data are interwoven throughout the text. Excerpts from the youths' narratives serve to elaborate and enlighten these data.

In chapter 8, I offer suggestions regarding how youths, parents, and the helping professions can negotiate healthy relationships between sexual-minority youths and family members. My concern is not only with individuals but also with the family as a context for healthy development of all members. As will become readily apparent throughout the book, research on the relations sexual-minority youths have with their parents has many shortcomings. The consequences of these imperfections on our understanding of sexual-minority youths and their parents and the proposal of a research agenda conclude this book in chapter 9.

ENDNOTES

[1] Aarons, L. (1995). *Prayers for Bobby: A mother's coming to terms with the suicide of her gay son.* New York: HarperCollins; Borhek, M. V. (1993). *Coming out to parents: A two-way survival guide for lesbians and gay men and their parents* (2nd ed.). Cleveland, OH: Pilgrim; Clark, D. H. (1997). *The new loving someone gay.* Berkeley, CA: Celestial Arts; Fairchild, B., & Hayward, N. (1998). *Now that you know: A parent's guide to understanding their gay and lesbian children* (3rd ed.). San Diego, CA: Harcourt Brace; and Griffin, C. W., Wirth, M. J., & Wirth, A. G. (1986). *Beyond acceptance: Parents of lesbians and gays talk about their experiences.* Englewood Cliffs, NJ: Prentice-Hall.

[2] Popular first-person accounts of sexual-minority youths include the following: Baetz, R. (1980). *Lesbian crossroads.* New York: William Morrow; Barber, W. K., & Holmes, S. (Ed.). (1994). *Testimonies: Lesbian coming-out stories.* Boston: Alyson; Due, L. (1995). *Joining the tribe: Growing up gay and lesbian in the '90s.* New York: Anchor; Heron, A. (Ed.). (1983). *One teenager in ten.* Boston: Alyson; Heron, A. (Ed.). (1994). *Two teenagers in twenty: Writings by gay and lesbian youth.* Boston: Alyson; National Lesbian and Gay Survey. (1992). *What a lesbian looks like: Writings by lesbians on their lives and lifestyles.* London: Routledge; Penelope, J., & Wolfe, S. J. (Eds.). (1989). *The original coming out stories: Expanded edition.* Freedom, CA: Crossing Press; and Saks, A., & Curtis, W. (1994). *Revelations: Gay men's coming-out stories.* Boston: Alyson.

[3] Savin-Williams, R. C. (2000). *An exploratory study of sexual-minority youths' relations with their parents.* Manuscript submitted for publication.

2

DIFFERENTIAL DEVELOPMENTAL TRAJECTORIES

SEXUAL ORIENTATION AS A CONTEXT FOR DEVELOPMENT

Considering sexual orientation as a significant context for child and adolescent development assumes that same-sex oriented individuals have meaningfully different life courses than do heterosexual individuals and raises a number of complex and controversial issues. For example, if differences exist between two individuals on the basis of their sexual orientation, what is the nature of those differences, and how did they come about? When did they first appear, and how long do they last? And, underscoring an ethical dimension, should these differences be recognized and celebrated? That is, can they and should they be eliminated or, alternatively, encouraged?

A thorough explanation of these issues is too large a task to be undertaken here given the limited objectives for this book. In brief, scholars have usually argued one of two positions: One, sexual minorities are similar to heterosexuals in all respects except for certain aspects of their sexuality or, two, sexual minorities are patently unique from heterosexuals because of that very same sexuality. With the first approach, developmental questions usually center on the degree to which gay and straight people resemble each other. The ways in which same-sex sexuality affects development are minimized. Those who embrace the second approach emphasize the disparities between gay and straight people. They are of two sorts: Those who argue that the very existence of same-sex attractions leads individuals to a unique life history and those who believe that biological or early psychosocial factors cause the distinctiveness of sexual minorities. Thus, because lesbian, bisexual, and gay people are treated differently by culture, they ultimately evolve unique developmental histories from heterosexual people, or they lead distinctive developmental trajectories because of their unique biological or psychosocial heritage.

Note that few in this debate are particularly concerned with how heterosexual attractions emerge or how the behavior, appearance, and emotions of heterosexuals are similar or dissimilar to those of sexual minorities.

Using as an example the purported difficult relations noted in the popular literature that gay sons and lesbian daughters have with their same-sex parent, the second approach should be clarified. Advocates of a *cultural* interpretation of sexual-minority development might explain the impaired relations as a direct result of the inevitable conflicts that emerge when children do not act out the gender ideal that their parents have for their same-sex children. They do not share a parent's sex-typical interests—for reasons that are of little interest to proponents of this view or are supposedly the result of random variations—such as team sports or cooking, thus creating strained relationships. In contrast, defenders of a *biological* perspective might place primary emphasis on scientific evidence that supports prenatal hormonal determinants for sex-appropriate or sex-inappropriate behavior. Sex atypicality, in turn, leads to conflicts with the expectations and demands of a same-sex parent.

This book avoids these debates by proposing an alternative developmental perspective. On the basis of research findings, clinical observations, and the personal experiences of sexual-minority youths, it is clear that sexual-minority youths are both the same as all other adolescents and unique as a group of adolescents. This more developmentally defensible position acknowledges the sameness and the diversity that characterize most lives. For example, gay and lesbian individuals might indeed have both sex-atypical neurological structures that inimitably shape their attitudes, beliefs, and abilities and age-appropriate conflicts with their parents that result from differing views about suitable gender behavior for the child. One must remember, however, that in most areas of biological anatomy and chemistry, sexual-minority individuals are indistinguishable from heterosexuals and that all parents and adolescents have periods of friction, regardless of the sexual orientation of the child.

What I propose is the existence of multiple developmental pathways, or trajectories, among sexual-minority children and adolescents. Diversity exists in many forms, especially in the ways in which sexual orientation shapes development. For example, some adolescents feel so driven by their sexuality that they disclose to their parents as soon as they are able to say the words to themselves; others vow never to tell their parents because they fear the repercussions of that disclosure (e.g., having to finance their own college education). We must acknowledge not only characteristics thought to distinguish heterosexuals and sexual minorities but also those within sexual-minority populations.

DIFFERENTIAL DEVELOPMENTAL TRAJECTORIES

Development is determined to a large degree by what has previously transpired in an individual's life, including genetic predispositions, environmental events, and their interactions. Yet, within any life history, turning points or critical incidents occur that set particular developmental processes or transitions in motion. One of these for many sexual-minority youths is their parents' discovery of the youth's sexuality. Wide variations exist concerning when, how, and why this occurs, thus supporting a perspective of diversity.

In its most general terms, a *differential developmental trajectories* perspective seeks to replace traditional conceptions of sexual-minority development that view an individual's life as progressing in an orderly series of ideal or typical stages. *Differential* is the variability within a single life, across multiple individual lives, and among diverse groups of individuals. *Development* refers to changes and continuities over time in an individual's life course across a number of domains, including biological, psychological, and social arenas. These processes may appear continuous with previous ones, or disconnected, and reflect both quantitative (in amount, such as increases in sexual libido) and qualitative (in kind, such as emotional understanding of whether the direction of the libido is toward females, males, both, or none) aspects. *Trajectories* accents the momentum and shape of development, which can appear linear, inverted, spiral, circular, or unpredictable.[1]

From this perspective, behavior is often driven by internal processes put into motion by biological systems, as well as by external events, including proximal factors such as friends and family and distal influences such as societal heterocentrism and homonegativism.[2] Sexual-minority individuals are not perceived as merely robotic or predetermined in their reactions to societal forces that converge on their lives but are, as researcher Laurence Steinberg wrote, "active, changing agents who select and affect the environments in which they participate." Consistent with Steinberg's view of developmental trajectories, diversity is created in individual lives because of the unique blend of determinants that are "in part charted for the adolescent by others or by society, [and] routes toward an endpoint that are chosen, or even created, by an active, self-directed organism."[3]

The focus advocated here is one that portrays sexual-minority individuals as both similar to others regardless of sexual orientation and unique because of their sexual orientation. This entails four types of investigations:

1. those that explore general characteristics and developmental processes of sexual-minority individuals that are similar to those that affect all humans;

2. those that distinguish same-sex development as dissimilar from the development of other sexual orientations;
3. those that describe variations among sexual-minority individuals based on a range of personal and social characteristics that remain constant or are transformed through the life course; and
4. those that explore the uniqueness of the individual, regardless of sexual orientation.

That is, in some respects, the lives of sexual-minority youths share commonalities with all other adolescents or subgroups of adolescents regardless of sexual orientation, with all other sexual-minority youths, with subgroups of such youths, and with no other adolescent who has ever lived. Thus, any presumption that sexual-minority individuals share identical developmental pathways becomes not only implausible but also a gross misrepresentation of their lives.

WE ARE THE SAME

The assertion that sexual-minority individuals are the same as heterosexual individuals in developmentally significant ways might appear self-evident but is frequently lost on those who portray sexual-minority youths almost as if they were alien beings—as unhealthy, unnatural, and undesirable. For them, concerned parents should be "on guard" with the moral courage, if not always with accurate information, needed to convince their vulnerable child that she or he could not be lesbian or gay. Their vested interest in designating the gay adolescent as unlike the heterosexual adolescent is straightforward and understandable. For example, in response to recent discrimination lawsuits, the Boy Scouts of America have maintained that a "homosexual" adolescent is a heterosexual boy who has been transformed by an early sexual experience or by the message that "gay is okay" given to him by "homosexual" role models.[4] Clearly, some individuals and organizations would be opposed to the perspective that in most respects sexual-minority youths are the same as most other adolescents.

The "we are the same" position has also been lost on some gay-friendly individuals and organizations who often cite a long litany of ways in which young sexual-minority youths deviate from their heterosexual counterparts. Perhaps this position is assumed to convey the pain of growing up gay, to point the finger of accusation at an uncaring mainstream culture, to justify resources for interventions with these youths, and to enter mainstream institutions to educate about the unique needs of sexual-minority youths. Media interpretations of these representations often portray being young, gay, and proud as an oxymoron—impossible to achieve in North American culture. These youths appear to be a weak lot, defenseless in the face of a troubled world. Are there no resilient, strong sexual-minority youths who have coped, survived, and thrived? If sexual-minority youths are at high risk for committing or attempting suicide, abusing drugs, prostituting themselves, and becoming infected with HIV, then how similar can they be to heterosexual youths? Studies that build into their research design a gay-versus-straight paradigm assume by their very nature that these are two separate populations of adolescents. One is "normal" and the other is not. Guess which is not.

In most respects sexual-minority youths are essentially similar to heterosexual youths, with comparable, although not always identical, biological and psychosocial developmental tasks. The very foundation of a differential developmental trajectories approach implies that adolescents are first, foremost, and always adolescents, and this fact must be remembered in any accurate rendering of their lives. An adolescent is an adolescent is an adolescent. Regardless of sexual orientation, adolescents have growth spurts, menses, nocturnal emissions, secondary sex characteristics, and acne; regardless of sexual orientation, adolescents must negotiate issues of attachment, intimacy, autonomy, individuation, and identity. For example, in an earlier publication I document that the timing of pubertal maturation of gay or bisexual male adolescents is identical to that of heterosexual youths and that late maturers, regardless of sexual orientation, were at a disadvantage on sexual and mental health domains.[5] A review of the literature demonstrates that lesbian and bisexual female adolescents vary little from heterosexual adolescents in self-esteem level, ego development, or self-concept.[6]

Although sexual minorities are more similar to heterosexuals than not, sexual orientation can be developmentally influential. In distinctive ways, sexual-minority youths vary from their heterosexual peers.

WE ARE DIFFERENT

By writing a book devoted to the voices of sexual-minority youths, I am assuming that sexual orientation is an important context for understanding how individuals come to be who they are. Thus, because of their sexuality, sexual-minority youths necessarily experience a substantially different life course than do heterosexual youths. Sexual orientation does not necessarily dictate the essence of what it means to be human, but it does serve to demarcate some aspects of development.

This is likely for both biological and psychosocial reasons. Although the evidence is far from definitive, especially regarding lesbians and bisexuals (of both sexes), sexual-minority youths appear to vary from heterosexual youths in their biological (genetic or prenatal hormone environment) makeup. For example, various studies have found that "homosexual" individuals differ from heterosexuals in particular aspects of their neuroanatomy, physiology, and physical features.[7] Differences have been reported in the hypothalamus, hormonal levels during prenatal life, penis size, and shoulder-to-hip ratios. Psychosocial research has documented that as a consequence of growing up nonheterosexual amid heterosexual family members, close friends, and societal institutions (e.g., schools and religious organizations) that presume and prescribe exclusive heterosexuality, sexual-minority adolescents are challenged to negotiate between being true to self and becoming what is expected of them. This task permeates their daily lives in ways not encountered by heterosexual youths when they express their sexuality. The consequences may be negative, such as increased levels of emotional distress and substance abuse,[8] or positive, such as feelings of specialness or creativity.

These differences, which have been presumed to exist only between sexual-minority and heterosexual populations, may also distinguish subpopulations of sexual-minority youths. This is the "hottest" and most promising area of research on sexual minorities.

WE DIFFER AMONG OURSELVES

The are-they-the-same-or-are-they-different debate must not, but often does, conceal the enormous diversity that is apparent within sexual-minority populations. Developmental trajectories may be unique to groups of individuals, regardless of sexual orientation, based on macro factors such as gender, race, ethnicity, and class, or micro factors such as personality characteristics or real-world experiences. For example, adolescent girls generally achieve higher levels of intimacy, sensitivity, and empathy in their close relationships than do adolescent boys, regardless of sexual orientation. Thus, it is to be expected that the romantic relationships of same-sex attracted women are more likely to evolve from same-sex friendships and to be characterized by emotional intimacy than are those among gay male youths.[9] Among various ethnic groups, Asian American sexual-minority youths are least likely to violate the taboo of disclosing to parents and to engage in same-sex activity at an early age.[10] Furthermore, within each of these gender and ethnic classifications of individuals reside further subgroups, which can be stable or fluid over time, based on any number of characteristics. Because of their personality style, sex-role behavior, gender identity, exposure to particular experiences, or personal belief systems, some sexual-minority boys are more similar to girls of all sexual persuasions than other boys, and some Asian Americans behave as if they were more White than Asian.

Examples of unique sexual-minority subgroups are boundless, and most have not been empirically verified. Growing up lesbian in Northampton, Massachusetts, is not the same as growing up lesbian in a small Missouri town. Being gay in a Puerto Rican family is not the same as being gay in a Mexican family. Some girls do not recall having early childhood same-sex attractions prior to identifying as lesbian but understand their sexual identity within the context of exposure to a college women's studies course or within a romantic relationship. Some boys are sex-centric, having sex with another boy before labeling themselves as gay, whereas other boys are identity-centric, declaring their same-sex status prior to engaging in gay sex. Some youths claim a bisexual, gay, or lesbian identity without sexual experiences. Others have had many same-sex encounters and do not identify as anything other than heterosexual. Some same-sex attracted individuals eschew a sexual identity label altogether. Other individuals claim a lesbian, gay, or bisexual label without same-sex attractions.[11]

With this level of diversity, it is a misnomer to declare a singular "gay lifestyle." Similarities across individuals exist, to be sure, but future investigations need to assess these in greater detail than has been done heretofore. This fact does not negate, of course, what any clinician or educator knows—the uniqueness of individual lives.

WE ARE EACH UNIQUE

This perspective, that every human being is unique insofar that no one like him or her has ever lived before or will in the future, is often lost in scientific presentations of data. It is the indispensable aspect of existence, however, for one venue of information—the life history accounts of youths that are narrated in "coming-out" books.[12] These histories are extremely popular among sexual-minority youths who are searching not so much to discover an identical tale but to find a story similar to themselves with which to identify. This process may well help alleviate feelings of alienation and isolation in ways sorely missed by more conventional methods of writing. As such, they serve an invaluable purpose.

DEFINITIONS

Several terms used throughout the book are defined here. These concepts have multiple shades of meanings, thus descriptions given below should not be construed as definitive for all contexts.

Sexual Orientation and Sexual Identity

When sexual orientation is considered as a context for development, the distinction between sexual orientation and sexual identity must be clear. The contrast between the two is often conceptualized as the distinction between an ever-present, invariant biological or psychological truth (sexual orientation) and a historically and culturally located social construction (sexual identity). Although this distinction oversimplifies both constructs, it is useful to clarify several developmental issues facing children and adolescents with same-sex attractions. For example, the differentiation between orientation and identity stipulates that an individual with a same-sex or an opposite-sex sexual orientation need not claim or acknowledge a similar sexual identity. A teenage boy with a same-sex orientation may engage in occasional sexual activity with girls to maintain his heterosexual veneer but consider himself bisexual. An adolescent girl who identifies herself as lesbian may in fact be bisexual in her sexual orientation but is afraid to claim this orientation as her identity because she perceives more communities for lesbian than for bisexual women.

Sexual orientation refers to the preponderance of sexual or erotic feelings, thoughts, and fantasies one has for members of one sex or the other, both, or neither. It is present from an early age, perhaps by conception if caused by genetic factors, during prenatal life if caused by biological or environmental factors acting on the developing fetus, or by age 5 if caused by psychogenic factors. Sexual orientation is generally considered to be immutable, stable, and internally consonant, although this is a matter of some contention among lesbian and bisexual women.[13] Sexual orientation is not subject to conscious control, influences but is independent of sexual conduct and sexual identity, and is multidimensional. Many individuals possess degrees of homoerotic and heteroerotic attractions and feelings; thus, homosexuality and heterosexuality may merely be the ends of a continuum on which we all fall. Others maintain that sexual orientation is a categorical variable in which people can be classified as heterosexual, homosexual, or bisexual.

Sexual identity represents a socially recognized category that names the perceptions, feelings, and meanings that an individual holds about her or his sexual feelings, attractions, and behaviors. The label occurs within a pool of potential sexual identities that are defined and given meaning by the culture and historic time in which one lives. Sexual identity is symbolized by such statements as "I am gay" and is thus a matter of personal choice. For some individuals, sexual identity remains fluid during the life course, probably not on a day-to-day basis, and is not necessarily consistent with sexual orientation, fantasies, or behavior.

Sexual Minority

Sexual minority is a descriptive term that refers to a wide range of individuals who apply diverse sexual identifications or behaviors to themselves. It includes all those who do not adhere to the perceived "normalcy" of heterosexuality. A more pedestrian definition is that sexual minority includes individuals who engage in a variety of sexual behaviors and identities that are seldom discussed in most homes. Included in this group are sadists, masochists, those who engage in anal and oral sexual behavior, all same-sex attracted individuals, and individuals who have any other conceivable identification or behavior that does not meet cultural standards of normal heterosexuality. This definition is somewhat inadequate because adult virgins (regardless of sexual orientation) and asexuals are sexual minorities and yet socially and religiously conservative groups would generally applaud them for this "moral" behavior.

In a more restricted sense, and the one used in this text, the term *sexual minorities* refers to individuals who report that they are gay, lesbian, bisexual, transgender, transsexual, unlabeled, or sexually questioning, or have same-sex attractions. When my reference point is solely to lesbian, bisexual, and gay individuals, these terms are used instead.

Heterocentrism and Heterosexism

Heterocentrism is the assumption that development "naturally" proceeds in a heterosexual direction. This perspective is so pervasive in culture that individuals unthinkingly act in ways that assume all individuals are heterosexual. Thus, girls are asked if they have boyfriends and when are they going to marry; boys are asked if they like the most recent *Playboy* centerfold and are seldom quizzed if they prefer the *Playgirl* alternative. When heterocentrism becomes judgmental, then *heterosexism* exists—girls who have boyfriends rather than girlfriends are considered to be better and healthier, and boys who are turned on by female rather than male images are believed to be more normal and better adjusted.

Homonegativity and Homophobia

Homonegativity refers to negative feelings, attitudes, and behaviors toward those with same-sex attractions. *Homophobia* is a popular term that is frequently used rather than homonegativity. However, I prefer to reserve this term for the more emotional expressions of negative attitudes toward homosexuality and gay people. Thus, the belief that homosexuality is not an equally viable way of life is homonegativity; to implement that belief by verbally abusing suspected gay people or by committing violent acts against perceived gay people constitutes homophobia.

Stage Models

Clinical and developmental psychologists first proposed *coming-out models* or *sexual identity models* over two decades ago. These theoretical constructions describe the advent of a same-sex identity through a series of invariant steps or stages by which individuals recognize, make sense of, give a name to, and publicize their status as lesbian or gay (bisexuality is seldom addressed). The reification of these "master" models to explain nonhetero-sexuality remains popular today.[14] Although diverse in conceptual underpin-nings, they are nearly universal in their stage sequences and assumptions regarding the ways in which youths move from a private, at times unknown, same-sex sexuality to a public, integrated sexuality. Healthy development involves movement along a predetermined developmental sequence with advanced status or maturity marked by the author as the attainment of the final stage.[15] For example, most models mark the onset of sexual identity development as the individual's first awareness of same-sex attractions, pre-sumed to occur in late childhood or early adolescence. This is followed some years later by a period of testing and exploration, during which youths seek information about similarly attracted individuals or engage in experi-mentation with same-sex sexual contact. After adopting a sexual-minority label and disclosing this to others, the person's final stages of identity development often entail disclosure to parents, romantic relationships, polit-ical activism, assimilation, and integration of one's sexual identity within other spheres of life. Development is thus generally perceived as linear, invariant, universal, inevitable, and predictable across individuals who share some real or hypothesized commonalities.

On the positive side, coming-out models have generated considerable interest in developmental issues regarding sexual identity, focused attention on lesbian and gay youths (because this is when most milestones are pur-ported to occur), and isolated aspects of development for further research. However, coming-out models have also had their downside.

Most profoundly, they are not true—at least in a universal sense. Although a linear progression is intuitively appealing, extant research sug-gests it seldom characterizes the lives of real sexual-minority youths.[16] Rather, considerable diversity exists among youths of different backgrounds, cohorts, and ethnicities regarding the paths taken to sexual-minority identification. Some of the most notable deviations from the standard model have been documented among women with same-sex attractions.[17] Perhaps this is to be expected, given that most coming-out models were derived from exclusively male samples. Lisa Diamond found little use for these male-oriented "master narratives" in her research with sexual-minority women.

Although coming-out models are inherently male-centric, recent research suggests that they do not even characterize the lives of current cohorts of males with same-sex attractions. For example, only 2% of male youths and none of the young women interviewed for this book followed the stylized sexual-identity models. Many did not use sex to help them figure out their identity but knew who they were prior to gay sex.[18]

Coming-out models simplify a complex, evolving process. One cannot understand the development of nonheterosexuality so easily. In critiquing such models, numerous researchers have called for a multidimensional approach to sexual identity development.[19]

Similarly, *grief/mourning stage models* have been proposed to describe the reactions of parents once they discover their child is lesbian, gay, or bisexual.[20] Once parents are confronted with the reality of their child's sexual orientation, these models suggest that a parent "coming-out" process is initiated "whereby parents are given the opportunity to restructure expectations and goals for the future life course of their children."[21] Parents supposedly react with symptoms of grief and mourning, progressing through a series of stages similar to those described by Kübler-Ross after the shock of learning of one's own impending death: denial, anger, bargaining, depression, and acceptance.[22] As is evident in chapter 3, these models are both simplistic and untrue.

CONCLUSION

The family of origin plays a pivotal role in the lives of sexual-minority youths, as it does for all youths. In this the reader will knowingly see the standard "adolescence" in many of the narratives that constitute the primary source of information for this book. These are the struggles faced by all youths growing up in American society as they negotiate new and old relations with family members. In keeping with a differential developmental trajectories perspective, also apparent are the unique concerns of youths who are not heterosexual. They too want to maintain good relations with their family and yet they fear that their "unconventional" sexuality will disrupt this goal.

For some youths, coming out to parents results in becoming alienated from their families, whereas for others, nothing is changed or the relationship improves once the secret is out. One possible way in which these variations can be understood is by examining subpopulation differences. In this book, disparities in gender development are emphasized—those encountered by daughters and sons in their experience with their same-sex or other-sex parent.

The personal lives reflected in these accounts attest to the combination of life circumstances that are marvels in their individuality, illustrating the diverse relationships sexual-minority youths and their parents have with each other—the essence of a differential developmental trajectories perspective.

ENDNOTES

[1] For earlier discussions of this perspective, see Savin-Williams, R. C. (1998). " . . . and then I became gay": Young men's stories. New York: Routledge; and Savin-Williams, R. C., & Diamond, L. M. (1998). Sexual orientation. In W. K. Silverman & T. H. Ollendick (Eds.), Developmental issues in the clinical treatment of children (pp. 241–258). Boston: Allyn & Bacon.

[2] Definitions of these terms are provided later in this chapter.

[3] Both quotes on p. 248 in Steinberg, L. (1995). Commentary: On developmental pathways and social contexts in adolescence. In L. J. Crockett & A. C. Crouter (Eds.), Pathways through adolescence: Individual development in relation to social contexts (pp. 245–253). Mahwah, NJ: Erlbaum.

[4] These arguments were made in a recent civil lawsuit, Roland D. Pool & Michael S. Geller v. National Capital Area Council, Boy Scouts of America, (1998) in which I served as an expert witness for the plaintiffs on the science of sexual orientation. Ultimately, the Boy Scouts dismissed the empirical evidence because it was not perfect or indisputable. For the Boy Scouts, moral authority took precedence over scientific authority.

[5] Savin-Williams, R. C. (1995). An exploratory study of pubertal maturation timing and self-esteem among gay and bisexual male youths. Developmental Psychology, 31, 56–64.

[6] See chapter 2 in Savin-Williams, R. C. (1990). Gay and lesbian youth: Expressions of identity. New York: Hemisphere.

[7] See chapters by Ellis, L. (1996). Theories of homosexuality and the role of perinatal factors in determining sexual orientation. In R. C. Savin-Williams & K. M. Cohen (Eds.), The lives of lesbians, gays, and bisexuals: Children to adults (pp. 11–34, 35–70). Fort Worth, TX: Harcourt Brace College; and Hershberger, S. L. (1998). Homosexuality. In H. Friedman (Ed.), Encyclopedia of mental health, Vol. 2 (pp. 403–419). San Diego, CA: Academic Press.

[8] This was a point I made in a 1994 review of the literature, Verbal and physical abuse as stressors in the lives of lesbian, gay male, and bisexual youths: Associations with school problems, running away, substance abuse, prostitution, and suicide. Journal of Consulting and Clinical Psychology, 62, 261–269. A more recent report with a nationwide, representative sample of adolescents found same-sex attracted youths had these kinds of problems. The study was conducted by Udry, J. R., & Bearman, P. (1997). Reducing the risk: Connections that make a difference in the lives of youth. Bethesda, MD: Burness Communications.

[9] Examples are available in Dubé, E. M., Savin-Williams, R. C., & Diamond, L. M. (2001). Intimacy development, gender, and ethnicity among sexual-minority youths. In A. R. D'Augelli & C. J. Patterson (Eds.), *Lesbian, gay, and bisexual identities and youths: Psychological perspectives.* New York: Oxford University Press.

[10] Dubé, E. M., & Savin-Williams, R. C. (1999). Sexual identity development among ethnic sexual-minority male youths. *Developmental Psychology, 35,* 1389–1399.

[11] Empirical evidence and examples of these points are provided in Diamond, L. M. (1998). The development of sexual orientation among adolescent and young adult women. *Developmental Psychology, 34,* 1085–1095; Dubé, E. M. (2000). The role of sexual behavior in the identification process of gay and bisexual males. *Journal of Sex Research, 37,* 123–132; and Savin-Williams, R. C. (1998). " . . . and then I became gay": Young men's stories. New York: Routledge.

[12] Many of these accounts are available in relatively cheap paperbacks and are a fascinating read. Without attempting to be comprehensive, several of these are referenced in endnote 2 of chapter 1.

[13] See discussion of the fluidity of some women's sexual orientation in Brown, L. S. (1995). Lesbian identities: Concepts and issues. In A. R. D'Augelli & C. J. Patterson (Eds.), *Lesbian, gay, and bisexual identities over the lifespan* (pp. 3–23). New York: Oxford University Press; Diamond, L. M. (1998). The development of sexual orientation among adolescent and young adult women. *Developmental Psychology, 34,* 1085–1095; Golden, C. (1996). What's in a name? Sexual self-identification among women. In R. C. Savin-Williams & K. M. Cohen (Eds.), *The lives of lesbians, gays, and bisexuals: Children to adults* (pp. 229–249). Fort Worth, TX: Harcourt Brace College; Kitzinger, C. (1987). *The social construction of lesbianism.* London: Sage; Kitzinger, C., & Wilkinson, S. (1995). Transitions from heterosexuality to lesbianism: The discursive production of lesbian identities. *Developmental Psychology, 31,* 95–104; Rust, P. (1992). The politics of sexual identity: Sexual attraction and behavior among lesbian and bisexual women. *Social Problems, 39,* 366–386; and Rust, P. (1993). Coming out in the age of social constructionism: Sexual identity formation among lesbians and bisexual women. *Gender and Society, 7,* 50–77.

[14] For example, within the last several years, the *Journal of Homosexuality* has published numerous articles in the following volumes addressing sexual identity models. Brady, S., & Busse, W. J. (1994). The Gay Identity Questionnaire: A brief measure of homosexual identity formation, 26, 1–22; Cox, S., & Gallois, C. (1996). Gay and lesbian identity development: A social identity perspective, 30, 1–30; Eliason, M. J. (1996). Identity formation for lesbian, bisexual and gay persons: Beyond a "minoritizing" view, 30, 31–58; Fassinger, R. E., & Miller, B. A. (1996). Validation of an inclusive model of sexual minority formation on a sample of gay men, 32, 53–78; Levine, H. (1997). A further exploration of the lesbian identity development process and its measurement, 34, 67–78; and Morris, J. F. (1997). Lesbian coming out as a multidimensional process, 33, 1–22.

[15] Theoretical models have included psychoanalytic, cognitive, symbolic interaction, and social learning perspectives. See Cass, V. (1979). Homosexual identity formation: A theoretical model. *Journal of Homosexuality, 4,* 219–235; Cass, V. (1984). Homosexual identity: A concept in need of a definition. *Journal of Homosexu-*

ality, 9, 105–126; Coleman, E. (1981/1982). Developmental stages of the coming out process. *Journal of Homosexuality*, 7, 31–43; Plummer, K. (1975). *Sexual stigma: An interactionist account*. Boston: Routledge & Kegan Paul; Sophie, J. (1985/1986). A critical examination of stage theories of lesbian identity development. *Journal of Homosexuality*, 12, 39–51; Troiden, R. R. (1979). Becoming homosexual: A model of gay identity acquisition. *Psychiatry*, 42, 362–373; and Troiden, R. R. (1989). The formation of homosexual identities. *Journal of Homosexuality*, 17, 43–73. McConnell, J. H. (1994) discussed additional limitations and uses of these stage models, in Lesbian and gay male identities as paradigms. In S. L. Archer (Ed.), *Interventions for adolescent identity development* (pp. 103–118). Thousand Oaks, CA: Sage.

[16] For a critique of these models, see Cohen, K. M., & Savin-Williams, R. C. (1996). Developmental perspectives on coming out to self and others. In R. C. Savin-Williams & K. M. Cohen (Eds.), *The lives of lesbians, gays, and bisexuals: Children to adults* (pp. 113–151). Fort Worth, TX: Harcourt Brace College; Eliason, M. J. (1996). An inclusive model of lesbian identity assumption. *Journal of Gay, Lesbian, and Bisexual Identity*, 1, 3–19; McConnell, J. H. (1994). Lesbian and gay male identities as paradigms. In S. L. Archer (Ed.), *Interventions for adolescent identity development* (pp. 103–118). Thousand Oaks, CA: Sage; and Morris, J. F. (1997). Lesbian coming out as a multidimensional process. *Journal of Homosexuality*, 33, 1–22.

[17] Recent evidence is available in Diamond, L. M. (1998). The development of sexual orientation among adolescent and young adult women. *Developmental Psychology*, 34, 1085–1095; Golden, C. (1996). What's in a name? Sexual self-identification among women. In R. C. Savin-Williams & K. M. Cohen (Eds.), *The lives of lesbians, gays, and bisexuals: Children to adults* (pp. 229–249). Fort Worth, TX: Harcourt Brace College; and Rust, P. (1993). Coming out in the age of social constructionism: Sexual identity formation among lesbians and bisexual women. *Gender and Society*, 7, 50–77.

[18] See recent publications by Dubé, E. M. (2000). The role of sexual behavior in the identification process of gay and bisexual males. *Journal of Sex Research*, 37, 123–132; Dubé, E. M., & Savin-Williams, R. C. (1999). Sexual identity development among ethnic sexual-minority male youths. *Developmental Psychology*, 35, 1389–1399; and Savin-Williams, R. C. (1998). " . . . and then I became gay": Young men's stories. New York: Routledge.

[19] Suggestions for alternatives are available in Eliason, M. J. (1996). An inclusive model of lesbian identity assumption. *Journal of Gay, Lesbian, and Bisexual Identity*, 1, 3–19; Eliason, M. J. (1996). Identity formation for lesbian, bisexual, and gay persons: Beyond a "minoritizing" view. *Journal of Homosexuality*, 30, 31–58; Morris, J. (1997). Lesbian coming out as a multidimensional process. *Journal of Homosexuality*, 33, 1–22; and Peplau, L. A., Garnets, L. D., Spalding, L. R., Conley, T. D., & Veniegas, R. C. (1998). A critique of Bem's "exotic becomes erotic" theory of sexual orientation. *Psychological Review*, 105, 387–394.

[20] Anderson, D. (1987). Family and peer relations of gay adolescents. *Adolescent Psychiatry*, 15, 163–178; Bernstein, B. (1990). Attitudes and issues of parents of gay men and lesbians and implications for therapy. *Journal of Gay and Lesbian*

Psychotherapy, *1*, 37–53; Borhek, M. V. (1993). *Coming out to parents: A two-way survival guide for lesbians and gay men and their parents* (2nd ed.). Cleveland, OH: Pilgrim; Bozett, F. W., & Sussman, M. B. (1989). Homosexuality and family relations: Views and research issues. *Marriage and Family Review*, *14*, 1–7; Brown, L. S. (1988). Lesbians, gay men and their families. *Journal of Gay and Lesbian Psychotherapy*, *1*, 65–77; DeVine, J. L. (1984). A systemic inspection of affectional preference orientation and the family of origin. *Journal of Social Work and Human Sexuality*, *2*, 9–17; Kübler-Ross, E. (1969). *On death and dying*. New York: MacMillan; Martin, A. D. (1982). Learning to hide: The socialization of the gay adolescent. *Adolescent Psychiatry*, *10*, 52–65; Myers, M. F. (1982). Counseling the parents of young homosexual male patients. *Journal of Homosexuality*, *7*, 131–143; Pearlman, S. (1992). Heterosexual mothers/lesbian daughters: Parallels and similarities. *Journal of Feminist Family Therapy*, *4*, 1–21; Robinson, B. E., Walters, L. H., & Skeen, P. (1989). Response of parents to learning that their child is homosexual and concern over AIDS: A national study. *Journal of Homosexuality*, *18*, 59–80; Strommen, E. F. (1989). "You're a what?": Family member reactions to the disclosure of homosexuality. *Journal of Homosexuality*, *18*, 37–58; Tremble, B., Schneider, M., & Appathurai, C. (1989). Growing up gay or lesbian in a multicultural context. *Journal of Homosexuality*, *17*, 253–267; Wirth, S. (1978). Coming out close to home: Principles for psychotherapy with families of lesbian and gay men. *Catalyst*, *3*, 6–22.

[21] Page 86 in Boxer, A. M., Cook, J. A., & Herdt, G. (1991). Double jeopardy: Identity transitions and parent–child relations among gay and lesbian youth. In K. Pillemer & K. McCartney (Eds.), *Parent–child relations throughout life* (pp. 59–92). Hillsdale, NJ: Erlbaum; see also Coleman, E., & Remafedi, G. (1989). Gay, lesbian, and bisexual adolescents: A critical challenge to counselors. *Journal of Counseling and Development*, *68*, 36–40.

[22] Kübler-Ross, E. (1969). *On death and dying*. New York: MacMillan.

3

RELATIONS WITH PARENTS

I first sensed that Richard was "different" when he was 9.

He never seemed to care for games young boys play. I would take him to baseball games, despite his protestations, and he would be somewhere out there watching the grass grow, or the birds soaring to the heavens. Richard was happier when he was in a corner reading, drawing, or making his own comic books. . . .

My heart sank. It was something I knew I had to face eventually. I had rehearsed a scene in my mind where Richard told me he was gay, and I was calm and understanding of it. But here it was, the moment of truth, and I felt confused. I also felt angry that he didn't trust me enough to let me know sooner.

But all I could manage for a reply at that time was, "That's okay," and left it at that. . . .

Yes, my son is gay, and that is just fine. That in no way changes the fact that he was the bundle of joy I held in my arms 28 years ago, or the child whose eyes followed the flight of the bird rather than the ball in the softball field, or the young man who continues to do me proud by his academic and professional accomplishments.

Richard is the same son that makes me happy simply by knowing that he is now truly free and happy.[1]

Elsie Uyeda Chung's written reactions to having a gay son were offered as a Mother's Day gift to other parents. Her experience is a common one among mothers of sexual-minority children in that she had early suspicions that her son was not "typical" of other children, later suppositions that the difference meant homosexuality, and a generally positive response to the "news." Her closing statement—that her son is the same as before she knew he was gay and that he is now happier and freer—is one that many parents articulate, if not immediately after they learn about the nonheterosexuality of their child, then at a later time.

Her story, however, is contrary to many popular self-help books composed for, and sometimes by, parents of gay children. These books often portray the child's act of disclosure as necessarily creating a crisis within the family that may never be fully resolved. Lesions in family relationships are inflicted with wounds that may not withstand later attempts to amend; parents likely encounter unique developmental issues not faced when all immediate members are heterosexual. The popular literature promotes the view that no task is more difficult or omnipresent for each affected parent, or riskier for family relationships, than the disclosure of same-sex desires by children to family members. The family's reactions can result in youths being disowned, thrown out of the home, or emotionally or physically harassed. From this perspective, because parents feel that their child has rejected them and all they have worked for, the development of healthy family relationships may be impossible to achieve.

In this chapter I review the popular and empirical literatures regarding the relationships sexual-minority youths have with their parents, including what is known regarding the importance of parents for sexual-minority youths and the association between disclosure to parents and the youths' psychological health. The focus then turns toward parents. First, attention is given to the various reactions parents have to their child's disclosure. To illustrate the nature of each, I provide exemplary narratives that are taken from news accounts, popular literature, and interviews of sexual-minority youths and their parents. Empirical research that addresses the nature of the reaction is also reviewed. The inclusion of both personal narratives and empirical research is intended to highlight the contrast between the two and to suggest ways in which they might inform each other. Factors that predict how parents react to the discovery that they have a lesbian daughter or gay son are also included.

Two final points: It is not my intent to discount the perspectives advanced by the personal stories of sexual-minority youths and their parents but to present data from empirical investigations that systematically address issues raised in these narratives. Second, attention is given only to heterosexual parents with sexual-minority children. This is not to deny that sexual-minority parents with sexual-minority children also exist, but as far as I can discern, no empirical investigation has addressed these family compositions.

POPULAR LITERATURE

Adolescents, regardless of sexual orientation, value their families because they provide "physical and emotional sustenance, connect us with our past, and provide a context within which we learn about the world."[2] Within this presumed loving milieu, individual members anticipate that they will be nurtured in their growth and development. Indeed, consistent with this view, most sexual-minority teenagers desire a close, positive relationship with family members—with the understanding that within the family they can preserve their personal sense of integrity, live according to the dictates of being true to self and honest with others, and express their sexual identity.[3] Yet, some youths admit to considerable anger because they were parented as if they were heterosexual and not as who they really are. This condition necessitates that some conceal their true identity until they feel safer; others, perhaps anticipating negative outcomes were they to be honest, sever emotional investment in the family to diminish the significance of possible rejection.[4] They may construct elaborate webs of deceit that result in limited communications, increased conflicts, and lost intimacy between themselves and family members.

Indeed, some of the most exacting decisions facing sexual-minority youths are whether they should reveal the nature of their sexuality to family members and, if so, when and in what manner. Resolving these dilemmas may very well challenge a youth's willingness to accept a newly recognized and labeled sexual identity. Thus, disclosure to the family may be one of the most arduous declarations of individuation yet faced by a sexual-minority youth.[5]

The popular literature on lesbian, gay, and bisexual youths and their parents focuses on these difficult prospects. These are embedded in compelling "coming-out" stories; self-help books for parents; and writings of clinicians, educators, counselors, and support professionals.[6] The accent is on the necessary trauma youths incur when they disclose to parents, or the consequences of not disclosing, and the stages that parents experience in coping with this unsettling news. No task is perceived as more intricate, treacherous, or omnipresent as disclosing to parents. Many youths in these stories who have not disclosed have few expectations that their parents will react in a positive, supportive fashion to the news that they have a lesbian, bisexual, or gay child. According to these accounts, parents expect their children to be heterosexual, and any contrary information will not be greeted with celebration. Perceiving few options other than to censor their same-sex attractions, youths believe that if they were to deviate from the heterosexual prescription, they would be implicitly or explicitly disowned and separated from their family of origin. This creates a situation in which they could be rejected, thrown out of the home, or physically or emotionally abused. One writer observed, "Gay people may be, in fact, the only minority in America whose families consistently reject them."[7] These youths and their parents are described by clinicians, educators, and mental health professionals as necessarily facing unique developmental issues not encountered by families in which all immediate members are heterosexual.

Once parents are aware of their child's nonheterosexual orientation, these popular tracts portray parental emotions and actions that cause considerable fear among lesbian daughters and gay sons. The spectrum of reactions has been characterized by a number of writers as similar to those experienced by individuals undergoing grief and mourning. Under such circumstances, sexual-minority youths may regret ever having disclosed to parents; relations become strained and perhaps irreversibly damaged. Whether the youths' fears of disclosure are real or imagined and whether parental reactions follow the grieving or mourning stages are discussed later in this chapter.

The validity of the information just reviewed is difficult to ascertain because relatively few pronouncements on sexual-minority youths and their families are derived from scientific empirical data. However, because the personal narratives are so opulent in their pathos, it is difficult to deny their truthfulness without fear of being charged with insensitivity and blindness. Indeed, the empirically unsubstantiated grieving stages have come to serve as sources of hypothesis generation for a limited number of empirical investigations of sexual-minority youths and their families. More commonly, however, we unquestioningly assume the information is true.

Thus, perhaps unwittingly, the personal narratives literature has contributed to the view that sexual-minority youth disclosures and parental reactions will be necessarily and universally traumatic. It is considered to be the norm rather than the exception for familial chaos to reign once the news is broken. Although few writers expressly defend the view that *all* youths have identical lives and that *all* parents experience identical symptoms and recoveries, their tracts implicitly make this assumption. Health care providers and other professionals often embrace these models without question, which then influences their subsequent treatment of bisexual, lesbian, and gay youths and their parents.

For their part, researchers have provided strikingly little usable data that address issues pertinent to sexual-minority youths and their families. Indeed, at times they have contributed to the outrageous claims made by popular literature—such as one half of all such youths are thrown out of the home once they disclose.[8] Although several studies examine whether adolescents come out to parents and at what age, virtually no empirical research investigates the decision-making process that adolescents undergo prior to revealing their sexual identity to family members, the effects such disclosures have on the youths and the family, and how their relationships change over time.

IMPORTANCE OF PARENTS

Relations with parents are clearly a source of concern for many sexual-minority youths. Damien Martin and Emory Hetrick, founders of the Harvey Milk School in New York City, the nation's first public school for youths at-risk because of their sexual orientation, and the Hetrick-Martin Institute, a New York City social and educational agency for sexual-minority youths, noted that the second most common presenting problem among youths who sought their assistance was relations with parents and other family members. Youths felt isolated and alienated, feared what would happen once the family discovered their homosexuality, and expected violence and expulsion from the home.[9] Knowing the parents' heterosexual expectations of them and their own deeply felt homoerotic desires led many youths to experience guilt, shame, anger, and rejection.

A youth who finally comes to the point when he or she can say to himself or herself, and perhaps to a best friend, "I'm gay" must subsequently confront very difficult decisions—whether, when, and how to disclose to his or her parents. Carolyn Griffin, Marian Wirth, and Arthur Wirth compiled accounts of parents' experiences with their children in *Beyond Acceptance: Parents of Lesbians and Gays Talk About Their Experiences.*[10] Many youths told their parents that they simply wanted to be loved and supported. Below are two of the youth's accounts:

> I was now one of those "terrible people." I took in the feeling that there was something dreadfully wrong with me—something so awful that if it was discovered, I might lose the parental love I was so dependent on for a good part of my existence. Or, because of this deeply awful thing about myself, I might be a source of great hurt to my parents. I longed to tell them and to be told I was loved, no matter what. (p. 160)

> I hope that you and Dad will just be supportive. And love me. I don't think that's a small thing. Just be my mom and dad—the same as you always have been. I guess that's what I want. I don't necessarily expect you to accept everything or to like everything about the gay life style. But I hope you'll try to understand another person's point of view and accept me as much as you do my brother and sister. (pp. 165–166)

Motivations for being "out of the closet" vary from child to child, but many of these youths long to be close to their families so that they can lead authentic lives. If they "keep the secret" from their parents, then time spent with the family is false, perhaps tense, and always less than ideal.

> We don't want to waste energy covering up the basic facts of our lives. Also, we want to be out because some of our greatest strengths and talents can only be expressed freely when we are completely ourselves. When we are not out, to our families . . . the constraint that goes into hiding and the inner conflict that daily drains our energy spells a real waste of human intelligence, creativity, and sensitivity. (p. 164)

Some parents appreciate that love, rather than revenge, motivates their child's disclosure. They too desire to maintain family relations that are positive and healthy for all concerned.

> I know it was difficult for Mary to tell us; perhaps the most difficult thing she's ever had to do. She told us because she cares so much for

us. She felt she had to tell us, and I think she wanted to tell us. She wanted us to share in her happiness. (p. 162)

Particularly insightful is the following parent, who sensed the dilemmas for both parents and children.

It takes a lot of courage for our children to tell us. Particularly if they're close to us. That might seem to be a contradiction. But I think it's hard even for those who've had easy, good relationships with their parents, because they don't want to jeopardize that. And they don't want to hurt us. They think and hope we'll accept it. But they're not positive. I think it's important to realize that it's very special, their coming out to us. It's interesting that all the parents I know are not sorry their children told them, though they may have been at first. Even though some of them went through hell, they still prefer to know. (pp. 161–162)

Of course not all parents want their children to tell them the truth. Mary Griffith felt numb after she was told, although for many years she had subtle suspicions that her son Bobby was different from his peers.

Bobby liked being in the kitchen with Mom, or rummaging through her costume-jewelry box in the bedroom, or playing with [his sister] Joy's things. Mary caught herself more than once shaping the word *sissy* in her mind, then quickly suppressing the thought. The idea of Bobby's being somebody society didn't approve of scared her, not only for Bobby's sake but also for hers. It didn't help when Granny would visit and scold Bobby for smearing on his mother's lipstick or messing with Joy's things. She warned her daughter, "Mary, if you aren't careful, this boy will turn out a sissy." (p. 45)[11]

After she discovered her son's sexual orientation, Mary did everything possible to hide this fact. "Not the church, not Granny and Grandfather, none of the others" should know. It was humiliating. "Worst of all, the revelation had blown apart the intimate familial contract; for all his family's protestations of love, the bubble had ruptured, and Bobby was on the outside looking in" (p. 78).

Her well-meaning campaign to save her son had merely helped drive him to his death. Bobby had believed the verdict pronounced by the people he most trusted and cared about: his own family. *And it was wrong!* The enormity of this revelation was almost harder to bear than the three years of doubt and grief that preceded it. She had been deaf to the agony of her own child, unresponsive to his caring, creative nature. All Bobby had needed was to be told he was perfectly all right just as he was. How blind, how stupid could she have been? she demanded of herself. What a monumental mistake! (p. 143)

Although these responses provide great fodder for the popular literature, I do not believe that they constitute the majority. In other families, the disclosure solidifies the relationship parents have with their child—and perhaps enhances their mutual intimacy and joy. Griffin, Wirth, and Wirth recounted one of these narratives from a mother.

> Everything that's important in your life that you share with someone you care about, intensifies your relationship. So it's made us closer even though we were close before. But if my daughter hadn't told me, and felt that she had to go her way on this, and I go mine, it would have been a barrier. Instead, knowing and sharing this has enriched our relationship. It also opens up a channel for other talk in the future. If we can share this kind of thing, then there is very little else she can't tell me. Or that I couldn't tell her. (p. 162)

If this hurdle is successfully negotiated and parents arrive at a joint resolution about having a gay family member, other sources of problems loom for a youth—how to tell brothers, sisters, grandparents, and the extended family.

> I also spoke about my sense of alienation from the family gatherings when everyone was together with their spouses and their families. The family gatherings were the worst times for me, because I had someone that I loved too, but I felt I couldn't say "Let me bring my partner. She's the one I really care about." So I felt I was the loner in the family. (p. 161)

A sister of an out gay brother was embarrassed at family gatherings because she wanted her family "to be more average. Like when we get together with the cousins, and they talk about their engagements and having children, and so forth" (pp. 123–124).

Thus far, the limited empirical research has focused on the difficult time youths have deciding whether to disclose to parents. This is seldom an easy decision, primarily because of the tremendous importance that youths place on their parents' acceptance. For example, 93% of college gay men in one study reported that coming out to parents was a "somewhat" to "extremely troubling" event for them. Among support group youths, this combined percentage dropped to 69% among gay males and 61% among lesbians, perhaps because a large percentage of these youths had already disclosed to parents.[12] Although coming out to parents ranked second to worries about AIDS among these support group youths, college gay men ranked it first, just ahead of terminating a close relationship. The fact that half of the college men characterized disclosing to parents as "extremely troubling" corroborates the view that until this event takes place it remains a central concern in the lives of many sexual-minority youths.

Although parents are often crucial players in their child's developing sense of self-worth, they may lose this esteemed position if youths perceive that they cannot confide the most intimate aspects of their life to them, particularly their struggles and feelings of discomfort with their sexuality. Indeed, similar to research with heterosexual youths, out sexual-minority youths reported that parents are critical determinants for current conceptions of the self. Among college gay men, only 15% rated a parent as currently the most important person in their life, considerably less than a gay male friend (54%) and somewhat less than a heterosexual friend who was aware of their sexual identity (25%).[13] In another sample of primarily college students, lesbians ranked relationships with parents 5th and gay men ranked parents 8th of 12 on a list of items important for self-worth. More important for both sexes were same-sex friends, career, academic success, and a romantic relationship; gay men also included physical looks and social life. Despite the *seeming* irrelevance of relationships with parents for current conceptions of self, more than 50% of the college students had at least weekly contact with their mother; contact with father was 33% (for daughters) and 42% (for sons).[14] This level of communication solidifies the significance of parents for lesbian, gay, and bisexual young adults.

Research findings suggest that although youths may find it tricky to counter their parents' heterosexual expectations of them, after coming out, most use other, more contemporary sources of sustenance. This should not imply, however, that they ignore their parents' opinions, especially when under stress. One study intimated that youths actively sought the support of their family when they experienced victimization and that the family extended sustenance when the child was injured or distressed. The family appeared to buffer the adolescent against the harmful effects of victimization, but only if the family support was high and the victimization that the adolescent faced was low.[15]

The effects that disclosure to parents have on a youth's life are not, however, systematically or definitively established. Several investigators have taken the initial findings demonstrating the importance of parents for sexual-minority youths one step further—exploring the effects of disclosure to parents on a youth's self-evaluation. Their findings, however, are not of one accord.

DISCLOSURE AND YOUTHS' SELF-EVALUATION

Research has thus far failed to unequivocally demonstrate that disclosure to parents is a reflection of either a healthy or an unhealthy mental status. Three seemingly contradictory outcomes regarding the relationship between disclosure and mental health have been empirically supported.

First, several studies indicate that those who disclose to parents are more unhealthy. In a study of primarily African American and Hispanic gay and bisexual males seeking assistance from the Hetrick-Martin Institute, those who had attempted suicide were more likely than nonattempters to have disclosed to parents or to have been discovered to be gay. Similarly, youths from urban support groups who had previous suicide attempts were more likely to have disclosed to a nonparent family member, to have positive relations with parents, and to have parents who are aware of their child's sexual orientation.[16] They did not differ, however, from nonattempters in how their parents reacted to the disclosure or in the distress they faced while discussing their sexual orientation with parents. The authors suggested that suicide attempters were more out to parents because the youths were aware of their same-sex attractions from an earlier age, which gave them a longer period of time in which to disclose, or because the youths' past suicide attempts sensitized parents to the reality that their child was suffering from issues directly related to his or her sexual identity. It is possible, however, that a third variable is responsible for the connection: a history of peer harassment drove the youth to both closeness with parents and suicidality.

The second alternative, that youths who disclose to parents score better on measures of psychological functioning, is based on three findings. College men who were open about their same-sex attractions less often feared verbal and physical harassment or worried about telling their parents, presumably because once the men were out, parents provided protection from being victimized, and the stress of withholding ended. One of the best predictors of a male youth's self-esteem in another study was the mother's (but not the father's) knowledge of his same-sex attractions. A third indication of greater psychological health is the finding that youths least likely to think of suicide were those whose mother and father knew their sexual orientation.[17]

Finally, research suggests that disclosure to parents is unrelated to psychological health. Among college men, life satisfaction was unrelated to general openness about being gay. Similarly, in a younger cohort of youths, self-esteem and all clinical scores on the Brief Symptom Inventory were unrelated to whether one was out to parents. In a third study, gay and bisexual men recruited through advertisements in gay publications, bars, social support groups, and university groups who had attempted suicide were no more likely than nonattempters to have disclosed to parents. Finally, among bisexual and lesbian women, parental knowledge and acceptance of their daughter's same-sex attractions were independent of her self-esteem level.[18]

The contradictory nature of these research findings typifies the literature on sexual-minority youths and their families. One major problem is determining directionality of causation. Research findings are generally correlational and thus are not necessarily informative of the causal pathway between disclosure and psychological health. For example, if one assumes that disclosure and psychological health are related, one could just as cogently argue that those who are functioning in a healthy manner are most likely to risk disclosing to family members as to contend that by outing oneself to parents one gains a measure of psychological health. Which comes first—high self-esteem or disclosure to parents—if indeed the two are related? The position taken in the Griffin, Wirth, and Wirth collection of parent narratives supports the earlier developmental genesis of self-esteem. They recount the story of Mike who "loves his parents, and they love him." After a hellish time coming to terms with his sexuality, Mike could finally say, "I am a homosexual, a queer, a faggot. I've always heard it is bad to be one of 'them,' but I know that I'm okay. No one will convince me that I am not" (p. 15). Griffin and colleagues conclude,

> Mike now has a bedrock feeling of self-worth which led to the decision
> to tell his parents. The telling itself was calm and uneventful. . . . His
> sense of well-being gave him the courage to be a leader in the fight for
> gay rights. (p. 15)

This is, however, mere speculation. That is, a satisfying relationship with parents might encourage youths to disclose to them or, perhaps equally likely, their relationship is satisfying because youths have disclosed to them. Perhaps both are true. A third possibility is that disclosure and mental health are connected through a "third" variable. Youths may be psychologically healthy because they grew up in a family context that celebrated being true to one's nature, including disclosing one's sexual self to family members.

The uncertainty of these distinctions is frustrating but indicative of a rich reservoir for future research (see chapter 9). Most basically, the research described above reflects the fact that relatively little is known regarding the youth–parent relationship in its most general terms. What is clear from several studies, however, is that parents are rarely the first person whom sexual-minority youths approach when questioning their sexuality.

FIRST DISCLOSURES

Several studies suggest that most youths come out to friends before family members. A recent Internet study of nearly 2,000 sexual-minority youths between the ages of 10 and 25 (mean = 18 years) revealed that youths were most likely to have disclosed to "my best friend" (76%), "friends at school" (66%), and "friends outside of school or work" (61%). Far behind were mother (49%), brother or sister (38%), and father (36%). In other studies, around 10% of youths first disclosed their sexual orientation to a parent, and when this occurred, it was almost always to the mother. The father was rarely the first person a youth told, although the initial disclosure can be to both parents simultaneously. Only 2 of 194 youths first disclosed to their father in one study.[19]

The first recipient is nearly always a same-age peer. Three quarters of community support group youths and college gay or bisexual men first came out to a friend. In three quarters of these cases, the friend was of the same sex, usually a best friend or someone the youth was dating or had dated. All youths had disclosed to a friend, but less than half had told a parent. A more recent study provides the first indication that the initial person may be another sexual-minority youth, perhaps because other same-sex attracted youths are now visible and hence available to become recipients of first disclosures.[20]

Surprisingly, age of disclosure to parents and how long after first disclosure youths tell parents are not always examined in research investigating the coming-out process. Several studies report that disclosure to parents follows the initial person by as little as 3 months or by more than a year. Even less is known regarding sexual-minority youths' relationships with family members other than parents, especially a youth's relations with siblings, grandparents, aunts, uncles, and cousins.[21]

PARENTAL REACTIONS

Mental health professionals who work with families that have been confronted with the reality of a child's same-sex orientation note that parents often react to the discovery that their child will not be fulfilling their heterosexual dreams with grief and mourning. These parents lament the passing of the child they assumed they had as well as their status as a "normal" family. Parents progress through a series of stages similar to those delineated by Kübler-Ross after the shock of discovering one's own impending death: denial, anger, bargaining, depression, and acceptance.[22]

According to grieving models, parents react in a less-than-ideal fashion after learning of their child's same-sex attractions. Although some eventually arrive at tolerance or acceptance, the literature is not clear about the proportion who make this transition. The process is not an easy one, and a period of uncertainty, disruption and, in more tempestuous cases, chaos characterizes the family.[23] Parent support groups use the inevitability of these grieving stages to help their members understand their feelings. They propose that when youths come out to their parents, a parallel parent "coming-out" process is initiated.[24] According to Daniel Mahoney, parents mourn

> the loss of the heterosexual identity of their child and their hopes,
> dreams and expectations for a traditional life for their lesbian or gay

child; the lack of grandchildren and the special relationship of being in a grandparent role; [and] their perceived lack of success as parents and as individuals.[25]

Empirical research, however, has seldom tested the validity of grieving models against the real-life reactions parents have on learning about the sexual-minority status of their child. Indeed, as will be apparent below, the limited evidence runs counter to these models. In the following pages, a review of germane studies and life history accounts illustrates the limited extent to which parental reactions to a child's disclosures have been investigated. The appropriateness of a model based on a sequential unfolding of grief and acceptance is rejected in favor of an approach that considers the reactions to be an array of *possible* initial responses.

Shock

Shock is one visceral response from parents that most frightens youths. Parents say ("You're not my child") or do (strike the child or sever financial support) things that will forever impair the parent–child relationship. In a national survey of over 400 parents, mostly mothers, just over one third experienced shock when they found out about their child's sexual orientation. In much smaller studies, the most frequent reaction is shock, followed closely by shame, guilt, and acknowledgment. But shock is not a universal reaction to the disclosure, and parents react with emotions characteristic of the full range of the grieving models.[26]

Parents might feel that the world as previously known has ended, resulting in extreme reactions. After being informed by her daughter that she was involved with another woman, one mother offered a dramatic response, "I'm going to kill myself," followed by an "angry insistence that she would never accept such a thing and that no girlfriend of Stacey's would be welcome in her home."[27] A mother of a gay son reported after an argument, "I begged him not to act on it, but he already had. . . . I had a feeling that was about the same as when somebody dies."[28]

Shock might not last a moment in time but occur over a protracted period in which overwhelming emotions intrude into daily life. The revelation is never far from consciousness.

> After reading the letter that Mary wrote telling us that she was gay, I couldn't think of anything else. I went about my daily work, but the thought of Mary's being gay was never out of my mind for an instant. I had difficulty sleeping at night, and the very second that I would wake, the thought would be with me. Over and over I kept thinking, "What are we going to do?"

Another parent felt that the

> word homosexual seemed planted across my forehead for days after
> Matt told us he was gay. It was the first thing I thought about in the
> morning and the last thing I thought about at night. I even dream
> about it.[29]

A parent's shock can come unexpectedly for the child. Stacey felt
guilty that she was ruining her mother's life by living out her selfish desires.
This initial reaction took many years of therapy to heal—helped in part by
the prospects that Stacey and her partner would provide the grandchildren
that her mother always desired.[30] Another young adult, Cathy, decided to
introduce her girlfriend Darlene to her parents, who had emigrated from
Korea, in the context of family inclusion (Darlene is a part of the family)
rather than as a statement of her individual identity.[31] The parents were
stunned and initially refused to recognize the relationship; however, they
kept communications open with their daughter.

Having prior suspicions that a son or daughter is different, unusual,
or not heterosexual, as did Elsie Chung who was quoted at the beginning
of this chapter, often ameliorates the shock value of the disclosure. In one
study, one fifth of fathers and nearly three tenths of mothers reported
suspicions that their son or daughter was gay or lesbian prior to finding out,
although many admitted that they did not want their suspicions confirmed.[32]
To suspect is one thing but to know is quite another. Although Mary Griffith
had many opportunities to observe the effeminacy of her son Bobby, she
was "dumbfounded" when she discovered her son's sexuality. "It was as if
a missile had blown through the roof."[33] Another parent knew but avoided
the inevitable.

> But at that time, I didn't consciously admit to myself that I had any
> idea of what was coming. I think I did know, down deep somewhere,
> but I just wanted to postpone what I perceived as difficult news, if even
> for a few minutes . . . I remember thinking, "Well, this is it. The die
> is cast, and what we feared has come to pass."[34]

One father admitted that he was clueless that his daughter was bisexual
until the fourth "hint." The first was that his daughter Carol did not visit
the family very often; the second, that Carol joined a women's group; and
the third, that she took a gay course.

> Then, one time, she wanted to go to a wedding in Eugene, and when
> I asked her who was being married, she gave me the names of two girls.
> . . . I said, "So I guess I'm to assume that you're gay, then." And she
> said, "Yeah." It wasn't really any big surprise to me because I had had
> too many clues. If you're hanging around with the gay community,

you've got to be gay, don't you? I'm not very smart, but I'm not completely dumb.[35]

The "suspicion" that heightens parents' awareness most often is a child's sex-atypical behaviors or interests, such as working on cars (girls) or playing with dolls (boys). Elsie Chung's son Richard did not appreciate the artistry of baseball. Mrs. Hite's daughter "had always said she really didn't like guys that well. It seemed to me that she went out with them mainly because the other girls did."[36] Another parent was also not surprised when she learned about her lesbian daughter.

> Once when Mary was three years old she asked, "Do I always have to be a girl?" When she was growing up she liked the companionship of boys her age. She always enjoyed athletics even though she was not that good. She was never very interested in dolls. I can still picture her as a little girl with a softball in one hand, a bat in the other, and a toy gun in the holster on her hip.[37]

Mary Griffith knew from an early age that her son Bobby was "different from other boys."

> Bobby was a gentle spirit, almost too good and too obedient, yet endearing and lovable. . . . He was not a cut-up, not given to roughhousing. He was content to be in the house coloring or playing with stuffed animals and dolls. Outdoors, he loved nature and paid more attention to the detail of natural settings than did any of the other boys. Once, at age three or four, he said, "Mom, when I woke up this morning I said good morning to all the trees and the forest."

With age, Bobby expressed his artistic interests through drawing and writing. Yet, Mary "reacted with embarrassment to his girlish way of swinging the bat, the flourish of his hand as he swept his long hair from his forehead, the doll he made for her one Christmas in junior high from scraps of lace borrowed from her sewing basket." In particular, Mary remembered Bobby's early pubertal fascination with the workout guru Jack LaLanne.

> [He] would rise early and sit at the tube for a couple of hours watching the muscular LaLanne go through his routines, then catch reruns after school. Mary noticed that Bobby merely watched, never joined in the routines. It annoyed her. "Bobby," she asked once, "why don't you ever do the exercises?" Bobby reacted with rare anger and walked out of the room.

Bobby's father noticed the same characteristics. Perhaps if he connected with his son by arranging joint "masculine" activities, then Bobby might be saved from homosexuality.

They hiked together on Mount Diablo, a lovely peak not far from their home. That outing was a disaster, most of it spent in silence or stilted conversation. Bobby talked about wanting to be a writer. Bob, strong on the work ethic, tried to discuss strategic career planning. Bobby zoned out, uninterested in the long view. Bob felt he was playing at being a father. Bobby apparently did, too. They both dropped into silence, wordlessly acknowledging that the whole effort was basically phony. After that, the rift between them widened: their interactions became polite, infrequent, awkward.[38]

In Bobby's parents' questioning minds, sex atypicality was associated with homosexuality and hence they were less shocked when their child disclosed to them. Other parents were surprised with the disclosure because their child was *not* sex atypical. "My son was 'all boy' the whole time he was growing up. He liked sports and fishing. He was a good pitcher in Little League." Cathy was "what you would expect a little girl to be. She played with dolls and had crushes on boys. She even dated a lot in high school. She chose to wear dresses and was very feminine."[39]

Beliefs that a child may be lesbian or gay—perhaps less so if bisexual— are often associated with childhood sex atypicality. Indeed, this assumed association has considerable research support, including cross-cultural evidence. Reviewing the literature, researcher Michael Bailey concluded, "To my knowledge no other childhood behavior is as predictive of an adult characteristic as atypical childhood gender identity is of male [and, to a lesser extent, female] homosexuality."[40] Whether and how this information influences parental reactions have not been empirically addressed. That is, do "suspicious" parents, who believe that something might not be "right" with their child's sexuality at a time when the child cannot name her or his sexual identity, modify their initial reactions to their child's disclosure?

Of greater interest, however, is whether shock is a common reaction of parents. A parent's heart may sink, as did Elsie Chung's, but little empirical evidence supports a dramatic, visceral reaction as a common response to a child's disclosure that she or he is attracted to same-sex others.

Denial and Isolation

Another reaction proposed by grieving models is for parents to deny the very information that they have just heard. That is, parents collect themselves sufficiently to realize, however briefly, the severity of their new knowledge and then deny the reality of their child's same-sex attractions. Denial, one of the most primitive psychological defenses, provides a buffer zone, a time for parents to regain their bearings and equilibrium. Their denial is usually an anxious one; perhaps at some level they know the truth but refuse to believe the information, dismiss the child's attractions as only a phase, or search for counterevidence.

Walter Fricke, Aaron's father, held onto the extremely limited counterevidence that his son was not gay. Despite his son's early timidity, femininity, and aversion to sports and his later identity problems when he became secluded from family and friends, gained weight (ballooning to 217 pounds at one point), and befriended "obvious" gay men, Walter remembered times that appeared to affirm his son's heterosexuality. "He had spotted a cute little girl exiting, so he made his way to the door, held it open, and smiled at the girl as she walked by. . . . His actions served as confirmation to me of a budding nine-year-old's impending heterosexuality."[41]

Not uncommonly, parents pretend that their child's self-disclosure never occurred. This is easier to implement if the child discloses at an early age; parents then believe that their early adolescent is just experimenting or in a rebellious phase. Or, by not acknowledging this aspect of their son or daughter, the parents believe that it will disappear. Still others, such as Mary Griffith, believe that the "problem" will readily disappear with the right circumstances. "Well, Ed, there's no doubt in my mind that God can handle this. God will help us, and he will heal Bobby." For his part, Bobby's father believed that his son only had to date more to "help him grow out of it."[42]

Fervent, zealous cultural proscriptions against homosexuality contribute to parents' denial. They have been reared with myths and stereotypes about gay people and the kind of life they are "condemned" to live, believe that homosexuality must play an exaggerated and central feature in their child's life, and are cut off from sources of support and images of positive gay role models. Mary Griffith knew little about homosexuality except what was taught by her church, which was with "overtones of a decadent and carnal secret ritual, a cabal somehow aligned with the satanic, condemned by her Bible and her church." She knew, "You can't love God and be a homosexual."[43]

This isolation from knowledge and support causes parents to feel as if they are the only ones who ever faced the devastation of having heterosexual dreams for a child dashed. One father's only impressions were negative.

> My image was that gays were people who picked up sex in the park. It was dirty and was done by people with strange mannerisms. Then I realized that I, myself, was now associated with gayness. My child was into something that repels a lot of people. I'm now part of it. [44]

Parents may believe that women become lesbians because they had been so hurt by fathers, stepfathers, brothers, and other men that they were unable to trust another man.[45]

It is difficult to assess how common denial is as a reaction to disclosure. In a cross-national survey of parents in a support group for families of lesbian, gay, and bisexual people, the most common initial feeling, reported by nearly three quarters of parents, was fear for the child's future. Other common feelings were sad (64%) and sorry (58%). However, only 35% reported that they "disbelieved" the news. Because the sample consisted principally of White, highly educated, liberal mothers of male children in their 20s and 30s, these findings cannot be generalized to other parents.[46] Perhaps they were too sophisticated to report what many popular accounts accent as a common reaction—anger and rage.

Anger

According to grieving models, denial can last only so long before counterevidence that the child is not going to be heterosexual becomes so overwhelming that a sense of control vanishes. The status quo is inevitably altered, and parents respond in a multitude of angry tones, from agitation to dismay and, in some cases, to rage. How common are these reactions is a matter of dispute. First is evidence from life history accounts.

One motivation for anger is based in the kinds of stereotypes that parents have about what it means to be "homosexual." Walter Fricke's views about gay people were antithetical to his personal values and hence a source of anger directed at his son for being the gay stereotype.

> Gays are, for the most part, irresponsible people who don't pay bills. Most of them have no loyalty to principles or moral values. Certainly not long term. Nothing challenges them, except their next partner. They appear to be happy on the surface, but sad with life in general. They drift into the job they hold rather than pursue it with diligence. They are unimpressed by ordinary persons.[47]

Anger may simply be generalized and irrational. One mother of a lesbian daughter was "filled with both anger at being told and gratitude that she had not told us earlier. Then I would get angry that she hadn't trusted us enough to tell us. My thinking and feelings made no sense at all." The mother and daughter had harsh words, especially after the mother was disapproving of the relationship her daughter and partner were developing. Was she purposely trying to hurt her daughter?

> I think Sarah expected too much too soon. Mark and I almost simultaneously blurted out, "How can we be happy about that? Find a man to love. Then we'll be happy." That was a very cruel thing. I can't speak for my husband, but I was trying to hurt her as she had hurt me. It's nothing to be proud of, a revelation like that, but it's the truth. After that there was no communication for some time.[48]

For these parents, their child has placed them in an awkward position in relation to friends, coworkers, and the community. Mrs. Hite originally worried, "What will people think if they know I've got a daughter that's along that line?" Eventually, however, she concluded, "Well, what the heck. Why do other people matter? They're my kids, and I like them however they are."[49]

These reactions can be mitigated under particular circumstances, such as when a child prepares the parent in advance of the disclosure. Additionally, as a defensive maneuver, parents often search for an external cause for their child's homosexuality, becoming irrationally angry at the perceived perpetrator. A bad second parent, an "alternative" peer group, a university, a gay teacher, or an ex-lover may be imputed. After Paul and Nancy discovered that their deaf son Tim was gay, they tried to find out who had converted Tim. "I know somebody got to you."[50]

Counter to these narratives, research has documented that relatively few parents display fits of rage and anger, physically or sexually abuse their child, reject their daughter or son, or eject the youth from the home after disclosure. Although youths might fear these initial reactions, especially from their father, few receive severe consequences. In a study of gay and lesbian young adults and parents of gays and lesbians (but not the parents of the gay–lesbian sample that was assessed), young adults reported that their parents rarely expressed anger or rejection. The parent sample gave even less credence to these reactions; rejection was the least common reaction both 1 week and 6 months after disclosure. Anger was the second least common reaction; it peaked during the first week after disclosure and then became relatively rare.[51] Guilt, acknowledgment, and acceptance followed shock as the most frequent responses. Compared with the gay and lesbian young adult ratings, the ratings by parents showed that parents experienced higher levels of shock and guilt as well as greater acknowledgment and acceptance. Both samples agreed that mothers felt greater anger and guilt, that fathers were more likely to deny and reject, and that the two did not differ on shame or acknowledgment.[52]

In several other studies, around 5% of youths suffered physical harm from parents or were thrown out of the home once they were open about their sexuality. For example, in a sample of Chicago support group youths, 3% reported that they had been thrown out of the home and were living in shelters or with friends.

Thus, instances of severe forms of parental anger are difficult to document in the empirical literature, although these are certainly the reactions that capture our attention when reported in the popular media. Perhaps more common are milder forms of anger, such as curtness, agitation, and raised voices—or the kind of anger Elsie Chung experienced—"that he didn't trust me enough to let me know sooner."

Bargaining

Bargaining is a parental reaction that attempts to postpone or alleviate guilt parents feel as a result of having a nonheterosexual child. It can also be a bid to eradicate the thought that this has come about because of their poor parenting skills. Religious parents may beseech God for just one supplication, a conversion of the child's sexual orientation, in exchange for promising henceforth to lead an observant life and give homage to religious laws and commandments.

Mary Griffith reassured her son that he need not be homosexual if he just simply prayed harder and tried to lead a better life.

> Bobby, we can beat this. If we trust in God. Homosexuality is curable with God's help. We've seen it on television, remember? It's not a natural thing. God will help you weed it out. Healing through prayer. That's the good news, Bobby.

Later, after Bobby failed to convert and committed suicide, Mary realized that her "bargain" with her son would have denied Bobby's very existence. "Bobby was loved, but was simply not okay. To be acceptable and accepted, he would have to change. It occurred to no one at the time that it might have been the family's responsibility to change, not Bobby's."[53]

Parents thus bargain with their child—renounce this temporary aberration or insanity and they will pretend it never happened, will not cut off financial aid, or will not throw the child out of the house. One father got down on his knees and begged his son not to act on his homosexuality: "You don't know for sure. You're too young" (p. 143).[54]

They ask their daughter or son to tell absolutely no one, perhaps including the other parent, and to never again discuss the issue. Parents then selectively edit details about the child when they are with others; with cryptic references, mysterious glances, and hidden hand signals and head nods, they maintain the family secret and preserve the family's social status. The fewer who know, the safer the parents feel; to them their situation is unique, a grievous burden to bear.

Sometimes the bargains have unintended consequences. Ruth asked her lesbian daughter Marsha not to tell her father "because I figured we'd have to pick her dad up off the floor or the ceiling or somewhere and take him to the hospital" (p. 4). Once Marsha's father found out about his daughter, he "was hurt by the fact that my daughter didn't trust me enough to tell me. I was very disappointed and began wondering just how shallow our relationship had been. Where had I failed? Why was she afraid of me?" (p. 4).

Quite often the "deal" is unrealistic because the child cannot fulfill the parents' wishes and still keep her or his integrity undiminished. The pact necessitates that the parents render their acceptance and love conditional—something a lesbian, bisexual, or gay adolescent might not be willing to tolerate. Parents might also recognize the unfairness of their demands.

> When my son first told me, I said, "I hope you're not going to tell anyone else." Then I began to realize that I couldn't impose that rule on him. We've all taught our children not to lie, yet we're tempted to say to our gay children, "Don't lie exactly, but live a lie." (p. 102)

Research has not addressed the extent to which parents bargain as a reaction to the disclosure. Some parents make pacts with God, fate, the spirits, or themselves and resolve to be good people if this burden were to be taken from them. Some attempt to change the child's sexual orientation, sending their daughter or son to a religious counselor or psychotherapist in futile attempts to proselytize or cure. Although it is not known how frequent these conversion attempts are made, they represent the way in which parents regard their child's sexuality, as a phase or illness, to be undone with the proper antidote. The failure of these secrecy efforts and negotiated settlements blocks potential sources of growth and support for all involved.

Depression

Depression and, in some cases, resigned tolerance are considered to be the anger experienced earlier turned inward, a guilt parents feel for not recognizing their child's "condition" early enough to change the outcome or for being the kind of parent that "causes" a child to be gay or lesbian. Walter Fricke believed that all parents feel this initial self-blame.

> When dealing with your child's homosexuality, it is difficult to avoid turning to God and asking whether this is the result of parental mistakes you made while raising your child. This is the heaviest burden that all parents of gay people have to carry at one point or another. . . . You think it is your fault because that is what you have been taught to think.[55]

Don's mother was struck with a devastating feeling that she had failed as a parent: "It's a blow to your ego to think you're such a competent and perceptive parent and then find you have a gay child. You think you know your child so well and then find out he knew this at a young age and didn't tell" (p. 5). In the same volume a father exclaimed, "Oh my God. My daughter is a pervert!" He felt that he must be "the world's biggest failure. Every father I saw was better than I was" (p. 7).

These parents appear to be susceptible to the now discredited psychoanalytic notion that homosexuality is caused by "family disturbance," especially close, dominating mothers and distant, aloof fathers. Parents read articles or books that cite bad parenting as the problem.

They said that there was usually an absent or rejecting father and a domineering, seductive, or binding kind of mother. I thought about how much Jack worked when the kids were small and the fact that I was the one who stayed home and took care of them. I twisted it all around and said, "Yes, maybe we are like that." (p. 7)

One mother second-guessed the time she spent with her son. "I was always much closer to Brian than my husband was. Brian and I often used to sit around and talk. I thought, 'Was that unhealthy?'" (p. 22).

Because Helen thought that homosexuality was a mental disorder, the fact that her son Craig was gay came as a "crushing blow—a gut level failure."

"What am I here for if I did this to my baby?" I didn't know how, I didn't know when, I didn't know what I had done. I searched through his growing-up years, but nothing seemed to fit what I'd read. Still, the finger of guilt pointed straight at me. . . . I wanted someone to take away my pain. I wanted someone to ease my burden of guilt. (p. 145)

Helen's pain became nearly unbearable as she "suffered the death of a dream." She grieved for her son, her role as an incompetent mother, and the opinions of her neighbors. Her mood bordered on depression because of her considerable shame and humiliation.

Several parents from Griffin, Wirth, and Wirth's collection reflected on their initial shame. One considered the worst scenario, "What if people gasped! What if they whispered behind my back! What if! What if! What if!" (p. 82). One couple found it

really hard for us to enjoy any kind of social contact with people for awhile. We got so tired of hearing people ask if Tony has a steady girl friend. Those kinds of questions were hard. So we withdrew inside ourselves. (p. 80)

Another parent recognized that "for the first time in my life I was ashamed of one of my children. I had always thought my kids were better than other kids that I knew. My feeling of superiority quickly vanished" (p. 82).

To thwart this perceived public scandal, parents distance themselves from formerly close relationships or isolate themselves and thus preempt the ostracism they feel will inevitably come. Mrs. O'Keefe had no friends who have gay children, "or if they do, they would never in the world admit it."[56] She could not tell anyone, or "I didn't tell anyone for quite a while, because you don't open a conversation with, 'Oh, by the way . . .'"

Some parents demand further evidence and with each piece of the puzzle in place they experience greater loss and sink into a deeper depression. Thoughts might turn to suicide. "It hurt so bad there were times when I was sorry I had to wake up and face the day. I often wished I could die" (p. 79). One set of parents believed that their world had come to an end.

"We had guilt feelings and thought that everything we had done with our children was wrong. For a brief time, we even thought about mutual suicide" (p. 2). Other parents consider the logical alternative: "Sometimes I even thought it would have been easier if my daughter were dead. I didn't think this very long or very often, but it does show how upset I was" (p. 75).

This internal grieving and sense of isolation could last for moments or much longer. One mother did not want her husband to know; she thus suffered alone for months. "I just went to pieces—inside, not outside—because Tom still didn't know. I thought, 'I can't go to work.' Then I'd think, 'I have to go to work. The bills are going to accumulate whether Jerry's gay or not. The world is going to go on too' " (p. 79). Another parent found herself crying after 6 months. "At first I cried all the time. I'd be at work and all at once I'd tear up. I wondered if I would ever get over that sad feeling" (p. 79).

One common source of grieving is for what might have been if the child had "chosen" heterosexuality—grandchildren. Stacey's mother, a Holocaust survivor, had to cope with her extended family's extermination, the illness and death of her son, and now the prospects that her only surviving daughter is a lesbian, and hence, in her eyes, barren.[57] Another parent had high hopes for her son to be the ideal family man. "I would certainly like to have normal family relationships with grandchildren. This part of it is a real heartbreaker" (p. 50).

Another potential depressing moment for parents is when their child's disclosure compels them to question their own sexuality. "For awhile there I wondered if homosexuality ran in the family. I have a brother who is gay and a son who is gay. I thought, 'Am I sure I'm totally straight?' It very definitely bothered me for awhile" (p. 84). Helen, Craig's mother, learned about "latent homosexuality" while in school.

> My understanding of this term was that a person could be sitting on an unknown time bomb that could go off if just the right set of circumstances came about. ... I remember thinking, "I have good women friends. Does that mean I could be gay?" (p. 145)

Finally, family members experience angst because the chaos centered on their sexual-minority child raises uncomfortable or long-suppressed issues surrounding the stability and health of the parents' marriage and of the family. One couple from Griffin, Wirth, and Wirth discovered the weakness of their marriage after the disclosure.

> Not only was my mothering role tested and found wanting, but so was my role as a wife. On top of thinking I had failed my son, I felt like I had failed John because his son was not the all-American boy. I needed John to reassure me about this and to convince me I wasn't a failure to him and the rest of the family. He couldn't do that. At that time

he wanted me to assure him that he wasn't a failure as a father. Neither of us could make the pain go away for the other. . . . For a while it looked like our world was full of roses. But after we found out that Craig was gay, all the roses wilted. Everyone in the family had a hard time. We went from having a perfect family image to being just a bunch of individuals who peeped out at each other and said, "Why don't you make it better for me?" None of us was able to do that. We all wanted to, but everyone was too weak. (p. 146)

Although several researchers have shown that one quarter to one half of parents experience guilt, shame, and depression after being told about their child's homosexuality, these emotions appear to decline quite rapidly after the first week of disclosure.[58] Any lingering sadness might reflect the kind of life they believe their child must now endure. Indeed, the most prevalent emotion experienced by parents—reported by three in four in one study—was fear for the child, ranking just ahead of sadness.[59] These two reactions may reflect the societal stereotypes parents endorse as they imagine only the sexual aspects of being gay and not appreciate the romantic, supportive relationships that their child is likely to develop with other gay women and men. They further believe that their child will inevitably be lonely in his or her old age or face discrimination that will result in leading a clandestine life. Within these reactions resides an acknowledgment and perhaps an acceptance that their son or daughter is not going to be heterosexual.

Acceptance

Acceptance with or without resignation is a process that might be instigated by support groups, educational materials, mass media presentations, and chance occurrences. Within months of her son's disclosure, Elsie Chung had joined Parents, Families, and Friends of Lesbians and Gays (P-FLAG), drawing "tremendous emotional support" such that the "experience of talking to one another about our fears and concerns opened our minds and allowed us to accept our children for what they are and respect whatever lifestyle they chose." Perhaps it is merely the passage of time and the growing recognition that all past efforts have failed—their child is still gay! Moving beyond their own pain and guilt, they consider the plight of their child.

I would like to think that I was kind and understanding as I reached out towards Craig, but I wasn't. I was hurting, and I didn't understand why it hurt so much. I didn't think about Craig for a good while. In fact it was some time before I realized what a traumatic experience he had gone through . . . There were no guideposts . . . We were in trouble, but we didn't know where to turn.[60]

According to progressive stage models, the parents' horrific imaginings have been replaced with a happier child, and this realization is sufficient for parents to move beyond their guilt, shame, anger, and sadness. Cathy's Korean parents gradually became more accustomed to her partner, in large part because they acknowledged the significance of the relationship for the happiness of their daughter. William Queen knew he had no choice but to accept his daughter: "And I know at this point if I had made any stink about it, I would have lost her completely. And I think that Carol's just a little more important than that." [61]

Acceptance thus implies that parents have minimized their mourning, willing to acknowledge and accede to their circumstances: as parents of a gay child. The child has a new negotiated place within the family with more honest and open lines of communication and understanding. Bernice Queen was ultimately grateful for the revelation of her daughter's same-sex attractions. "I think Carol and I are closer now that she's told me, because she is able to be more honest with me." [62]

These developments encourage a son or daughter with a romantic partner to bring that person to family gatherings. Stacey's mother grew to appreciate her daughter's new partner, Maggie, in part because she could see how happy Stacey was. Maggie became a regular at family dinners. However, Stacey's mother still wanted to keep her daughter's sexuality a private, family matter until Stacey demanded Maggie be invited to a family wedding. This family crisis was finally resolved and now the mother hugs and kisses Maggie and is willing to entertain the thought of the couple having a child, her grandchild. [63]

Their story illustrates an important point: Initially acceptance can be tentative or quickly revoked. Walter Fricke learned to accept his son's sexuality but he still "prayed for change."

> There are two sides of me and both of them hope that deep within Aaron there is a latent heterosexual screaming to be free. . . . My son, however, disregards, as a waste of his time and my money, my standing offer to hire a female prostitute for him. My other side is the God-fearing side, which believes that when all else fails, try the strength of prayer. This is the side that goes to bed at night praying that Aaron will not be gay the next morning . . . If my attitude toward Aaron's homosexuality seems harsh and nonaccepting, consider that there are parents who, in their desire to change their gay children, do not stop at prayer.

Walter Fricke learned, however, to pray for himself and his own self-understanding. Before his death he had learned the limitations of his prayers to convert his son: "At this point, if Aaron became heterosexual overnight, I would seriously consider entering the priesthood." [64] Another parent too realized that full acceptance had not yet been achieved.

I would like to get to the point where I can feel that her homosexuality is as natural for her as heterosexuality is for me. I'd like to get to the point where homosexuality isn't all that important in our life with Mary. It won't be easy to do, and I don't know if it'll come to that. But I hope so.[65]

Over time parents become increasingly desensitized to the issue and are thus "given the opportunity to restructure expectations and goals for the future life course of their children by revealing to others that they have a gay or lesbian child."[66] The movement toward acceptance of their child's sexual orientation is motivated in part by the fear that if they do not they will lose their place in the child's life. William Queen's ultimate statement of acceptance was somewhat less than a ringing endorsement of his daughter—but it was a very pragmatic one.

I look at the thing this way. I could have lost my daughter to drugs, to destructive political activism, to any number of things. I could have lost her and not had her anymore in my life. If I had been bullheaded and said, "no daughter of mine is going to be like that," I really could have lost her. No different than if she had been in a car wreck. I don't think being gay is all that big a thing.

His wife, Bernice, assumed a similar perspective: "Much better that than pregnant. I sincerely felt that. I love Carol very much, and if this was to be her lifestyle, I knew that I was going to have to learn to accept it."[67]

Some parents understand that relatively little of significance has really changed. After "sitting by myself," one parent quickly realized her only option.

He's still the same son who asked me for five dollars this morning; he's the same boy who was here for breakfast, who took out the trash, who wrecked the car. His sexuality doesn't have anything to do with his integrity or his ability to love or his worth. . . . I would have lost the things we have shared and all our closeness. He's a loving, honest, and wonderful son. He told me he was gay, and he's still a loving, honest, and wonderful son. I don't think you have to be anything but full of love to learn to accept your child.[68]

Parents may even take an active stance to improve the status of all sexual-minority youths. After the death of her son, Mary Griffith began a 3-year process of learning about her son through reading his personal diaries, talking to other gay people and their parents in P-FLAG, and self-analysis. Through the reconsideration of her religious beliefs, she came to accept her gay son and her role in his death. Mary Griffith became an activist, speaking to both gay and nongay groups, appearing on television and other media sources to talk about her experiences, marching in pride parades, and trying to save other families from the heartache she experienced. She had a story to tell, "the power of ultimate truth," to "touch a life early on, before a tragedy happens."[69]

In research studies, youths have been less likely than parents to perceive a positive change in parent–child relationships following disclosure. Parental acceptance levels, as reported by youths, range from 10% to 70%, depending on factors such as sex of the child and the parent, whether youths are drawn from support or collegiate groups, how long after the coming out that acceptance levels are stressed, and year of data collection. The lowest level was given to gay and bisexual male hustlers and street youths in a study conducted nearly 15 years ago: Just 10% of fathers and 21% of mothers were positive about the youths' homosexuality. Most studies, however, report acceptance levels to be just under 50% for both parents, although few differentiate acceptance levels in accordance to how long parents have known. One would expect that the longer parents have known, the higher the acceptance level.[70]

Parent samples, however, report higher levels of acceptance. Following disclosure, over 80% of mothers and 60% of fathers in one study noted improvement in their relationship, over 20 percentage points higher than that reported by youths. In another sample of parents, 97% stated that they now accept their gay child. This acceptance level is likely higher than that reported by youths because of the selective nature of the sample—parents in a support group, the mandate of which is to assist parents in reaching acceptance. One would expect that parents who gravitate toward joining a support group that has the explicit goal of gaining acceptance of their child's sexuality would be more likely to benefit from it than the average parent. Although this study is limited in its generalizability, it offers hope to parents that although they might struggle with their child's homosexuality, eventually family unity can be achieved. A sample of young adult men supports this view: Relationships with mother and father often deteriorated following disclosure but significantly improved thereafter.[71]

Although the research is optimistic regarding the eventual outcome of family relationships once disclosure has taken place, questions of biased samples remain. Parents are selected from support groups and not from representative populations of parents with sexual-minority children. One could argue that parents not in support groups are those least likely to accept their gay child and that youths who disclose do so because they are fairly certain that their parents will eventually come to accept them. Youths without this expectation are not included in research because they have not yet disclosed. They may realistically expect not acceptance but rejection from their parents.

The range of first parental reactions to the disclosure of their child that he or she is gay or lesbian is vast. In the limited samples available, some parents reject their child and react with shock and denial; many others respond with knowing inevitability, acceptance, and unconditional love. They do not *move* toward acceptance as stage models propose; a positive response *is* their initial reaction. This characterized Elsie Chung, who had fleeting notions that her son was not heterosexual. Once he confronted her, she knew the information to be true. If shock, denial, anger, bargaining, and depression follow disclosure, they are certainly not universal, and perhaps not even the most common, features of parental reactions.

Much of the popular literature is not so optimistic. Because of preexisting negative attitudes and stereotypes of gay people and the heterocentric assumption that heterosexuality is normative and best, it maintains that few adults initially or eventually attain the status of a proud, self-professed parent of a gay, bisexual, or lesbian child. This is why social science research is needed—to document that such parents exist and to discover how they achieved this status. Despite a few leads, relatively little is known about those who reach this pinnacle.

FACTORS INFLUENCING PARENTAL REACTIONS

Factors that predict how parents react once their child discloses to them are poorly understood. One speculation is that their response depends on *how* they discover the child's same-sex attractions—whether they are told directly by the child or indirectly by others. However, one study found that whether parents were told directly by the son (two thirds of mothers and one half of fathers), someone else told them, they asked their son, or they discovered by accident was insignificant in determining parental reactions.[72] This issue deserves additional study, especially if focused on whether parents had suspicions about their child's sexual orientation prior to disclosure.

Another speculation is that the child's age when the discovery occurs determines parental reactions. Parents are more likely to deny the permanence of the acclaimed sexual identity if their child discloses to them at a young age; if their child discloses during young adulthood, then their denial is less likely to occur because they feel a diminished ability to control the youth's sexuality. Although research has not tested the hypothesis that reactions of parents are more severe if the child is not an adult—largely because too many other intervening variables, such as sample recruitment bias, are not controlled—it is an important consideration when reviewing research.

Alternatively, the age of the parents might influence their reactions to having a gay or lesbian child. In one study, young parents were more likely to accept their sexual-minority child and have a positive relationship with her or him. Perhaps young parents are more likely to be influenced by modern conceptions and visibilities of sexual minorities. A good parent–youth relationship was predicted by considerable telephone calls or personal visits while the youth was in college and the high self-esteem of the youth. Because the study was cross-sectional, issues of causation are questionable. That is, perhaps frequent contact was the result and not the cause of the positive relationship.[73]

Other factors that have been proposed to affect parental reactions to gay, lesbian, and bisexual family members include the family culture, parenting style, religion, ethnicity, and sex-role orientation.[74] None of these variables have been systematically pursued. Most modestly, research has investigated the attributes and beliefs of parents that might influence their reactions to the disclosure of their child. One suggested that adherence to "traditional family values" is an important variable predicting whether a youth comes out to parents and what the outcome of disclosure will be. Adolescents who grew up in a family that embraced the values of traditional religion, marriage, and children were most likely to perceive that their parents were disappointed with their homosexuality. However, youths in the disapproving families were not therefore less likely to come out to their parents or to do so at a later age.[75] In another study, gay sons who reported that their mothers had traditional sex role attitudes and that their fathers rated high on religious orthodoxy perceived that their parents were more accepting of them. The authors speculated that the parents' emphasis on family unity enhanced their ability to come to terms with the family crisis.[76]

By contrast, mothers who appeared to have the most difficulty accepting their lesbian, bisexual, or gay child were those least exposed to the external world. For example, few nonaccepting mothers in one study had a college education, friends other than their extended family, or worked outside the home; most were relatively inexperienced with gay people, culture, and politics. The author argued that parents with these characteristics often retain rather robust dogmatic stereotypes, misconceptions, and conservative values, all of which impede their ability to accept their child as nonheterosexual.[77] Many parents report that prior to their child's disclosure they had no understanding of homosexuality, held common stereotypes, or never thought about it. Some parents—whether this number is small or large is difficult to determine—become barricaded in negative reactions and are unable to move forward.[78]

Additionally, a small-scale study concluded that non-White families may regard homosexuality negatively, contributing to increased rejection or intolerance of gay, lesbian, and bisexual family members. The notion that homosexuality is a White disease coupled with traditional religious beliefs, adherence to sex-role stereotypes, enmeshed kinship ties, and expectations that all children marry and procreate leads some ethnic-minority parents to deny their child's homosexuality. The authors focused, however, on "success stories"—occasions in which youths were not rejected and the parent–child relationship remained intact. These parents ameliorated the conflict between their cultural values and homosexuality by "(a) prioritizing and reinterpreting values, (b) finding precedents, and (c) externalizing the blame." These flexible, open-minded parents willingly communicate to keep their family intact.[79]

Although sexuality is generally not discussed in traditional Asian homes, the Asian American parents of lesbian daughters and gay sons interviewed in one study were aware of but chose to ignore gay issues prior to their child's disclosure. They acknowledged that the openness of modern North American culture allowed their child to express what was already present. Many equated traditional sex-role reversals with homosexuality but did not thus participate in verbal debasement or assume judgmental attitudes toward their child. Initially, they admitted, their attitudes were not positive and they worried about what neighbors and community members would think of them. Although few believed that their ethnic community would accept their child, the importance of maintaining family cohesion led many of these Asian American parents to ultimately accept and advocate for their sexual-minority children.[80]

Far too little is known about factors that predict parental acceptance or rejection of sexual-minority children. The important variables may be characteristics of the parent, the child, their relationship, or the larger culture in which they live. Research that addresses these issues holds great promise to help us understand how to improve the relationships sexual-minority youths have with their parents.

CONCLUSION

Elsie Chung, whose story began this chapter, would appear to be an exception because she did not pass through the stages of shock, denial, anger, bargaining, depression, and acceptance once she discovered her son's same-sex attractions. Research has generally agreed with Elsie's experience rather than with grieving stage models. Although these stage-like emotions are present in some parents after they discover the news, what has not been addressed by investigators is the process by which shock evolves into acceptance, or the existence of these responses as discrete developmental events that predict which parents will respond in which way.

Only one published study has attempted to trace the evolution of parental reactions—and this from the perspectives of both youths and parents. Adital Ben-Ari studied 32 Israeli gay and lesbian young adults and 27 parents who were not, however, the parents of the youths in the study. Both the youth and parent samples reported temporal drops in shock, denial, shame, guilt, anger, and rejection and marked increases in acknowledgment and acceptance, which ranked as the most frequent reactions from both mothers and fathers one month following disclosure. Over time the rank ordering of responses, which was nearly identical for the young adult and parent samples, changed relatively little. These results indicate that if the grieving stages were experienced, they characterized only some parents, were in mixed or random order for others, and only briefly if at all existed for the majority of parents. For example, denial and anger were never more common than acceptance. Thus, although most parents accepted their child, little is known about how they got there or how much time they took.[81]

This study highlights major problems with current research. Although all empirical findings reported in this chapter are important in understanding parent–child relationships, they do not directly address the process that parents experience in accepting their sexual-minority child. Clearly, under-researched but potentially a rich source of information is a clarification of the sequences of reactions and emotions that parents have after discovering their child's same-sex attractions and the factors influencing this process. Particularly noteworthy are indications that parents characterize themselves as more accepting than sexual-minority youths report their parents to be; that despite reports in the mass media, extreme negative reactions and rejections appear to be relatively rare; and that most parents accept their child relatively quickly after disclosure. In general, considerably more needs to be known about both the short- and long-term consequences of coming out for both youths and parents.

Except for those who propose that parents experience Kübler-Ross's grieving stages after learning of their child's same-sex attractions, I know of no alternative model that helps us to understand the process by which parents come to internally resolve the reality of having a sexual-minority child. Empirical support for grieving models is so limited as to cast doubt as to their validity. At the most general level they may be correct in that with time parents react with less shock, denial, shame, guilt, anger, and rejection and with more acknowledgment and acceptance. However, although these negative responses may be common first reactions, many parents initially acknowledge and accept the child's same-sex attractions. Only a very broad developmental pattern can be discerned from the available data, not a conceptualization of a universal five-stage grieving model.

From my reading of the popular literature and the empirical data, parental reactions to the disclosure appear to be individualized, diverse, and complex. For example, one young woman in the present study reported that her mother had multiple and complex reactions to her daughter's sexuality. In this regard, she may be the most typical of all mothers.

▽   At first she was fine, struggling to hold back tears. Then proud of me for being able to stand up and be different, but then disappointed that I had not told her first. She was worried about AIDS and if I would be hurt by it, but then said it probably wouldn't affect me because I'm bisexual, unless I had sex with boys, which was what she wanted, but not if it meant getting AIDS. She had read that bisexual men were at risk for AIDS and that bisexual women often hooked up with bisexual men. She cried, we shared, we talked, she ignored the issue—all of this over a week. She was struggling with it, I knew this—nothing extreme like kicking me out or disowning me, but the end of her dreams.

   She was just trying not to be judgmental, although she was judgmental. She values heterosexuality and she wants me to be that, but she also wants me to be what I am, my own person. She wants me to be a politician and she is afraid this would hurt. She wants to protect me. I reminded her that I'm black and a woman and I've dealt with so much in my life. Can't I handle this one more thing?

It would be exceedingly difficult to characterize this mother's response in terms of universal grieving stages.

In a small-scale interview study, Daniel Mahoney noted that although disclosure by a child creates an initial period of crisis, subsequent movement is dependent on particular, at times random, events. The chance of these events, such as the outcome of telling a friend or attending a P-FLAG meeting, occurring is difficult to predict and determined largely by individual style and motivation rather than by some inherent epigenetic grieving sequence.[82]

The implication of these observations and the research reviewed in this chapter is that the critical events that shape the timing and manner by which parents reconstruct their new identity as parents of a sexual-minority child do not depend on an unfolding of a universalized process but on idiosyncratic or random developmental processes or events. Thus, the most accurate generalization that can be made regarding the factors that portend the reaction of parents to the news is "unpredictable," hardly an ideal scientific position. However, a positive prior relationship between parents and child may be the best omen for a healthy resolution. Even well-educated, liberal parents can initially react negatively and with rage, especially if they have a poor relationship with their child, while conservative, religious parents who love their child unconditionally can respond in an accepting, loving manner when informed about their child's same-sex attractions. Perhaps more important than factors that predict the initial response to disclosure are those that lead to healthy long-term relationships.

CHAPTERS THAT FOLLOW

In the next four chapters, I "deuniversalize" these issues to present what is currently known from the empirical literature and from a sample of sexual-minority youths about the ways in which families negotiate the process of having a sexual-minority member. The narratives are from two studies I conducted concerning identity development among youths with same-sex attractions.[83] The appendix briefly describes these studies.

One point needs to be emphasized. To some readers, the youths' interpretation of their parents' reactions cited in the narratives might appear unfair or insensitive. For example, some youths perceive a mother's or father's reaction to the news of their sexuality as ill-wrought when in fact the parent is struggling to respond as best as she or he can. The parent still loves the child and wants to be supportive but has stereotypes and considerable fear for the child's difficult future. These potential differences in construction of events reflect some of the second-guessing that sexual-minority members may have about out-group motives, as well as the differing perceptions of statements that often characterizes minority–majority issues more generally. Again, I want to emphasize that the narratives are the perceptions of youths and may or may not reflect the realities of their family members.

ENDNOTES

[1] From her article, My son is gay . . . , on page 1 in the May 9, 1998, newsletter, *Hokubei Mainichi* (San Francisco).

[2] Page 416 in Hancock, K. A. (1995). Psychotherapy with lesbians and gay men. In A. R. D'Augelli & C. J. Patterson (Eds.), *Lesbian, gay, and bisexual identities over the lifespan: Psychological perspectives* (pp. 398–432). New York: Oxford University Press.

[3] Borhek, M. V. (1988). Helping gay and lesbian adolescents and their families: A mother's perspective. *Journal of Adolescent Health Care, 9,* 123–128.

[4] Anderson, D. (1987). Family and peer relations of gay adolescents. *Adolescent Psychiatry, 15,* 163–178.

[5] D'Augelli, A. R. (1991). Gay men in college: Identity processes and adaptations. *Journal of College Student Development, 32,* 140–146.

[6] See examples in Borhek, M. V. (1993). *Coming out to parents: A two-way survival guide for lesbians and gay men and their parents* (2nd ed.). Cleveland, OH: Pilgrim; Coleman, E., & Remafedi, G. (1989). Gay, lesbian, and bisexual adolescents: A critical challenge to counselors. *Journal of Counseling and Development, 68,* 36–40; Fairchild, B., & Hayward, N. (1998). *Now that you know: A parent's guide to understanding their gay and lesbian children* (3rd ed.). San Diego, CA: Harcourt Brace; Heron, A. (Ed.). (1994). *Two teenagers in twenty: Writings by gay and lesbian youth.* Boston: Alyson; and Strommen, E. F. (1989). "You're a what?": Family

member reactions to the disclosure of homosexuality. *Journal of Homosexuality*, *18*, 37–58.

[7] Page 1 in MacDonald, G. B. (1983, December). Exploring sexual identity: Gay people and their families. *Sex Education Coalition News*, 5, pp. 1, 4.

[8] One example of a popular writer making this claim is Woog, D. (1997, October 28). Our parents. *The Advocate*, pp. 23–34.

[9] Page 174 in Martin, A. D., & Hetrick, E. S. (1988). The stigmatization of the gay and lesbian adolescent. *Journal of Homosexuality*, *15*, 163–183.

[10] Griffin, C. W., Wirth, M. J., & Wirth, A. G. (1986). *Beyond acceptance: Parents of lesbians and gays talk about their experiences.* Englewood Cliffs, NJ: Prentice Hall. Quotes for the next few pages, unless otherwise designated, are from this volume.

[11] The story of the Griffith family, especially of Mary Griffith, and the suicide of their gay son and brother, is recounted in Aarons, L. (1995). *Prayers for Bobby: A mother's coming to terms with the suicide of her gay son.* New York: HarperCollins.

[12] See data presented in D'Augelli, A. R. (1991). Gay men in college: Identity processes and adaptations. *Journal of College Student Development*, *32*, 140–146; and D'Augelli, A. R., & Hershberger, S. L. (1993). Lesbian, gay, and bisexual youth in community settings: Personal challenges and mental health problems. *American Journal of Community Psychology*, *21*, 421–448.

[13] D'Augelli, A. R. (1991). Gay men in college: Identity processes and adaptations. *Journal of College Student Development*, *32*, 140–146.

[14] Savin-Williams, R. C. (1990). *Gay and lesbian youth: Expressions of identity.* Washington, DC: Hemisphere.

[15] Hershberger, S. L., & D'Augelli, A. R. (1995). The impact of victimization on the mental health and suicidality of lesbians, gay and bisexual youth. *Developmental Psychology*, *31*, 65–74.

[16] D'Augelli, A. R., & Hershberger, S. L. (1993). Lesbian, gay, and bisexual youth in community settings: Personal challenges and mental health problems. *American Journal of Community Psychology*, *21*, 421–448; and Rotheram-Borus, M. J., Hunter, J., & Rosario, M. (1994). Suicidal behavior and gay-related stress among gay and bisexual male adolescents. *Journal of Adolescent Research*, *9*, 498–508.

[17] These results are reported in D'Augelli, A. R. (1991). Gay men in college: Identity processes and adaptations. *Journal of College Student Development*, *32*, 140–146; D'Augelli, A. R., & Hershberger, S. L. (1993). Lesbian, gay, and bisexual youth in community settings: Personal challenges and mental health problems. *American Journal of Community Psychology*, *21*, 421–448; Pilkington, N. W., & D'Augelli, A. R. (1995). Victimization of lesbian, gay, and bisexual youth in community settings. *Journal of Community Psychology*, *23*, 34–56; and Savin-Williams, R. C. (1990). *Gay and lesbian youth: Expressions of identity.* Washington, DC: Hemisphere.

[18] Studies include D'Augelli, A. R. (1991). Gay men in college: Identity processes and adaptations. *Journal of College Student Development*, *32*, 140–146; D'Augelli, A. R., & Hershberger, S. L. (1993). Lesbian, gay, and bisexual youth in community settings: Personal challenges and mental health problems. *American Journal of Community Psychology*, *21*, 421–448; Remafedi, G., Farrow, J. A., &

Deisher, R. W. (1991). Risk factors for attempted suicide in gay and bisexual youth. *Pediatrics, 87,* 869–875; and Savin-Williams, R. C. (1990). *Gay and lesbian youth: Expressions of identity.* Washington, DC: Hemisphere.

[19] The Internet study was conducted by !OutProud!, The National Coalition for Gay, Lesbian, Bisexual and Transgender Youth and Oasis Magazine. (1998, March). *!OutProud!/Oasis Internet Survey of Queer and Questioning Youth.* Studies confirming the rarity of first disclosure to parents include D'Augelli, A. R., & Hershberger, S. L. (1993). Lesbian, gay, and bisexual youth in community settings: Personal challenges and mental health problems. *American Journal of Community Psychology, 21,* 421–448; D'Augelli, A. R. (1998, February). *Victimization history and mental health among lesbian, gay, and bisexual youths.* Paper presented at the Society for Research on Adolescence, San Diego, CA; and Herdt, G., & Boxer, A. (1993). *Children of Horizons: How gay and lesbian teens are leading a new way out of the closet.* Boston: Beacon Press.

[20] D'Augelli, A. R., & Hershberger, S. L. (1993). Lesbian, gay, and bisexual youth in community settings: Personal challenges and mental health problems. *American Journal of Community Psychology, 21,* 421–448; Dubé, E. M. (2000). The role of sexual behavior in the identification process of gay and bisexual males. *Journal of Sex Research, 37,* 123–132; and Savin-Williams, R. C. (1998). *". . . and then I became gay": Young men's stories.* New York: Routledge.

[21] D'Augelli, A. R., & Hershberger, S. L. (1993). Lesbian, gay, and bisexual youth in community settings: Personal challenges and mental health problems. *American Journal of Community Psychology, 21,* 421–448; D'Augelli, A. R. (1998, February). *Victimization history and mental health among lesbian, gay, and bisexual youths.* Paper presented at the Society for Research on Adolescence, San Diego, CA; Savin-Williams, R. C. (1998). *" . . . and then I became gay": Young men's stories.* New York: Routledge; and Sears, J. T. (1991). *Growing up gay in the South: Race, gender, and journeys of the spirit.* Binghamton, NY: Harrington Park Press. For discussion of relationships with nonparent family members, see Demo, D. H., & Allen, K. R. (1996). Diversity within lesbian and gay families: Challenges and implications for family theory and research. *Journal of Social and Personal Relationships, 13,* 415–434; and Savin-Williams, R. C., & Esterberg, K. G. (2000). Lesbian, gay, and bisexual families (pp. 197–215). In D. H. Demo, K. R. Allen, & M. A. Fine (Eds.), *The handbook of family diversity.* New York: Oxford University Press.

[22] Kübler-Ross, E. (1969). *On death and dying.* New York: MacMillan.

[23] These stages are described in many sources, including the following: Anderson, D. (1987). Family and peer relations of gay adolescents. *Adolescent Psychiatry, 15,* 163–178; Bernstein, B. (1990). Attitudes and issues of parents of gay men and lesbians and implications for therapy. *Journal of Gay and Lesbian Psychotherapy, 1,* 37–53; Borhek, M. V. (1993). *Coming out to parents: A two-way survival guide for lesbians and gay men and their parents* (2nd ed.). Cleveland, OH: Pilgrim; Bozett, F. W., & Sussman, M. B. (1989). Homosexuality and family relations: Views and research issues. *Marriage and Family Review, 14,* 1–7; Brown, L. S. (1988). Lesbians, gay men and their families. *Journal of Gay and Lesbian Psychotherapy, 1,* 65–77; DeVine, J. L. (1984). A systemic inspection of affectional preference orientation and the family of origin. *Journal of Social Work and Human Sexuality, 2,* 9–17;

Martin, A. D. (1982). Learning to hide: The socialization of the gay adolescent. *Adolescent Psychiatry*, *10*, 52–65; Myers, M. F. (1982). Counseling the parents of young homosexual male patients. *Journal of Homosexuality*, *7*, 131–143; Pearlman, S. (1992). Heterosexual mothers/lesbian daughters: Parallels and similarities. *Journal of Feminist Family Therapy*, *4*, 1–21; Robinson, B. E., Walters, L. H., & Skeen, P. (1989). Response of parents to learning that their child is homosexual and concern over AIDS: A national study. *Journal of Homosexuality*, *18*, 59–80; Strommen, E. F. (1989). "You're a what?": Family member reactions to the disclosure of homosexuality. *Journal of Homosexuality*, *18*, 37–58; Tremble, B., Schneider, M., & Appathurai, C. (1989). Growing up gay or lesbian in a multicultural context. *Journal of Homosexuality*, *17*, 253–267; and Wirth, S. (1978). Coming out close to home: Principles for psychotherapy with families of lesbian and gay men. *Catalyst*, *3*, 6–22.

[24] See discussion of this possibility in Boxer, A. M., Cook, J. A., & Herdt, G. (1991). Double jeopardy: Identity transitions and parent–child relations among gay and lesbian youth. In K. Pillemer & K. McCartney (Eds.), *Parent–child relations throughout life* (pp. 59–92). Hillsdale, NJ: Erlbaum.

[25] Pages 24 and 25 in Mahoney, D. (1994). *Staying connected: The coming out stories of parents with a lesbian daughter or gay son.* Unpublished master's thesis, University of Guelph, Guelph, Canada.

[26] See, respectively, in Robinson, B. E., Walters, L. H., & Skeen, P. (1989). Response of parents to learning that their child is homosexual and concern over AIDS: A national study. *Journal of Homosexuality*, *18*, 59–80; and Ben-Ari, A. (1995). The discovery that an offspring is gay: Parents', gay men's, and lesbians' perspectives. *Journal of Homosexuality*, *30*, 89–112.

[27] This case is taken from Iasenza, S., Colucci, P. L., & Rothberg, B. (1996). Coming out and the mother–daughter bond. In J. Laird & R. Green (Eds.), *Lesbians and gays in couples and families* (pp. 123–136). San Francisco: Jossey-Bass.

[28] Page 1 in Griffin, C. W., Wirth, M. J., & Wirth, A. G. (1986). *Beyond acceptance: Parents of lesbians and gays talk about their experiences.* Englewood Cliffs, NJ: Prentice Hall.

[29] Pages 76 and 77 in Griffin, C. W., Wirth, M. J., & Wirth, A. G. (1986). *Beyond acceptance: Parents of lesbians and gays talk about their experiences.* Englewood Cliffs, NJ: Prentice Hall.

[30] Iasenza, S., Colucci, P. L., & Rothberg, B. (1996). Coming out and the mother–daughter bond. In J. Laird & R. Green (Eds.), *Lesbians and gays in couples and families* (pp. 123–136). San Francisco: Jossey-Bass.

[31] Liu, P., & Chan, C. S. (1996). Lesbian, gay, and bisexual Asian Americans and their families. In J. Laird & R. Green (Eds.), *Lesbians and gays in couples and families* (pp. 137–152). San Francisco: Jossey-Bass.

[32] Robinson, B. E., Walters, L. H., & Skeen, P. (1989). Response of parents to learning that their child is homosexual and concern over AIDS: A national study. *Journal of Homosexuality*, *18*, 59–80.

[33] Page 76 in Griffin, C. W., Wirth, M. J., & Wirth, A. G. (1986). *Beyond acceptance: Parents of lesbians and gays talk about their experiences.* Englewood Cliffs, NJ: Prentice Hall.

[34] Page 2 in Griffin, C. W., Wirth, M. J., & Wirth, A. G. (1986). *Beyond acceptance: Parents of lesbians and gays talk about their experiences.* Englewood Cliffs, NJ: Prentice Hall.

[35] Pages 87 and 88 in Baetz, R. (1980). *Lesbian crossroads.* New York: William Morrow.

[36] Page 119 in Baetz, R. (1980). *Lesbian crossroads.* New York: William Morrow.

[37] Page 26 in Griffin, C. W., Wirth, M. J., & Wirth, A. G. (1986). *Beyond acceptance: Parents of lesbians and gays talk about their experiences.* Englewood Cliffs, NJ: Prentice Hall.

[38] The last four quotes are on pages 44, 46, 52, and 95 in Aarons, L. (1995). *Prayers for Bobby: A mother's coming to terms with the suicide of her gay son.* New York: HarperCollins.

[39] Both quotes are on page 27 in Griffin, C. W., Wirth, M. J., & Wirth, A. G. (1986). *Beyond acceptance: Parents of lesbians and gays talk about their experiences.* Englewood Cliffs, NJ: Prentice Hall.

[40] Page 76 in Bailey, J. M. (1996). Gender identity. In R. C. Savin-Williams & K. M. Cohen (Eds.), *The lives of lesbians, gays, and bisexuals: Children to adults* (pp. 71–93). Fort Worth, TX: Harcourt Brace College.

[41] Page 62 in Fricke, A., & Fricke, W. (1991). *Sudden strangers: The story of a gay son and his father.* New York: St. Martin's Press.

[42] Pages 76 and 78 in Aarons, L. (1995). *Prayers for Bobby: A mother's coming to terms with the suicide of her gay son.* New York: HarperCollins.

[43] Pages 52 and 53 in Aarons, L. (1995). *Prayers for Bobby: A mother's coming to terms with the suicide of her gay son.* New York: HarperCollins.

[44] Page 152 in Griffin, C. W., Wirth, M. J., & Wirth, A. G. (1986). *Beyond acceptance: Parents of lesbians and gays talk about their experiences.* Englewood Cliffs, NJ: Prentice Hall.

[45] Baetz, R. (1980). *Lesbian crossroads.* New York: Morrow.

[46] Robinson, B. E., Walters, L. H., & Skeen, P. (1989). Response of parents to learning that their child is homosexual and concern over AIDS: A national study. *Journal of Homosexuality, 18,* 59–80.

[47] Page 24 in Fricke, A., & Fricke, W. (1991). *Sudden strangers: The story of a gay son and his father.* New York: St. Martin's Press.

[48] Both quotes on page 78 in Griffin, C. W., Wirth, M. J., & Wirth, A. G. (1986). *Beyond acceptance: Parents of lesbians and gays talk about their experiences.* Englewood Cliffs, NJ: Prentice Hall.

[49] Page 120 in Baetz, R. (1980). *Lesbian crossroads.* New York: William Morrow.

[50] Page 3 in Griffin, C. W., Wirth, M. J., & Wirth, A. G. (1986). *Beyond acceptance: Parents of lesbians and gays talk about their experiences.* Englewood Cliffs, NJ: Prentice Hall.

[51] See, respectively, Herdt, G., & Boxer, A. (1993). *Children of Horizons: How gay and lesbian teens are leading a new way out of the closet.* Boston: Beacon Press; and Ben-Ari, A. (1995). The discovery that an offspring is gay: Parents', gay men's, and lesbians' perspectives. *Journal of Homosexuality, 30,* 89–112.

[52] Ben-Ari, A. (1995). The discovery that an offspring is gay: Parents', gay men's, and lesbians' perspectives. *Journal of Homosexuality, 30,* 89–112.

[53] Pages 77 and 98 in Aarons, L. (1995). *Prayers for Bobby: A mother's coming to terms with the suicide of her gay son.* New York: HarperCollins.

[54] Unless noted otherwise, all quotes with page numbers are from Griffin, C. W., Wirth, M. J., & Wirth, A. G. (1986). *Beyond acceptance: Parents of lesbians and gays talk about their experiences.* Englewood Cliffs, NJ: Prentice Hall.

[55] Page 94 in Fricke, A., & Fricke, W. (1991). *Sudden strangers: The story of a gay son and his father.* New York: St. Martin's Press.

[56] Page 135 in Baetz, R. (1980). *Lesbian crossroads.* New York: Morrow.

[57] Iasenza, S., Colucci, P. L., & Rothberg, B. (1996). Coming out and the mother–daughter bond. In J. Laird & R. Green (Eds.), *Lesbians and gays in couples and families* (pp. 123–136). San Francisco: Jossey-Bass.

[58] Ben-Ari, A. (1995). The discovery that an offspring is gay: Parents', gay men's, and lesbians' perspectives. *Journal of Homosexuality, 30,* 89–112; and Robinson, B. E., Walters, L. H., & Skeen, P. (1989). Response of parents to learning that their child is homosexual and concern over AIDS: A national study. *Journal of Homosexuality, 18,* 59–80.

[59] Robinson, B. E., Walters, L. H., & Skeen, P. (1989). Response of parents to learning that their child is homosexual and concern over AIDS: A national study. *Journal of Homosexuality, 18,* 59–80.

[60] Page 144 in Griffin, C. W., Wirth, M. J., & Wirth, A. G. (1986), *Beyond acceptance: Parents of lesbians and gays talk about their experiences.* Englewood Cliffs, NJ: Prentice Hall.

[61] Page 88 in Baetz, R. (1980). *Lesbian crossroads.* New York: William Morrow.

[62] Page 92 in Baetz, R. (1980). *Lesbian crossroads.* New York: William Morrow.

[63] Iasenza, S., Colucci, P. L., & Rothberg, B. (1996). Coming out and the mother–daughter bond. In J. Laird & R. Green (Eds.), *Lesbians and gays in couples and families* (pp. 123–136). San Francisco: Jossey-Bass.

[64] Pages 92–93 and 95 in Fricke, A., & Fricke, W. (1991). *Sudden strangers: The story of a gay son and his father.* New York: St. Martin's Press.

[65] Page 74 in Griffin, C. W., Wirth, M. J., & Wirth, A. G. (1986). *Beyond acceptance: Parents of lesbians and gays talk about their experiences.* Englewood Cliffs, NJ: Prentice Hall.

[66] Pages 217–218 in Herdt, G., & Boxer, A. (1993). *Children of Horizons: How gay and lesbian teens are leading a new way out of the closet.* Boston: Beacon Press.

[67] Page 96 and 91 in Baetz, R. (1980). *Lesbian crossroads.* New York: William Morrow.

[68] Page 17 in Griffin, C. W., Wirth, M. J., & Wirth, A. G. (1986). *Beyond acceptance: Parents of lesbians and gays talk about their experiences.* Englewood Cliffs, NJ: Prentice Hall.

[69] Page 145 in Aarons, L. (1995). *Prayers for Bobby: A mother's coming to terms with the suicide of her gay son.* New York: HarperCollins.

[70] Remafedi, G. (1987). Male homosexuality: The adolescent's perspective. *Pediatrics, 79,* 326–330. For example, recently this was reported to be 51% for

mothers and 27% for fathers (sex differences for adolescent participants and length of time parents have known were not reported); see D'Augelli, A. R., Hershberger, S. L., & Pilkington, N. W. (1998). Lesbian, gay, and bisexual youth and their families: Disclosure of sexual orientation and its consequences. *American Journal of Orthopsychiatry, 68,* 361–371.

[71] Ben-Ari, A. (1995). The discovery that an offspring is gay: Parents', gay men's, and lesbians' perspectives. *Journal of Homosexuality, 30,* 89–112; Cramer, D. W., & Roach, A. J. (1988). Coming out to mom and dad: A study of gay males and their relationships with their parents. *Journal of Homosexuality, 15,* 79–91; and Robinson, B. E., Walters, L. H., & Skeen, P. (1989). Response of parents to learning that their child is homosexual and concern over AIDS: A national study. *Journal of Homosexuality, 18,* 59–80.

[72] Cramer, D. W., & Roach, A. J. (1988). Coming out to mom and dad: A study of gay males and their relationships with their parents. *Journal of Homosexuality, 15,* 79–91.

[73] Savin-Williams, R. C. (1990). *Gay and lesbian youth: Expressions of identity.* Washington, DC: Hemisphere.

[74] Bozett, F. W., & Sussman, M. B. (1989). Homosexuality and family relations: Views and research issues. *Marriage and Family Review, 14,* 1–7; Morales, E. S. (1989). Ethnic minority families and minority gays and lesbians. *Marriage and Family Review, 14,* 217–239; Newman, B. S., & Muzzonigro, P. G. (1993). The effects of traditional family values on the coming out process of gay male adolescents. *Adolescence, 28,* 213–226; Strommen, E. F. (1989). "You're a what?": Family member reactions to the disclosure of homosexuality. *Journal of Homosexuality, 18,* 37–58; and Tremble, B., Schneider, M., & Appathurai, C. (1989). Growing up gay or lesbian in a multicultural context. *Journal of Homosexuality, 17,* 253–267.

[75] Newman, B. S., & Muzzonigro, P. G. (1993). The effects of traditional family values on the coming out process of gay male adolescents. *Adolescence, 28,* 213–226.

[76] Cramer, D. W., & Roach, A. J. (1988). Coming out to mom and dad: A study of gay males and their relationships with their parents. *Journal of Homosexuality, 15,* 79–91.

[77] Pearlman, S. (1992). Heterosexual mothers/lesbian daughters: Parallels and similarities. *Journal of Feminist Family Therapy, 4,* 1–21.

[78] Ben-Ari, A. (1995). The discovery that an offspring is gay: Parents', gay men's, and lesbians' perspectives. *Journal of Homosexuality, 30,* 89–112; Boxer, A. M., Cook, J. A., & Herdt, G. (1991). Double jeopardy: Identity transitions and parent–child relations among gay and lesbian youth. In K. Pillemer & K. McCartney (Eds.), *Parent–child relations throughout life* (pp. 59–92). Hillsdale, NJ: Erlbaum; Muller, A. (1987). *Parents matter: Parents' relationships with lesbians daughters and gay sons.* Tallahassee, FL: Naiad Press; and Robinson, B. E., Walters, L. H., & Skeen, P. (1989). Response of parents to learning that their child is homosexual and concern over AIDS: A national study. *Journal of Homosexuality, 18,* 59–80.

[79] Page 262 in Tremble, B., Schneider, M., & Appathurai, C. (1989). Growing up gay or lesbian in a multicultural context. *Journal of Homosexuality, 17,* 253–267.

[80] Hom, A. Y. (1994). Stories from the homefront: Perspectives of Asian American parents with lesbian daughters and gay sons. *Amerasia Journal, 20*, 19–32.

[81] Ben-Ari, A. (1995). The discovery that an offspring is gay: Parents', gay men's, and lesbians' perspectives. *Journal of Homosexuality, 30*, 89–112.

[82] Mahoney, D. (1994). *Staying connected: The coming out stories of parents with a lesbian daughter or gay son.* Unpublished master's thesis, University of Guelph, Guelph, Canada.

[83] The completed one is my 1998 book, " . . . *and then I became gay:" Young men's stories* (New York: Routledge) and the planned manuscript is tentatively titled, " . . . *and then I kissed her:" Young women's stories.*

4

DAUGHTERS AND MOTHERS

Pam

Mom was the second person I told, about 3 months after I told my best friend—the one I had the crush on. I felt it was important because this was my first committed relationship in my life, the real thing after so many false starts and bummed realities. And of course I wanted to share it with her; if I brought my girlfriend home, well, she'd have to know. I mean she would know no matter what I said because she knows me like no one else, and I just can't keep secrets from her. We share everything and always have.

I brought Jen over, the same weekend that I wanted to tell her, for support in case Mom freaked out or I needed someone to calm me. So the first night Jen and me were talking in my bedroom and the walls are really thin, some kind of plywood, and I think Mom figured it out, maybe at least with the conversation that we had; at least I hope it wasn't because of the sex we had! I was 17 and Mom knew that Jen and me had been together a lot during the last month and that I had stayed over at her house and now here she was over a lot at other times.

I was super nervous, though Jen told me to just come out and tell her, but I couldn't go to school so I called Mom at work and she asked if there was anything I wanted to tell her. I said in as normal of a conversation tone as I could that I was "with" Jen and that I liked her; that we were dating. She said she was happy for me and that it was very fine. I told her that it was very strong and that I didn't know if it would ever happen again. She asked how it was compared with my relationship with Scott and I told her it was 10 times more intense, though Scott and I were still good friends. And she was very understanding, saying that it only happened once for her as well, and supportive, almost casual, not shocked. Later she told me, "I had suspected it since you were 10. It's a good thing if you're okay with it."

She has remained as I would have suspected—supportive, very supportive. I felt she already knew because she's so liberal socially and politically and she seems to have a special relationship, almost like a straight gaydar, with gay people. She has had this special relationship with a gay man friend—the only other man beside my father that she says that she has ever loved, a man my father was jealous of and wouldn't let visit the home. He recently died, maybe of AIDS, and she was very upset with it, really out of it, crying, depressed—maybe the only man she really loved. She saw him whenever she could for many years before he died. One interesting "warning" she gave me was saying, "You don't have to identify yourself as lesbian, but you do have a choice if you want to be monogamous." I wonder if that was related to his death. That I was shocked by!

She likes my Jen and is even okay with the commitment ceremony we've planned for next August, except she wants us to wait because we're so young and she wants us to be for sure. She wants us to live together first to make sure of our commitment—just like a hetero couple! She and Dad will pay for the ceremony and will play whatever role we want for them in the ceremony, like giving away the bride or groom—whichever we decide.

Nancy

One of my college friends was visiting me at home during the summer, and while I was at work one day she e-mailed a friend on my mom's computer, only something went wrong and so she did not send it. It related how bad my mother was going to react to the news that I was queer. When she [my mom] got home that night and read her e-mail and saw the unsent message she went ballistic, only I was unaware, didn't know what was going on. She was maybe most upset because the e-mail bashed her for being the kind of mother who won't be supportive of her daughter. She is screaming at me and gives me a month to leave the house, and I'm just floored. She said how much I disrespected her and that I was not worthy to live there and how all my friends weren't any good. And I'm just trying to figure out what's wrong! She finally tells me about the e-mail, which I didn't know about.

She gets a little calmer and asks me if it's true, and it never occurred to me to deny it because we share everything, and I said that it was. She starts giving me ultimatums and says I can't return to Smith [College] for my sophomore year but I have to go to the local community college or the University of Connecticut and live at home. For a month I was in trauma, wondering if I'd get to go back to school, and really just shocked at how Mom reacted to all of this. I didn't expect her to love the fact that I'd not be having babies, but I never thought she'd take away my college education! So I started calling everyone I knew and gay organizations to raise money for my college education. I wasn't panicking because somehow I knew I was going to go back to Smith and be with all my friends.

At the time, anyways, I was going to therapy with them [parents] about our generally bad recent relationships, and we talked about it and that helped some. Mom agreed to let me go back to Smith but put conditions on me returning—like losing weight, dating males, and growing my hair long. As if any of those had anything to do with anything! So I agreed for peace, knowing I wasn't going to do any of those things. She is still not so great, but a little better.

We used to be best friends and then we moved to the point of her not even wanting to see me. Now we've moved to a different place, in part, so we can talk again about anything, except about gay issues. I want to talk to her about my girlfriend, and so once when I asked her if I could talk to her about some problems we were having, and she said absolutely not. I don't want to rock the boat until after I graduate, so I keep a low profile. You know she's from a rural, conservative area, and there were always lots of racial and homophobic slurs in her home. She's still trying, but she has a ways to go.

Wendy

Well, no, and no plans to tell her. She is very traditional Catholic woman; she probably only slept with one man in her life, my dad. She hasn't seen much of the world but spent her life in her kitchen and her home. She is strong person who had difficult life, and she clings to her Catholic faith to get by. She's from small town in North Dakota and did not finish schooling so she could marry Dad. She had no real young adulthood or career and not exposed to things that most people have.

We've never been real close. She wanted me to succeed, I guess, but she also couldn't understand why I didn't want her life, why I had to go so far away to college, why I don't come home more often. Maybe she felt like I rejected her in some way. We're okay now at least, but I've moved away from her, her life, her religion. She'd say my lifestyle was wrong, sick, confused, not because she knows but she'd be parroting these lines from her Bible. Not that she would know but she's been taught these things by her religion. That's the bottom line, always is, every issue, doesn't matter what it'd be about. She'd say these ridiculous things, at least ridiculous to me, and then we'd argue and she'd be hurt because daughters are not supposed to rebuke their mothers. I can't argue with her because I can't stand to see her hurt, and she shows it a lot. She knows that and that's her defense.

Once, not long ago, when I was home after undergraduate, I decided to open up her mind and plant the seed of idea, about gay friend of mine who was having lots of problems with family. This family was lot like ours, a point I knew she'd get. They were kicking him out because he was gay, putting him out on streets. He tried to live with friends, but didn't work out. He attempted suicide and was now in hospital. She was very compassionate toward him, and I knew she'd be. But she did not speak about him being gay though I told her this was what it was about. Just plant seed because he too is Catholic and comes from large family. I think she knows family so can identify with them. That was Step One, but I don't know when I'll do Step Two.

In her own way she wants me be strong, independent, freer than her. But for me to be that way may threaten her just too much. I just can't predict how she'd react. She can't disown me or ignore me because her religion won't allow that. I may never tell her, leading my East Coast life and her, well, the Midwest life.

We expect close, intimate bonds between mothers and daughters, and a recent survey of youths' relations with parents documents that most daughters believe that they have excellent relationships with their mothers.[1] Whether this attachment and intimacy are maintained once a daughter informs her mother that she will not be replicating her mother's heterosexuality is unknown because few researchers have addressed it. For Pam, this mutual trust was solidified following her disclosure; Nancy's mother, however, was overwhelmed by the news and reacted in a destructive fashion. Wendy, who does not have an intimate relationship with her mother, has long-standing doubts about her mother's ability to handle disclosure—and she is unwilling at the present time to test the accuracy of her knowledge.

THE RELATIONSHIP BEFORE DISCLOSURE

Scientifically, little, if anything, is known about the unique relationships young women with same-sex attractions have with their mothers prior to the disclosure of their sexuality. Researchers Bell, Weinberg, and Hammersmith reviewed the pre-1970s research and identified only a few small-scale, clinically oriented investigations.[2] Their study, conducted with lesbian and heterosexual adult women recalling feelings they experienced two to four decades earlier, reported that same-sex oriented women more often recollected negative, hostile relationships with their mother, characterized by lower levels of warmth, communication, and identification and less desire to be like their mother. Other than this 30-year-old study, little scientific evidence exists contrasting the relationships same-sex and other-sex oriented women have with their mother.

When quizzed about their childhood relationship with their mother, the young women I interviewed describe a variety of bonds, as might be expected. Three themes emerge: relationships that are supportive, distant, and conflictual.

Supportive Relationships

The vast majority of the young women are similar to Pam and Nancy in that they have warm, supportive, and intimate childhood familiarity with their mother, and this closeness and trust often encourages them to disclose to their mother. "Well, I wanted to share it with her and, well, she'd have to know. So did I really have a choice?" Young women frequently speak about this intimacy—how regularly they talk about common concerns and how central this relationship is to their sense of self and well-being.

∇   We've always been very close, very close, and talk about everything. No secrets from her! She was this way with her mother and sisters. I tell her everything that is going on for me, and I always will. I can't imagine it being any other way. If she has problems then we talk; if I have, we talk—or we talk about other people's problems!

This gave me hope in coming out to her. Shortly thereafter I told her I was dating Naomi because I wanted to share it with her and why Barrett disappeared from our home and Naomi appeared. But you know, she seemed to know it before I did!

This familiarity between mother and daughter can border on merger or enmeshment and lead the daughter to not disclose in order to establish boundaries between them. One daughter fought to maintain some sense of independence.

∇   We are great friends, and she would deal with it well. We are not as close as she wants us to be, but too much for me. She's always had me as a confidante, and I've not wanted it to be so much.

If they were to be as intimate as the mother desired, then the daughter would have to disclose. "I've tried to separate us. We look alike and have the same mannerisms. I want at least one secret from her!" Another youth, trying to recover from falling in love "with the woman I couldn't have," decided that she could not also cope with her overprotective mother if she were to share with her why she was "so depressed."

∇   I love her, but she is very overprotective, and this interferes with our relationship. She just doesn't let things go, and she goes where I don't want her. I think I'll never tell her because it would just make it more difficult—but she keeps asking what is wrong, all these questions. I know I'll tell her and then somehow expect her to take care of it all.

Distant Relationships

Although most daughters report a high level of intimacy with their mother, notable exceptions can be found, including relations that are distant and formal. Wendy felt that she and her mother have never been close; they live in two different worlds. One youth commented, "The issue would never come up. We don't usually talk about sex or anything personal so it would seem a little weird to talk about it. It would take awhile because she is a very private person."

Young women with a remote mother–daughter relationship sometimes find it difficult to predict their mother's reactions. One daughter, an Asian American, who just became aware of her attractions to other women, does not believe that the superficial relationship between her and her mother could withstand such shocking news.

∇   It's all so new, and I have no idea how she'd react, but probably not good because it'd be out of the blue for her. I just can't fathom it, and she couldn't either. She has not reacted well when I don't date an educated Asian man.

Conflictual Relationships

The mother–daughter relationship ranges from the supportive to the conflictual, the latter of which can occasionally escalate into true abuse. Fewer than 10% of the mothers are described as abusive by their daughters. In all cases of severe conflict, alcohol or mental illness is a prominent precursor, persuading daughters to elect silence or to disclose at a distant, "better" time.

∇   I never realized it growing up that she was addicted to alcohol and other substances all her life. There was a time when I took care of her after she passed out in the evenings. She and Dad were emotionally abusive to each other and me. She could be quite mercurial, manic one moment and depressed the other. I walked tippy-toed all the time. She just wasn't there for me.

For the vast majority of the young women, disclosing to their mother is the most important developmental milestone after self-labeling. By and large, they agree with the young woman who, on reflecting why she now has a positive sense of self as a sexual minority, simply said, "The most important thing was acceptance from Mom."

WHETHER MOTHERS ARE TOLD

Few mothers of sexual-minority women fail to recognize that their daughter has same-sex attractions. Among current cohorts of adult sexual-minority women, up to 90% believe that their mother knows or suspects; among younger women, the rate is about 80%.[3]

Nearly two of three young women, or 63% of the interviewed youths, had come out to their mother. This is somewhat lower than what is reported in research conducted during the past decade with lesbians and bisexual adolescents in urban support groups.[4] Although it is difficult to separate the effects of cohort from the unique recruitment venues of this study, the evidence supports the position that young women today are more likely than earlier generations to disclose to their mother and to do so at an earlier age.

Only once in my interviews did a youth recant her disclosure following an unexpected maternal hostility. She retracted the lesbian statement and is currently waiting for a better time, if one should ever arise, to tell her mother.

∇   I knew growing up that she never wanted to deal with sex issues, especially past puberty, so we never had this what-the-blood-is-all-about talk. She is very immature about sex. She always seemed frightened by the topic. Call me naïve, but I somehow thought she could handle the information, so I told her I was a lesbian. She was so negative, hurt, so I told her I was just kidding, and she seems to have believed me. I have no desire to hurt her, to cause her pain. I hate it that she assumes that I'm heterosexual.

Although this story reflects two common themes for remaining closeted observed in several of the narratives—daughters do not want to hurt their mother and the fear of what she might do if she were to find out—it does not highlight the most common.

REASONS NOT TO TELL

Little empirical data exist explicating the reasons young lesbians and bisexual women decide not to disclose to their mothers. In the present sample, among the 37% of nondisclosers, one half report that it is not a good developmental time—they are not ready to tell their mother or they feel their mother is not ready to hear the information. Nearly one quarter have not yet "got around to telling her." Others have not disclosed because they do not want to hurt her or because of their mother's fervent religious beliefs or ethnic identification; only rarely do they report that they fear negative reactions. No one suggested a lack of closeness as a reason not to disclose. This last point will assume heightened significance when daughters' relationships with their father are discussed in the next chapter.

Not the Right Developmental Time

Most daughters recognize that eventually they must tell their mother, or that she "already has to know" or "will know by some power she has as a mother." Their relationship is too close not to tell her. Reflecting on whether she plans to tell her mother, one young woman sighed, "I never got around to it. I mean, she must know. She knows everything about me!" If the daughters do not come forth with the information, then the mothers might force the issue. Some daughters suspect their mother really knows but "is just forcing, even daring, me to tell her. You know, like she's been acting very strange lately. She like makes these slightly homophobic jokes, and it bothers me. Why doesn't she just say it!?" Another notes that her mother makes jokes, in a serious way, "that half my friends are gay."

In response to such "subtle" pressure, most daughters eventually come out. Those who do not most often cite as the reason, "the time is not yet right," for her, the mother, or their relationship. One young woman had the golden opportunity to disclose, but at the last moment she diverted the conversation. The time was not right for her because she had just started the process of exploring her sexuality and was not prepared to confront the task of exposing herself to her mother.

▽ I almost did. She asked me last summer why most of my friends were gay! She then told me about her friend's lesbian daughter and wanted to connect me up with her, as a "friend" she added at the last moment. Then she very haltingly says, "I've been meaning to ask you, are you, are you, are you . . . you know. It'd be okay with me."

I had the opportunity! I didn't jump. So I didn't say "yes" or "no," just, "Don't worry." She'll feel like I lied to her by omission when I eventually tell her. She'll be so mad at the lie. It'll change our relationship. I'll have to educate her, and then she'll be fine. She wouldn't shout at me but avoid it by focusing on the lie.

Why didn't I tell her when I had the chance?! It's just too new for me. I want to be more sure, to know this is really my fate. I can't say I am and then take it back!

Or, daughters perceive that the time is not right for their mother. She simply will not tolerate nonheterosexuality, or she will make subtle, or perhaps not so subtle, homophobic remarks that reveal her personal views about homosexuality. Occasionally, the lack of respect runs both ways.

▽ Once I tried to start a conversation with her to get her feelings about such things, talking about this bisexual girl I met. And she said, "Bisexuals don't exist." This floored me, so I asked what she meant, and she said that it was all just a phase—"All women have this." If I told her about me she'd say, "Don't be so silly." She'd not take me seriously but would just be annoyed. She always thinks I'm "silly" and that she knows the ways of the world when she really is the naïve one. Who ever told her that bisexuals don't exist? She's been listening to some weird people or thoughts in her head.

Have Not Gotten Around to It

A second reason for not coming out to one's mother is typified by the youth who said, "I'd be willing to. She'd be very positive, but I have no plans to tell her because there's not reason to." That is, these youths have yet to discover a reason to disclose or they have simply "not gotten around to it." When probed as to why they have not done so, these young women could not articulate a reason. It is not that they expect a negative reaction or that they are not close to their mother; most feel that their mother will be neutral at worse and most likely positive.

∇   I'd have no problem telling her, but it just hasn't happened yet. I was thinking of telling her maybe before college. My mom would still love me and won't disown me. She's not comfortable with homosexuality, but she still loves me.

When one reads further into their accounts, several of these young women are motivated in part by a desire not to hurt their mother. This constitutes the third most frequent reason for not disclosing.

Wants Not to Hurt Her

Daughters also do not disclose because to do so would hurt their mother or cause her to worry. They loathe the thought that they might be responsible for causing her pain. Perhaps she has had a difficult life, so why give her one more thing about which to worry?

∇   My mother is always worrying about random things. Like if I was to go skydiving she'd like worry. She worries so much, like whether Dad will keep his job, if the stock market will fall, if her friends will reject her—like there is no point in adding more to her life. She would be okay with it—like not disown me or anything. She'd accept me, tell relatives, and then ask them if they thought she'd done anything wrong. She'd like worry about it destroying my professional life and my political life. So I don't like tell her.

Youths do not want to be saddled by the guilt of their mother's self-blame or worry about her worrying.

The following bisexual daughter has the perfect setup—a great relationship with a liberal, open, and pro-gay mother. Yet, she remains closeted because she cannot bear hurting her mother by revealing that she has not been the perfect daughter.

∇   This is the ridiculous thing—that I haven't told her. My parents are these liberal, hippy parents, and I am 99% sure she won't have any problem with it. So why don't I tell her? Don't know, except I haven't, and no deadline works. I just don't want to think about it. She knows everything about me, my sexual encounters—well with guys—and just everything. So why can't I tell her?! I've tried hinting, but she just won't take the hint. She's had gay friends. She'd probably just say something like, "Go exercise the heterosexual side of yourself."

Well, she probably knows anyway, so I'll probably just confirm it over Christmas. Vaguely she has to know. Like I'll say little things, like I took a women's studies class so when they bought my little brother trucks I told them they ought to buy dolls, unless of course she was afraid he'd grow up to be gay! She said, "Of course you're right," and she bought the dolls and told me, "I don't care what my kids are as long as they are happy."

That should be enough, right? Yet, she'll be sad at night, and I wonder if she's sad because I'm gay. She'll be okay in front of me, but when I'm not looking she looks sad. She feels guilt and sadness over so much that has happened to me. How could I do this to her? I've had so many girl crushes, and if a girl talks to me I won't tell her about it. Yet, I dated a guy for 2 weeks while in California, and I called home and told her I was dating this cute guy. I felt so guilty when she was so happy for me. Why would I tell her that and not about the girls I have crushes on? Why hurt her?

She tells me absolutely everything about her life, and she thinks I tell her everything, and generally I do, but about this, well, no. My god, she marched in the '60s for civil rights and then women's rights, but not for gay rights. Is that the reason? Is it that I don't trust her because she didn't march for gay rights? I just can't be responsible for failing her. She's just been the perfect mom, and I've not been the perfect daughter. No, if she had marched for gay rights I still couldn't tell her. But over Christmas I'll tell her. This is my deadline—so call me next New Year's.

Mother's Ethnic and Religious Objections

Similar to Wendy, some youths prefer not to reveal their same-sex attractions because they know their mother's cultural identification or religious beliefs will preclude them from being supportive. Closely knit ethnic families may pressure daughters to marry within the ethnic community, have children, and contribute to the community's growth and solidarity. To counter these ethnic and religious issues is a very daunting task.

∇   Her ideas are very Chinese, and her plan for me is to meet a nice Chinese boy and marry, have two children, keep house, and be there when he gets home every night. She's from the old school of Chinese life and will remain that way. Nothing changes her, at least until her mother dies. I had trouble with her even when dating a Jewish boy. I would not have her approval, and it would be difficult. When I tell her she'll say I decided to do this and I can decide not to do this. She'll tell me to remember my grandmother and why I choose to hurt her.

∇   I've begun to test the waters. I asked how she likes *Ellen* and she does, but when she saw the interview with her she said it was not meant to be. God did not create this. This was a good indication to me of how she would react.

I've hinted that I like a girl, and she knows about my special bonds to women, but she does not realize what this really means. I have a very close relationship with her. There is no point of telling her unless I had a very serious relationship and wanted to settle down with her. She'd be furious, disgusted a lot. She was born in Cuba, and her only knowledge is that it's bad. It'd be hard to explain to her as a good thing.

∇   I wouldn't [tell my mom] for two reasons. One, if I did I would be permanently grounded with no contact with my friends. She already suspects something, so I can't go on sleepovers. She thought something might be going on so me and my friends couldn't see each other for 2 months. I'm involved in Green Peace, but she thinks it's a lesbian front organization because so many feminists are in it, so she won't let me go to meetings because she's afraid I'll meet the lesbian community.

Two, they would blame my sister [a lesbian]. I'd not be allowed to talk to her or her friends. Like when my sister is here Mom makes sure our doors are open all the time. Is she afraid we'll have sex or that she would convert me?!

My mother is extremely dysfunctional. My sister is the only one who has really understood me, and I've needed that safety zone. I feel stripped of my privacy. Mom would give me the "you are going to hell" bit. She'd cry and pray and make it very difficult for me. She'd say the rosary for me. She can't say more than five sentences without Jesus or Mary in it. She pushes her morality on others. I have zero respect for her and no tolerance, and I don't hide it.

These cultural and religious inhibitions encompass several of the other reasons—fear of negative reactions, fear of hurting their mother, not developmentally the right time—but have, in addition, the unique problem that these reasons are wrapped in strongly felt maternal ethnic and religious traditions.

Fear of Negative Repercussions

Although fear of negative repercussions is a common theme in the coming-out literature, it is rarely expressed in my interviews with these young women. Several youths, however, believe that their mother might hurt herself or them, physically, mentally, or financially, if she were to know. If daughters are fairly certain of these outcomes, then this knowledge will usually prevent them from sharing with their mother. Wendy views her mother as a traditional, small-town-oriented religious woman who does not understand modern life or concepts. The possibility that she would understand her daughter's sexuality is so remote that Wendy has no plans to disclose.

Although the fear is seldom of physical harm, in the case presented below the daughter expresses anxiety that disclosure might lead to an extension of the physical abuse she received as a child. She also wants to avoid feeling guilty if her mother were to die from the news; she insists on finishing her college career, and this would not be a foregone conclusion if she disclosed.

▽ I haven't told her, but every once in a while when I'm angry with her or something she's done, or when she becomes physically abusive toward me, I want to blurt it out. Yet I don't want to tell her that way, to be like her, yet at times I want to hurt her like she hurts me. I don't know how she would react; it's hard to tell because she's bipolar [manic–depressive], sometimes on medication, and I don't know what to expect given that.

She has heart and other physical problems. It is scary to think about what might happen if she got really angry, and I don't want to be responsible for that. [During my childhood], she had total reign [over my Dad], and I never want to have that kind of relationship with my partner. She had Dad in the palm of her hands.

Whatever, I have no plans to tell her until they pay for college. Maybe I'll wait until I graduate next year, have a job, and am more independent. She wouldn't support me financially; she'd have Dad withdraw support. That's more than I can handle right now.

It'd be awkward. She'd try to convince me to be heterosexual, and then go on about what it would do to Dad, the church, my younger brother, my grandmother.

The basis for these perceptions varies but is often premised on the young women's belief that their mother will ignore the issue, either consciously or unconsciously, or will explode once she knows, spewing vendettas, insults, and threats. This conviction prevents one young woman from coming out to her mother, although she "almost" disclosed on several occasions. Ultimately, however, she decided against it.

▽ I was going to tell once, so I called to talk and when I got close, then she hung up on me. I know that I won't get anything from her. She won't react very well. I feel she would use it to discredit me with my sisters and drive a wedge between us.

At one point she said the guy I dated for 3 years was gay and I said, thinking now was the time, that it was not terrible, if he was happy. Alarmed—I think she was baiting me—she said half screaming, "How would you like it if some big fat bull dyke liked you?" I said that I'd be honored and then in near panic she says to me, "Tell me it's not true about you!" Now was not the time to tell her.

Reasons for not disclosing are sometimes simple, sometimes complex, and sometimes difficult to categorize. Within any one stated reason varying motivations exist, some of which are readily apparent (e.g., fear being cut off financially) and others that are hidden or elusive (e.g., desire to be the perfect daughter). The following youth experienced complex circumstances.

▽   I almost did a thousand times. I know that she must know already. We've talked about the issue in the abstract, and she has met my lesbian friends and likes them. She's met my Swedish girlfriend, and she is so obviously lesbian.

I have a much closer relationship with her than with Dad, and so if I told her and not him then that would be something else he would say I didn't share with him. I don't want to tell him yet. He is much more conservative, and I don't want to jeopardize that relationship.

I almost told last year, but I didn't want to deal with Dad. She's had 2 years to deal with my questioning, and so I'm sure she'd be okay with it. She'd love me no matter what and would support me. Her concern would be the hardships for me and how others would react.

When will young women say the words? From the narratives, two consistent themes emerge. One, daughters disclose when they have a committed relationship with a woman and want to bring her home to share this joy with their mother. "Only when it matters in my life, like an involvement that is monogamous and might lead to marriage." Until this time, tension often characterizes the mother–daughter relationship; the daughter is waiting for the right excuse to talk openly about herself—or she may want to continue the charade as long as possible, especially if she fears negative reactions.

One young woman who is only out to her closest friends best expresses the second theme. She needs more certainty about herself and what her attractions mean before sharing them with someone as important as her mother. "She would not disown me, but I could never tell her, not until I come out to myself. She'd not go bonkers." Against this backdrop of young women who cite reasons not to tell are those who find sufficient reasons to disclose.

REASONS TO TELL

Despite these reasons not to disclose, most young women who volunteer to participate in research on growing up with same-sex attractions find the right developmental time or overcome religious, ethnic, or cultural barriers to tell their mother about this most intimate aspect of their life. Why? Nearly two thirds of the disclosed young women I interviewed respond with answers that have as their basis a loving, caring bond between mother and daughter. Either the daughter makes a conscious decision to share this most intimate aspect of her life or her mother asks her about her sexuality. The two acts are sometimes inseparable. Alternatively, the youth is outed by another, or she fears she will be, or it is the right developmental time to come out.

Wants to Share Her Life

Pam's experience is relatively common: Being in love with another woman, she *had* to share this new development with her mother: "She knows me like no one else, and I just can't keep secrets from her." Similarly, another youth told her mother a few months after she came out to herself because, "I wanted her to know this amazing woman I was in love with and to know about me and not have to hide."

Daughters are primarily motivated to maintain or improve the exceptional emotional intimacy they currently have with their mother, although at times their goal is to increase or repair a daughter–mother relationship that has ruptured over time. Perhaps communication has degenerated or persistent anxieties and tensions have eroded their daily interactions. Under these circumstances, coming out represents an attempt to reclaim or salvage their intimate relationship. One youth and her mother talk every Sunday morning, at which time they exchange life stories and "chat about nothing." During one of these routine calls the mother's questioning left an indelible impression on the daughter's memory.

▽   So she says to me, "You sound so happy today."
    You see, I just got this date with this incredibly hot girl on the rugby team. I was so happy because it was my first date with a girl, and I had actually asked her out. This was a major step for me, and I knew I wanted to share this with Mom. But how?
    Her next question comes out of nowhere, "How is rugby?"
    "I love it," and I'm thinking, "Where in the hell did that come from?" Maybe here's my opening.
    Then she asks, "Are there a lot of dykes on the team?"
    This floored me because she never speaks this way! How could she even know about such things? I was taken aback and knowing that I can never lie to her, I said, "Yeah. Does this bother you?" Here is my chance to tell her! "Good question. I'm kind of attracted to girls, and I always have." Silence on the other end, and that's my coming-out-to-mother story!

This narrative highlights the special bond between mother and daughter, which can be so ubiquitous that the mother essentially knows before she is told. Her question of whether there are any dykes on the team is a communication to her daughter that now is the time for the daughter to "own up" to her sexual attractions. Occasionally, young women simply shrug their shoulders to the question and say, "Well, she has to know sometime." Most commonly, they believe that their mother already knows and that eventually they have to tell her, given the closeness of their relationship. One youth cannot imagine not telling her mother. "I told her when I had my period, and the next day everyone knew! People I hardly knew asked me how hard was it? Any cramps? Much bleeding? There are no secrets or nothing sacred in our family! You think I have a choice to tell her?! I told her because she knew. I knew that; she knew that." In other cases, the mother is more direct.

Mother Asks

A common perception among youths is that their mother intuitively knows when something is "not right" with her daughter. This emotional sensitivity frequently informs a mother about her daughter's sexuality. Indeed, one third of the youths disclose, not by admission or choice, but because their mother poses the question by hinting, probing, demanding, suggesting, or cajoling the information. The mother sets the stage or even forces the issue sooner than her daughter might have desired.

Pam's mother seemed to know why her daughter was telephoning her at work—"She asked if there was anything I wanted to tell her." She had suspected since Pam was a child. A mother "knowing" long before her daughter does is not an uncommon occurence. One daughter finally responded to her mother's hinting by telling her "so I could get her off my back. She said she had known for years!" Another daughter was upset with her mother for not telling her that she, her mother, is a lesbian: "It would have made my life a whole lot easier if she had told me." Similar to Nancy's mother, a mother asks because she suspects.

∇   Fall semester of my freshman year we went to a talk about sexuality sponsored by the Dean of Students, like an info-commercial on student life. Part of that, there was a zap [a panel of youths answering questions] by the gay group on campus, and Mom began asking questions of the students. I'm real embarrassed because she's asking so many questions, naïve ones.

  Afterwards I'm correcting some of the false things she said about gay people and she asks me, "Anything you want to tell me?" I divert her by rushing her to supper, but later that night she asked again more directly, and I told her. I had planned to tell her anyway that weekend because she was dropping so many hints before I left home—like warning me about women on athletic teams and saying there were so many groups on campus for everyone and on that list she included Bi-GALA [Bisexual–Gay and Lesbian Association].

A sense of not having control over the disclosure process is not unusual, and many young women are not happy with this disempowerment. "Actually, she asked what was going on between Ling and me. I pussyfooted around and then admitted we were in a relationship. I wasn't ready yet to tell her, but I had no choice."

Outed by Another

This feeling of losing control can be even more dramatic when coming out occurs completely unexpectedly—as is true for 15% of the daughters interviewed. In their circumstances, someone "outed" them, either accidentally, as in Nancy's case, or as a malicious act, as the following story documents. This narrative is the most direct act of sabotage I recorded in my interviews.

∇   This jealous ex-friend, my best intense friend during my "Utopian Year" when I fell in love, and what ultimately ended that Utopian Year, goes into my room and "finds" the letters Jessica had written me. She searched my room and "accidentally" found them in the false bottom of my trunk. She said she had a vision from God which told her where they were.

    She shared these with her parents and my sister. They all freaked out, and all four went to the Christian counseling center to ask what they should do and got a game plan. She took me on a picnic and told me she found out about me and Jessica but wouldn't say how. I forced it out of her, and she told me about the letters. That evening, as they had planned it, my sister said that I had to tell our parents or the four of them would. I felt like a caged animal; no where to run. I waited a week while Jessica was on vacation. I told her I had to tell my parents. I sat them down at 10 p.m. and said, "I'm gay."

More accidental and less volitional is a situation in which a young woman "outed" herself when she joined a women's self-defense class with her mother. On the application form in response to a question about "current stresses in your life," the daughter wrote, "Coming out as bisexual." She did not realize that her mother had to co-sign the application. Later her mother asked her if there were any "stresses" she wanted to share.

Perhaps the most "hurtful" aspect of unsolicited outings is the sensation that young women have that they will lose control of their life. Most want to tell their mother and have full intentions of doing so, but in their own time. They are robbed of this resolve and feel that the relationship with mother suffers as a result.

Is the Right Time

At some point a daughter, just over 10% in the current sample, feels it is developmentally the right time to come out to her mother. For various reasons, the desire to disclose becomes stronger than the desire to hide. One "right" time is going away to college.

∇   I told her over Fall Break. There was this wall between us, and this restricted what we talked about. Also it restricted what I wanted to do at home, like talk at my high school gay/straight alliance, march in the gay pride parade, and bring girls home. These are all important to me, and I wanted to feel free to do them.

It wasn't the thought that she would disown me. Some of my friends have that problem, and so they swear they'll never tell until after they graduate. Relative to them I'm lucky. She's not that comfortable with homosexuality and it might stump her, but she still loves me.

Another young women disclosed because she knew that she would need her mother's support.

▽   I was missing my girlfriend a whole lot after we broke up, and I knew I couldn't do the 3 months at home without having someone to talk about it with. By saying it out loud then we could talk, quit pretending, and I could survive the summer without a relationship.

Fear of Being Outed

One of the perils of not disclosing is the possibility that someone else might "beat me to it" and thus cause problems in the mother–daughter relationship. Less than 10% of the young women, under dire threat of exposure, decide to disclose before she is "outed" by another person or the media. One young woman feared her "lesbian aunt will slip up and tell her mother." Another dreaded that her brother, an upperclassman at the same college she is attending, would discover her involvement in lesbian campus events. "I just can't continue hiding with my brother here. He's going to read about me in the student newspaper sooner or later." Possible media exposure convinced another young woman.

▽   I wanted to be able to talk freely with her and not be careful that I might disclose something accidentally. With my activism at school someone could call, or a newspaper could call—I was in the *Boston Globe*, and someone could show her the article. Many of my friends just assume I'm out so they might not be discreet. We have a great relationship, the kind of relationship that we can tell each other anything, and I don't want to ruin that. She'd have been hurt if someone else told her and not me.

The attachment between mother and daughter is of such importance to some young women that they do not want to jeopardize it by withholding personally critical information. If her mother is to eventually hear it, then "setting the record straight" must come from the daughter and not someone else.

Even though a young woman discloses to her mother with the best of intentions, such as to deepen their relationship, coming out does not always result in the intended consequence.

∇   My reasoning was stupid, and now I regret it. I fell for this woman, and she came out to her mother and it turned out okay, so I decided I had nothing to lose because I have a good relationship with my mother. I thought maybe my mother would let her come home with me over Break. I wanted my mother to be more a part of my life. Well, now she's less a part and getting lesser every day.

Daughters might not know their mother as well as they think they do and thus can be surprised when she reacts in a very negative fashion. This is Nancy's story—she would never have guessed that her mother would threaten her college education and force her to live at home. However, as will become apparent below, most decisions to come out appear to be correct, at least when judged by the mother's initial reaction. Before coming out, daughters must decide when and how to disclose. As expected, nearly as many answers to these questions exist as there are daughters who disclose to their mother.

WHEN AND HOW MOTHERS ARE TOLD

Young women attending urban community groups tend to disclose to their mother while still living at home, averaging just after their 17th birthday.[5] This is earlier than that reported by the young women I interviewed who disclosed just prior to their 19th birthday (mean age = 18.7 years). In this regard, Nancy represents the "norm," Pam is early, and Wendy, still not out to her mother at age 23, is on the late side. The youngest age of disclosure was 14 years; several young women have not disclosed as they approach their 25th birthday.

Two of the youths came out to their mother before they disclosed to anyone else, including their best friends. Other researchers also report that on rare occasions, the mother is the first person to be told about a young woman's sexual identity.[6] A mother is nearly always told before a father—there are only four exceptions in the present study. It is worth noting that although young women are out to their mother before their father, the disclosure to her usually occurs on average 1 year after she first discloses to a best friend.

Of the 48 youths out to their mother, 28 told her directly, usually during a planned or unplanned conversation. Others were out because their mother asked them about their sexuality or someone else outed them. In several situations a daughter was outed accidentally.

Direct Disclosure

Examples of direct disclosure were provided in the last section. These conversations, however, might not necessarily occur face to face. For instance, one youth initially intended to come out in person to her mother during a 6-hour car drive home from college. Last-minute fears brought about a change in these plans.

∇   I was afraid of her reaction and unsure of her and us. So I told her over the phone before she came up. I first asked how she felt about gay issues. She said she had no problems with it. "To each his own, but I wouldn't."
    "How would you think if I was bisexual?"
    She was quiet, clearly not happy, "Whatever works for you."
    The ride home was a bit tense, and she didn't ask a word about it.

Indirect Disclosure

Some young women elect not to tell their mother directly, perhaps because they anticipate that they will "chicken out" on seeing her initial reaction, they want to maintain control, or they fear that she will respond in a negative manner. Although letters were the indirect disclosure of choice of previous generations, they appear to be decreasing in popularity. Uniquely, one young woman wrote her mother a long, "in-depth letter about my sexuality on Parents' Day at church. I felt she has to know and this seemed like an appropriate time." She did not know whether she could confront her religious mother face to face, to see her hurt and to then be reproached by her.

One elaborate, indirect coming-out technique involved a youth retaking control from her intrusive and manipulative mother. Feeling neutralized in her family by a mother who refuses to share power with her oldest daughter, the young woman carefully designed the disclosure process.

∇   When I was 17 and being a very cheesy, romantic English type, the week before my girlfriend went away to college I was writing her like an 80-page tome on our relationship. It was really a good-bye letter, and though I was locking everything up on my computer, I had thrown away drafts of the letter in my recycling bag.
    I had the original bound in crushed velvet to give to Nell, but Mother was very curious about what I was spending so much time doing in my room. I knew she was a snoop. She took what I had written from recycling, bound it, made three copies, and was going to give one to the priest and one to Dad.
    She never approached me with what she had done, but I found these three copies under her bed. Yes, snoop begets snoop! I wrote a long letter because I knew Mother would show Dad a copy of it. Then I put a copy of *Now That You Know* [a self-help book for parents] on each bed. I had been to P-FLAG meetings so I knew about this sort of thing. Mother never talked about the letter or the book to this day.

One increasingly common indirect technique for coming out among younger generations involves sending parents electronic messages. For some young women, e-mail has emerged as a viable method for communicating difficult information.

▽ I was freaking out, stressing at school, boyfriend problems, and every-thing with the woman who had rejected my overtures, and it just tumbled out as I was e-mailing her. In the mess I told her. I clicked "send" before I could think about what I was doing or take it back. It was easier because I did not have to see her face. I quickly turned off the computer, knowing I couldn't control how she reacted but I could when I found out how she did—which felt like I had some control. I didn't turn it on for days after that.

Mother Asks Based on Suspicions

Some youths never have an opportunity to disclose to their mother, either directly or indirectly, because they are challenged in advance by their mother. To understand the reasoning behind a mother's suspicions requires interviewing her directly. In this absence, several possibilities can be gleaned from the narratives of daughters. One common impetus for questioning is an increasing awareness and concern by a mother that her daughter is developing an unusually intense relationship with a "best female friend."

▽ I was walking with Mom in the park, and she was talking to me about some of her problems. But I just couldn't concentrate on them and kept bringing it back to Brit. Finally she backed me into a corner, "What's with all this about Brit? Brit said this. Brit did that. It's Brit, Brit, Brit!" In anger I told her that this Brit thing was about my best friend.

She had been questioning me about why we were spending so much time together and calling each other. She said I wasn't being myself lately, like distant and hiding something from her. We were both upset, and I was trembling when I said, "What do you think is going on?"

"Maybe you're experimenting."

"Maybe so, or maybe it's more than that."

"Don't beat around the bush," she screamed. "Tell me what's go-ing on!"

At this point I just decided now or never was the time. "So you really want to know? Well, yes, we're involved."

Mothers might also understand that particular cues from their daugh-ter's social world indicate that she is not heterosexual. It is not difficult for mothers to link these "unusual" friends, social and political sensibilities, and interests with their daughter's sexuality. These "hints" might be rather obvious, such as a daughter taking a gay studies course in college or having lesbian literature in her possession. One mother read her daughter's journal and discerned the incriminating evidence; another discovered her daughter talking in a lesbian computer chat room. Sometimes the evidence is of dubious quality.

∇   I had really wimped out on Coming Out Day big time. She told me later she had been suspicious because of my lesbian friends and my political stuff and, get this, because I listened to the Indigo Girls! As soon as she made this ridiculous comment I sarcastically told her, "Well, you listen to them and you're not lesbian." She was also a big Joan Baez fan in her day. Well then, maybe she is! She certainly has lots of women friends.

∇   She knew long before I even came out to myself. Once my sophomore year in high school we were in the mall, and I stopped by a men's shoe store to look at the display boots because I really wanted boots. She asks, "Are you a lesbian?" I just said, "Motherrrr!" I didn't deny it.

Then once my grandparents were over and we were watching some 20/20 show in which it had the straight people versus the queer people, and I was cheering on the queer people. She then took me aside and told me how horrible and wrong queer people were and got very graphic about how they did sex with their tongues. She's psycho!

A third source of suspicion that leads mothers to pose the sexual identity question to their daughter involves stereotypes they embrace associating sex atypicality with lesbianism. Mothers notice particular behaviors or appearances and associate them with unconventional sexuality. One daughter reported that her mom "freaked out that I had become so masculine. She allowed it at first because she said I'd outgrow it, or else I'd become a lesbian." Her mother asked many leading questions, about her rugby shirt, her short hair, and her pierced eyebrow. "Then she asks me, 'Why don't you dress like a girl?!' She was so afraid that I'd be a butch, but this isn't me. I was a ballerina at 7!"

As should be apparent from the narratives in this chapter, many disclosures are not well planned or thought through in advance. Mothers explicitly or implicitly elicit some disclosures with poor judgment or little regard for their daughter's well-being. In other cases, however, the process of revealing one's sexuality is set in motion by a daughter long before the actual verbal disclosure.

∇   I had prepared her for this earlier by leaving enough clues since 10th grade. But we just never spoke. Then I began talking about my lesbian friends and their loves. I knew what I was doing. So it was in the back of her mind. When the time came and I had a girlfriend and brought her home from college, it was obvious. The first conversation we had about it was only last year. I told her about my girlfriend and that I was bisexual. It was clear that she had already come to terms with it on her own. It's our way of talking about personal issues.

Not all disclosures include naming an identity. Despite the excellent relationship Pam has with her mother, she could not say she is a lesbian but that she is "with" Janet and that they are dating. Young women, for personal or political reasons, often do not want to use the "L" or "Bi" word. One youth loathed the bisexual label because it "emphasizes the sexual aspect," so she told her mother that she was "dating a woman." The hesitancy to embrace particular words can also reflect a young woman's political rejection of any label for herself or her sexuality that restricts who she can be. Youths may also believe that their mother will respond less harshly to more benign descriptors, that terms other than *lesbian* will be less shocking. Preferred alternatives are usually descriptions of behavior or feelings: She "has a crush on a girl" or is "not completely attracted to males."

One other variation is young women who do not recall a single conversation or moment in time when they came out to their mother. Rather, through a series of conversations they reveal the nature of their sexuality.

∇   This is what we do, she and me, talk. So, yes, I'm sure that I told her
     I slept with a girl and that I was probably gay. She probably even asked
     if I was gay, and I said "Whatever." She told me it was normal to fall
     in love with a girl. She could always tell when I had a crush on a girl,
     and I think she doubted it was a phase. Whatever was fine with me
     was fine with her.

Another youth's mother asked her if she was experiencing "problems with her sexuality" while she was still in junior high school. After initially denying it, the daughter later confirmed that she was less than certain about it.

∇   So by this point she definitely knew. She asked if I wanted to see a
     psychologist to help me out. Actually, at first I told her that I didn't
     know, though I did, so it was a gradual process of telling her. She could
     understand how women could love women but not with males loving
     each other.

The initial reaction of mothers to their daughter's coming out ranges from relative acceptance to hysteric outrage. The popular image is of the latter, although the common reality is actually much closer to the former—mothers might not like the news but nevertheless love and support their daughter.

MOTHERS' INITIAL REACTIONS

The widespread horrific image is perpetuated by research that focuses on the victimization of lesbian, gay, and bisexual adolescents, which is most often conducted with at-risk urban support group youths. One of the most interesting studies in this genre is of adolescents living at home. Lesbians were threatened with physical violence and were the recipients of verbal abuse and attacks more often than were gay sons. The most frequent perpetrator was their mother. Despite these findings, mothers were generally more accepting than fathers of their daughter's sexuality.[7]

According to the young women in the present study, mothers respond with a range of emotions on learning about their daughter's sexuality. Pam's mother was happy and supportive; Nancy's was so outraged that she nearly severed the dyadic relationship. Because the reactions that receive the most "press" are those of Nancy's mother, nondisclosed daughters' expectations of how their mothers will react are likely affected. Although I cannot deny that indeed some mothers react in an extremely emotional, disturbing fashion, the more important, though seldom-addressed question is how common are these outrages?

Expected Versus Actual Reactions

Among young women who have not disclosed to their mother, the average expected response is midway between neutral and slightly negative, including expressions of denial ("It's only a phase") and self-blame.[8] Few predict that their mother will reject or physically attack them, and nearly one in three anticipates her mother will be supportive. However, that expectation is insufficient to provoke a disclosure.

Among those who have disclosed, the average initial response was slightly better than what the undisclosed expected—barely more negative than positive, but certainly not horrific. Indeed, the most common reaction, reported by 25% of the young women, was positive and supportive; nearly as many mothers were very supportive. However, nearly 10% of mothers were perceived by their daughter to have reacted with emotional volatility, threats to cut off financial aid, or attempts to send them to conversion therapy. Four percent of daughters were rejected or physically attacked by their mother.

Positive Initial Reactions

Full acceptance of her daughter's same-sex sexuality is seldom an easy task for a mother. She may want to be "totally cool about it" yet feel frightened by this unfamiliar territory, disappointed that the heterosexual dreams she has for her daughter will not materialize, or fear for the safety of her daughter who must survive within a hostile world. One mother "took it as a normal thing and asked if I wanted to see a counselor to help me out. I knew this meant that *she* needed to see someone because she was stressed about it." Another mother apologized for being so emotional, "but I knew it was because she loved me and wanted my life not to be hard."

She was not surprised by her daughter's revelation because, according to the daughter, "She knows I've always been open to exploring all types of feelings." The mother was uncertain, however, about *how* she should respond, as well as what this meant about her own performance as a mother. Another mother was not surprised because she had long suspected; as a result, she reacted very positively, almost to the dismay of her daughter!

∇ She is my closest friend, and I trust her. I knew she would not throw me out. Yet, I was scared; strange for her not knowing this about me. Sooner or later I'd have to tell. "Oh, I know!" She guessed this when I was 3 and knew by first grade. So, why didn't she tell me!? I could have killed her! I took my jaw off the floor. Such agony for so long over the decision to disclose. She knew all my life. She had talked to friends and relatives, to get support and perspective. By the time I was ready, she was past ready.

Positive responses from mothers are often accurately predicted. The daughter of a lesbian mother initially reported that her mother was cautious rather than ecstatic—"Are you really sure?"—as she had originally thought she would be. The mother later belied this disinterest by excitedly telling her lesbian friends that she has a lesbian daughter. They were delighted but "jealous because they too wanted one, but theirs were all straight." Her mother still dreads the reactions of those who assume that she has made her daughter a lesbian by raising her in a lesbian household.

Daughters who have politically liberal parents, live in a family in which gay issues are freely discussed, and have gay family friends are those most likely to trust that their mother will not "freak out" with the disclosure—although this does not always hold true. A mother might be comfortable with gay friends but not with a gay daughter. In one family it helped that a mother's lesbian sister struggled mightily to come out several years earlier.

∇ Since she was 14 she knew about her sister so she understood how women can love each other. She had seen her sister being depressed and didn't want me to have the same problems. She was scared about the trouble I would have in life. She put a card on my pillow that night saying, "I love you for you." No matter what happened, I knew I could always come home.

The best predictor of maternal acceptance among the young women is having an open, honest, caring relationship with their mother. One mother was accustomed to the creativity and openness of her daughter. They had discussed many historic and contemporary issues and were the best of friends. Once told, "She was totally receptive and supportive. She was laughing, totally comfortable. It was like, 'Oh this is new'—like she said with my studying Zen Buddhism."

Mothers' support, however, can also be conditional. Before they fully accept their daughter's sexuality, particular compromises must be negotiated. For example, one Orthodox Jewish mother expressed annoyance with her daughter's sexuality but immediately switched "to a happy face when I said I hadn't had any sex." With this implicit compromise that the daughter would not act on her attractions, the mother could more readily fulfill her religious dictate to love and support her daughter without violating her religious obligation to view same-sex behavior as against God's will.

Another mother was initially "very cool towards it until I agreed not to tell my naïve and troubled younger brother." She demanded further concessions—the youth could not date a particular girl because the girl's mother was in the same social group as the mother. "She made it subtle, 'It'd be a lot *easier* if you chose *not* to have a relationship with her.'" Although the mother professed to be supportive, the daughter felt betrayed because her mother was more preoccupied with her own social status than in accepting her daughter's sexuality.

Neutral Initial Reactions

Counter to what daughters often expect, the "average" mother does not noticeably react in either a positive or negative way. Are these the ones who have known for years and thus already have come to terms with their daughter's same-sex attractions? One young woman who e-mailed her mother received the following sparse electronic response: "Glad you told us." Another youth sensed no noticeable change in the relationship after the disclosure: "We did not speak about it for a year except I knew I was her daughter and she loved me and if I'm happy then it is okay. Maybe she's always known so this was no news. I mean, if she already knew, then what has changed?"

The mother's reaction might also be relatively neutral because she is not significantly invested in her daughter's life. Although rare, several daughters received a limited response from their coming out because, "Well, she has her own problems." Another youth reported that she and her mother seldom share aspects of their lives. She told her mother during one of her sporadic trips home. "She nodded and then asked me how school was going."

Negative Initial Reactions

To fully represent the range of possible reactions, the most disturbing responses must be documented—despite their infrequency. Although the following narrative involves both parents, the mother was the driving force creating the hideous situation that perhaps permanently destroyed the mother–daughter relationship.

∇   This was when I was a freshman. Over the phone I told her [that I am bisexual], and she is quiet, and I added, hopefully, "I still like boys." It didn't help. She was embarrassed, ashamed, shocked, and then it went downhill.

She ordered me to come home, so I came home to face the music. Both my parents are alcoholic, and Mom was drunk when I got home and talking about how disgusting I was. "I hate you! You're selfish. When did you know?" I told her as soon as I had sex with a boy I knew this was not what I wanted for my life. The next morning she announced I had two choices: back to Northampton and be straight or never welcomed home anymore. I told her I'd "be straight," but that was just so I could go back.

I returned and just kept doing my regular things, and then she called and announced that they were coming up that weekend. She threatened to pull me out of school because she believed Northampton was making me this way. "You don't know yourself. You don't know what is going on." They accused me of being on drugs—and I guess I was drinking a lot. Next day she calls my housing director demanding that she keep an eye on me and lock me in my room if necessary. Well, she's a lesbian herself, and after she told me the story she said, "See you at Sheila's [lesbian bar]!"

If I came home with them I'd lose my first year. She is very controlling, manipulative, and abusive, and she can get out of control. I'm frightened of her so I went to get my stuff before they arrived, and I moved my stuff out of my dorm room, leaving a letter that said I was not coming home with them now or for the summer and was taking time off to be by myself, work, live, be independent. They weren't amused.

They called around, found me, and demanded [over the phone] that I come home with them. When I said I wouldn't, they said they're coming to get me. I was getting really drunk.

When they came the first thing she said was, "Get in the fucking van! You need to come home and get fixed. You're such a fucking mess. Look what people have done to you! You're a mess! You're sick!" I eventually gave in and began loading the van and then my network of friends started to come by and advised me that I could call a counselor or the campus police. The counselor said "don't go home" because I was 18 and not a minor. They refused, wouldn't leave, so I called the campus police and had them escorted off campus. And that's where it stands today. We barely talk.

Other young women face unpleasant situations as well, including one who was harassed by her screaming mother who screamed for days. The shrieking was about everything, in part because the mother feared that she was losing the most precious relationship in her life. Further reflecting her self-absorption was her embarrassment about being known as the mother of a lesbian.

▽   I called a family meeting and told them. Told them I was lesbian, and if this was a problem for them I was prepared to leave and stay with a friend, if they can't deal. Mother went white and stark cold. When I told her she just looked away; she couldn't look me in the face. It scared her out of her freaking mind. She screamed lots of questions; said it was unnatural. Everything imaginable, such as, "What happened to you as a child? Why do this to me? To hurt me? To rebel against everything we've taught you? How can you do this to your brothers? How can I step outside the house?"

I answered these questions for days at the top of my voice. I had been well trained as a peer counselor, but I was unprepared for this huge screaming match that lasted all night long. It was pretty messy. It was very bad. She cried and said how sad she was and that a part of her that was me died in her. For the next 2 weeks, if I entered a room she'd leave. Wouldn't talk to me except bare necessities.

She said she was most upset because I had hid something from her, that we always share everything and how dare I not tell her. "Who have you told before me? How could you tell someone outside the family?" This is all very weird to me. We have a couple of lesbian family friends, but her daughter, well, that is another thing! She thought I was being influenced by older women and LBQ [campus support group]. She wanted me to see a therapist, but it had to be a heterosexual one so I wouldn't get dragged further in.

She got so upset because I kept interrupting her. She usually sits me down and lectures me for hours, but I wouldn't let her this time. I stood up for myself and was vocal to her. "This is not my daughter. This is not the daughter I raised, to be respectful, to honor her mother. No, this is not my daughter!"

This last paragraph suggests the operation of an additional dynamic—the need of some mothers to exert power or control over their daughter. These mothers appear extraordinarily upset by this breach in relative power—the ultimate realignment of their relationship. This change might well threaten her sense of integrity and self-concept as "mother." Another youth recalled her mother demanding,

▽   "Don't shave your head." Where did she get that? I wasn't the daughter she thought she had? What had she expected? That I'd shave my head, gain 50 pounds, dress in leather, and buy a motorcycle? Does she think she's not my mother? I mean, she knows me and that's not me.

Other mothers react less with overt anger than with denial. "Her reaction was to say it was a stage, that all females have emotional relationships with girls, that we're all born bisexual, and that I'd been socially conditioned to be loving toward everyone." Another young woman was hoping for an "okay-that's-cool" response but instead received a dismissal, something she was unprepared to refute.

She didn't take me that seriously. She said very little, "How do you have sex with her?" A day later she said to forget about her. She thinks it's only a sexual thing and once the novelty goes away it'll be over. "Don't be out about it or identify as such, or be political about it."

Whether these mothers truly experience little anger or this is simply their style of managing conflict remains unknown. The next step is to interview them directly. What is clear from the daughters' perspective is that of all responses, denial is the most difficult to address. How can one confront denial? How can one convince her mother that it is not a phase? That she is serious about this matter?

Many mothers experience particularly unique difficulties with bisexuality, in part because in most cases they are well aware of their daughter's history of heterosexual relationships. They either disbelieve her same-sex attractions or assert that she should forget the girls and concentrate on the guys.

∇ She didn't believe me! "You may think you are, but you're not." I was not anticipating this. She said something I thought I'd never hear from her lips, "You've not had enough sex with boys." Well I had, but I couldn't tell her that because it was casual sex, and I knew what she thought of that.

She was disappointed and worried that the rest of the family would react badly. Worried about me not having children. She was glad I told her because I'm her daughter, and she will always love me. I knew she'd never say "get out of the house." She had put so much hope on me, me being her only daughter.

She's always accused me of bad judgment and being smart and independent, and this bisexuality, in her head, was all about these things. She was afraid I'd be lonely. She wants me to switch schools to get away from the lesbians, or that I should take time off because of stress. So ridiculous!

She says if I'm bisexual then I ought to be dating guys and forget women. She's starting to accept it, struggling, but not ready to accept it yet. She wants me to get counseling. She wants the outcome for me to realize that I can have homosexual feelings but can connect with males and thus date them.

The bisexual myth that a daughter has *equally* strong attractions to males and females often implies to parents that their child can simply choose boys and forget the girls. Other misconceptions are apparent in the following narrative:

∇ I don't tell her if I'm dating a woman, which has not happened much. She hasn't done her homework, so she doesn't understand that just because I'm dating a man doesn't mean my bisexuality disappears. She asked questions like, "Does this mean you have to have males and females all the time? At the same time? You can't marry?" She thought being bi meant I'd be promiscuous, having both boys and girls, and so I had to educate her. I told her, "No, I see myself as monogamous. I want one life partner, like you."

It's really frustrating. I can't get that across to her. I've not managed to convince her that if I'm dating either a man or a woman it'd not make me less bi. She hides behind, "Well, she's dating a guy so there's still hope."

The variety of ways that mothers react to the disclosure of their daughter's same-sex attractions comprise information that is clearly far richer than any "average" or reductionistic modal statistic can convey. From "you're not my daughter" to "I'm proud of you," mothers react in ways that span all conceivable responses. Although few mothers openly celebrate the disclosure, fewer reject their daughter because of her sexuality. Even the most accepting mothers, however, fear that their daughter will experience a more difficult life. The family is one thing; the world is another.

Yet, if the focus is only on the initial maternal reaction, much of what is significant about the disclosure process is missed. Empirically, what occurs after the initial disclosure is uncharted territory. The following narratives represent a sampling of this diversity.

RELATIONSHIPS AFTER DISCLOSURE

Following the initial disclosure, the mother–daughter relationship can go one of several directions. Progressing from an initially positive base, it can remain positive, deteriorate, or improve. Or, it can persist from an initial negative reaction and stay bad, degenerate, or recuperate, even if so slightly. Finally, the relationship after disclosure can be relatively neutral and stay that way or go in either a positive or negative direction. Although these possibilities ignore the more complex and nuanced aspects of a parent–child relationship, they afford a starting point for discussing what occurs following the initial maternal reaction.

In a review of the scientific literature, I found no study that followed parents over time, comparing their initial reactions to later ones. The closest to this methodology is one study that asked a small sample of parents to retrospectively report, in general terms via a preset checklist, how they reacted to their child's disclosure 1 week, 1 month, and 6 months after disclosure, as well as their present reactions. However, because the author reported only summary statistics, the ways in which any individual parent changed over time were not possible to discern.[9]

The Relationship Continues

In my interviews with young women, over 60% reported that the mother–daughter relationship has essentially stayed the same from the initial disclosure to the present time. This stability most often characterized those relationships in which the mother's initial reaction was positive or neutral (80% of all such reactions). Furthermore, only one third of the most negative initial responses remained very bad; most improved somewhat (one half) or considerably (one sixth).

The most common permutation, that the mother's initial response is positive and their relationship has stayed positive since the disclosure, is represented by one mother who reacted "fine, positively, not shocked and no screaming. There's been no real change, although the issue does not come up much." This response is consistent with the way she reacts to most of her daughter's personal issues. The lack of change does not always imply, however, that the relationship has remained at the status quo—for example, that the mother has not struggled to educate herself—or that no notable shifts have occurred. One mother of a young woman did "lots of reading and became a part of P-FLAG and edits their newspaper and does diversity training at work. All this within a month!"

Many daughters who describe a dyadic relationship that has remained positive over the years also report a long history of sharing close, intimate moments with their mother. Not uncommonly, the mother is also familiar with sexual-minority issues, has lesbian or gay friends, or has liberal political and social ideals.

∇   Mom helped me come out when she and I talked about most people being on a continuum, and this helped me realize I was on it by having a relationship with a woman. This allowed me to be more aware and accept that side of myself.

I can talk about my girlfriends and sometimes she'll ask, though usually more than I want her to. She is a strong supporter of gay rights. She worries most about me being beaten up, me being so open on campus and in the media.

Similar to Nancy, whose narrative begins this chapter, young women may become frustrated that their mother is making little, if any, progress toward understanding their sexuality and wish that she would move a little faster toward acceptance. "Relative to her on other issues, it hasn't been great," recalled one youth. She cherishes the advancement her mother has made, but expects further growth.

∇   We've continued to talk more about it, and she's met my girlfriend Mary. It is still hard for her, but she said she might go to a P-FLAG meeting. I talk a lot to her and tell her I appreciate her progress. But I can get pretty pissed at her when she backslides.

Like when she visited last month was okay until she understood that I planned to stay the night at Mary's apartment. "You stay the night, and she might take advantage of you." What?! She thinks I ought to date more people, by which she means men.

She wants to be good, but is not quite there yet. I don't want to shove it in her face, but she doesn't try to control the sexual practices of my sisters and their boyfriends, so why me? She wants to be there for me, especially because Dad can't—they're competitive in who can be the best parent, so I work this to my advantage.

Time might not, however, always work to the youth's advantage. Over the years a daughter can develop lofty expectations for her mother's acceptance, and when she does not advance adequately the mother–daughter relationship suffers. In the following narrative, a daughter is severely annoyed that her highly educated mother cannot overcome her homophobia.

▽   I am really disappointed for her not doing things like reading literature. Like she never went out and tried to find anything. My mother is a woman who researches everything, and she never went out and even looked at a book about bisexuality, even the ones I gave her. They're untouched. I say Stonewall, and she doesn't know what I am talking about.

How dare you not understand me! When I do gay and lesbian work on campus I would really like to share it with her, but I don't feel like I can because I don't feel like it matters to her. So it doesn't matter one twit to her all the leadership stuff that I do here. There has been no real change, and we don't talk about it unless I start the conversation.

Another daughter anticipated continuing support after her mother initially reacted very positively. However, that was the last affirmative response she received. Most perplexing to the daughter is, "Why the silence?" Perhaps enough time has not transpired.

▽   We're sitting in a Borders parking lot. A sale table of books, and I bought one on the gay movement. We got back in the car. She asked, "Is there anything more to this than personal freedom issues?"

Here was my chance for honesty. "Yes, I guess so."

"Really? I had the feeling." Took real guts for her to bring it up. She was ready for the answer. She was quiet. "Have you ever dated a woman?"

"I think about it a lot."

"It's not something I would hope for you. I want an easier life for you, but if you choose it then I can get used to it."

There has been no mention of it since. It's there in her head. I guess I just have to wait.

Negative initial reactions can stay bad. Neither time nor any other factor appear to alter the negativity.

∇ She is still very cold toward me and just minimal caring. She doesn't call. I have to call her. I've told her I still have attractions for guys, and she wants me to marry this guy I've dated. She keeps asking me how Thomas is and how happy it would make her if I were to marry him. Never any conversation about women, so I just tell her what counts. She'll never bring it up. She just brackets that part of my life off, so I've given up hope for her.

One factor that thwarts improvement following an initially negative response is the presence of traditional religious beliefs, especially within a context of pronouncements that homosexuality is necessarily against God's design. Some religious groups instruct their congregants, parishioners, or converts not to acknowledge a child's nonheterosexuality. One youth initially feared that her family would sever all ties; although this has not transpired, "She thinks I will get out of it and is praying for me. We just don't discuss things because her views are her church's and they're not changing." As evident from other narratives in this book, religion need not be a detriment to loving and supporting a child, regardless of her sexual attractions.[10]

One young woman interprets her mother's inability to transcend this obstacle as an expression of envy or jealousy. Either the mother is envious of her daughter's freedom and ability to pursue egalitarian relationships with other women or the mother mourns her own lost opportunities because she does not pursue her erotic interests.

∇ I suspect that Mom is like me, and this bothers her. She's very butch, a tomboy, and all my friends who see her tell me she has got to be a dyke. If she lived in a more open environment then maybe she'd been. But now I feel she's taking it out on me—she's jealous of my living the life she couldn't, so she's got to give me a hard time.

   If we lived in a small town like she did, then maybe I'd still be in the closet like her. You know, once she "confessed" to me after drinking too much one night that in college she was attracted to women. Damn! I wished I would have asked her more, like how so or why didn't she act on it physically. But I was so dumbstruck I didn't say anything else, and now it's too late to ask. Maybe she is annoyed because I've gone and done what she couldn't.

Another deterrent to progression toward acceptance for some mothers from ethnic families is fear of how they will be perceived by *their* parents if the latter were to discover that their child has produced a lesbian or bisexual daughter. For many ethnic minorities, the family serves as an essential stronghold of the culture; it is a support system that insulates against societal oppression and maintains cultural purity and history. If a young woman neglects her responsibilities as mother and wife, she is stigmatized, as are those who raised her. One young woman noted that her family's strong ethnic heritage inhibits her mother from advancing in her attitudes toward homosexuality. In her culture, loyalty to the *familia* comes first.

∇   On mother's side we're Mexican with a strong emphasis on family, and if I came out as lesbian to them, then not only am I the sick one but also her for being a bad parent. This older generation, I have nothing to say to. Mom doesn't want me to tell them, and because she spends all of her winters in Mexico, I respect her wishes. I don't want it to get back to the small town where she lives. To Mom, family is so important. I took away her dream of having grandchildren. Mom said I can't tell Grandmother because she'd have a heart attack.

The institution of *familia* also, however, protects young women, as noted by writer Oliva Espín: "Latin families tend to treat their lesbian daughters or sisters with silent tolerance: Their lesbianism will not be openly acknowledged and accepted, but they are not denied a place in the family, either."[11]

Little evidence of progress after a disclosure might also reflect a mother–daughter relationship that was so severely impaired before the coming out event that relatively little can improve the bond thereafter. Although there is little scientific evidence to suggest that same-sex attracted young women are any more likely than heterosexual women to suffer abuse, neglect, and bad relations with their parents, similar to all other populations of young women, they have their examples. One daughter doubts that her relationship with her mother will ever reach a "normal level."

∇   I can't say to her today that I have a girlfriend because that would be shoving it up her ass. She thinks it's disgusting and that I'd be flaunting it. She can't hear about my problems or my life. It was like I was reborn that day, or maybe it was like my graveyard in her eyes. I want to be comfortable with her but I can't; there is more than just my sexuality that is playing in here. There's abuse and a history that goes way back. I've not lived with either of them [divorced parents] since that time.

The second most common trajectory is a mother–daughter relationship that improves over time. The narratives permit some understanding as to why their bond becomes stronger and more intimate.

The Relationship Improves

Over one third of all young women report that the mother–daughter relationship is enhanced over time. This positive slope is most likely to occur when the initial reaction is "very negative." Most resistant to improvement are relationships in which the mother initially denies her daughter's same-sex attractions or suggests that she is only passing through an adolescent or women's studies phase (20% got better). Although many of the young women report progress in their relationship with their mother, far more desire or expect it.

No one factor is responsible for improving mother–daughter relationships. However, the aspiration of both dyadic members to maintain a close bond is a powerful motivator. The relationship between Nancy and her mother improved ever so slightly, perhaps because of the historic closeness of their union—it was something neither wanted to forgo. As a result, each was willing to compromise to maintain it. Any attempt to explain a mother's progression in her attitudes toward her daughter must examine not only the mother's transformations but also changes in the daughter that contribute to a healthier mother–daughter relationship, such as greater tolerance, understanding, or willingness to grant her mother time to adjust, adapt, and ask questions. Because the present study of sexual-minority young women did not interview mothers, I am limited to daughters' interpretations of the makeover of their relationship.

Daughters often believe it is the consequence of time and love. Indeed, several daughters note that it simply took time for their mother to move beyond her initial shock and disappointment to discover that she, the daughter, has essentially remained the same person. Mothers remind themselves that their daughter is still their daughter, and they do not want to lose her. Besides, nothing significant has really changed. One mother eventually accepted her daughter's sexuality.

∇   She won't be flying any banners in parades anytime soon, but if I was in a relationship she would support me. Of course, she still hopes I'll find a man to suit me, but she would invite my girlfriend home on Christmas if I had one. This is a monumental shift for her.

The other change agent—love—manifests itself in various ways. A mother might worry about her daughter's happiness, life, and future but ultimately accepts her daughter because she loves her.

∇   Mother got a little teary eyed, but she's a phenomenal woman. She did really well, and now I can talk to her about anything, my girlfriends, being a lesbian—anything! She went to a couple of P-FLAG meetings, but it turned out not to be for her. She's not a gay pride sort. I couldn't ask for a better situation.

Other than time and love, young women frequently hypothesize several other factors that move their mother toward tolerance or acceptance, such as the daughter becoming involved in a same-sex romantic relationship. This was true for Pam as well as for others.

∇   She didn't like take me serious. I had to have this torrid romantic relationship to solidify it in her mind. Then she believed me. Made it concrete. She thought I was being hasty about being queer, and lesbian sex was my cop out on life. Now she sees differently and is more comfortable with the concept.

This all started when I like broke up with Sarah. She saw me crying. I was not comfortable telling her about Sarah. This would make me really a lesbian in her eyes. She was fine with it, great. She even said to remember there were other fish for me!

Now she is helping me plan the wedding commitment with Judi. She realizes it is not a stage anymore. Still, she is uncomfortable with my "lifestyle." It doesn't fit hers. She has definitely gotten better about it. She mentioned it in the family newsletter, the ceremony. She now believes it doesn't reflect badly on her, and I'll have a good life with Judi.

This change from an emphasis on sex to relationships reflects the mother's understanding about what being attracted to women means for her daughter. It can result in increasing comfort and support.

This comfort can also be enhanced if the mother meets her daughter's nonheterosexual friends. The exposure to "not straight" women who are neither "freaks" nor stereotypes can instill in her a sense that being a sexual minority does not lead to the dire consequences about which she might have fantasized.

∇   She has come a long way. She eventually visited me in Boston and met my queer friends—she thinks all of Boston University is gay! It moved her. She met my girlfriend, which was weird because she is interracial, and all she could say was how tall she was. She had only considered me marrying a Greek. It is hard for her, and she fears for my safety and how society will treat me. It helps that she sees my friends so happy and confident. Occasionally she'll lapse and say it is a phase, but then will say she met a girl who's perfect for me.

Finally, daughters also note that their mother is better able to support them after she overcomes feelings of shame and guilt that it is her "fault" that her daughter is not heterosexual and anxiety that other family members will blame her. Mothers can be freed from self-blame if *their* parents and siblings are not shaming.

∇   We don't talk about it much today, but if I say I'm spending lots of time with a particular person of the female persuasion then she begins to question me in a negative way. I'm trying to educate her, and there's been progress. She's in a better place but not fully accepting yet. She keeps thinking that she failed some way, perhaps by not having a father around for me.

The big break came last summer when Mom told my grandparents about the commitment ceremony, and they're coming to the ceremony. She was hedging until Grandpa said, "So what?" He's fine with it, and so you know Grandma is too. That was it. Not her fault. I mean you can't take the South out of the woman entirely!

Although daughters articulate factors they believe transformed their mother, they have greater difficulty recounting the exact process by which their mother reached acceptance. One daughter speculates that her mother "went through all the classic P-FLAG stages that they tell you about." However, her interpretation of this process is not exactly consistent with P-FLAG literature—no initial shock or depression, but quick acceptance (see chapter 3).

∇   She was absolutely okay with it, calm at first, but perhaps confused. Couple of days later she was freaking out, visibly uncomfortable. She calmed down. She was most upset because I was having sex so she asked me not to have sex, but, hey, we were teenagers!

  She sent me to a shrink, not to convert me but to help me out. I went to three worthless sessions, and then said I wasn't going unless she was going to P-FLAG. I didn't want me to be the only one working through things; she had to do her share.

  She was scared, but now she's great. Mom loves my partner, and they go out shopping together. She even bought me and my girlfriend a brass bed and lingerie. She could not be more supportive. We are closer than ever, and she has been adopted by my gay friends.

These transformative processes can be slight adjustments or major renovations in the relationship. Regardless of how the transition in the mother's acceptance is provoked, what is most important to her daughter is simply that a change occurs, even if it is not complete.

∇   She feels more comfortable than she did, but she is still silent and reserved. She is also more friendly with my girlfriends, although we don't talk about my relationships. There is a gap but not a huge one. She invited my girlfriend to stay at the house, which is a huge step. She was very polite to her, which is small progress also. She is afraid of raising too many objections because she's afraid of never seeing me— I'd be with my girlfriend all the time.

  She is neither supportive nor abusive, just ignores it. Occasionally she'll send me some religious pamphlets about the topic. She is great with babies and other things she can control but can't deal with adults, like me. Although our relationship is now not great, I'll take it. For example, my car is covered by [queer] bumper stickers, and she used to tell me to back up in the driveway to cover up my stickers so the neighbors wouldn't see. Now she has stopped that.

The process of change can appear to be a minor tweaking, so seemingly insignificant that a youth is unaware that any progress has been made. Then, a seemingly innocent encounter illustrates the depth of transformation that her mother has undergone.

∇   She said I couldn't be bisexual but that I'd have to choose between lesbian and heterosexual! Almost as if it would have been easier on her if I had said that I was a lesbian! Here I thought saying bisexual would soften the blow. She thinks bisexual means "have not made up your mind yet." She asked me not to tell anyone else in the family because we are very religious.

     There was no mention of anything for months after this, and this hurt because I don't like hiding and I wanted more acceptance. But I left her alone and told no one else in the family. Just pretended we never had the conversation.

     Then two months ago I had to move to a new apartment, and she and my brother came to help me. One of my best friends is a lesbian who's very butch, and she mentioned a woman she was attracted to, "the hottest chick I've ever met." Mom smiled, thinking she meant me!

     Later that day Mom asked, "Is this friend your 'special friend?' Am I asking too many questions? I thought about what I said, and I apologize for not being more accepting. I want you to be happy."

     But what really broke my heart was when she said she had woken up for two weeks crying, until she talked to my cousin and this helped her come to terms.

Alternatively, dramatic changes in the mother's perspective and behavior are sometimes evident. However invoked, conversions occur in cases that begin with rejection and advance to tolerance and in cases that progress from neutrality to unimaginable support. One such mother, whose initial reactions were the most severe of those reported by the young women—a situation in which the parents moved their daughter out of the home and placed her with her grandmother in another town—eventually "came around."

∇   Mom was initially angry and silent. The next day she said that I had to realize that I can't baby-sit for the neighbors, and I said I knew this. She forced me to go to the Christian counseling center and supported Dad that I had to move out because I was a bad influence on my sisters and brothers.

     The summer after getting kicked out of the house I tried to patch things up in my relationship with her. I had blamed them for everything and had been very bitter. So I apologized and tried to convince her that I had not changed and was not an evil person. It tore her apart because I'm still her child. She agreed with Dad in kicking me out, but now she didn't want me out of the family or to the intensity of him or in pushing me away. When I was at my grandmother's and visiting home it was a little better. I'm still the same person was my message.

     She can't relate to my lesbianism. Jessica and me had a commitment ceremony last year, and I invited her, and she said she couldn't come. Then I told her not to come as "mother of the bride" but as a guest, and she did. She can hug me and doesn't blame me for wanting a partner with equal power. Her religion says it is wrong, but she loves Jessica and welcomes her whenever she sees her. She'll get there. I just want tolerance, and I can get this from my mother. Acceptance is a bit of a stretch right now.

Another impressive adjustment in a mother's attitude occurred after she experienced an unspecified "self-revelation." She and her daughter had always been very close, and this news startled her into uncharacteristic behavior. The key catalyst to acceptance was participation in a parent support group.

▽ At first she wanted to tell absolutely no one—although she then told Dad and eventually all of her relatives, including her four sisters, before I had a chance to. It was weird for awhile. I couldn't predict her. She wanted to know why I had to be so politically involved, wearing freedom rings, and why so visible.

Then what a change! She found, on her own, the P-FLAG group and cried all during the first meeting. During the second she felt better and then brought me to the third. Then she took me to the Pride March and held the banner for P-FLAG! She volunteered to be interviewed for the newspaper and had our picture with our names in the *Miami Herald*.

She really came out herself, as the mother of a lesbian. She came to an "Ellen Party" we had at the sorority and said she loves me and all my "queer" friends—she actually used that word! She even offered to set up a halfway house for "baby dykes" who had no home to go to over breaks and holidays. She can talk easier with my friends than I can!

Of course not all relationships improve with time or stay the same. The trajectory most feared by young women is the one in which the relationship worsens after coming out.

The Relationship Deteriorates

Although relatively rare, the dyadic relationship can deteriorate, sometimes to the point that communication and support no longer occur. One daughter received an initial e-mail response from her mother stating that she was "glad" for her; the second e-mail was not as positive.

▽ She said she was hurt, didn't accept it as a choice, but would love me. So I thought things were cool, but on my first visit home in person I brought my girlfriend, which might not have been a good move. She was stunned, shocked, and her mouth hung open. Second time, *sans* girlfriend, Mom cried. She was angry at Dad for being nice to me. Third time I was sick so Mom could take care of me and that was great for her. Fourth time she was warm one minute and then silent; cried and then happy. Just no reason for the switch, like in mid-sentence. I don't know what to expect on the fifth, but it's getting more dangerous.

Perhaps the most difficult stumbling block preventing a mother from accepting her daughter was noted in the last section—her belief that she is at fault for the daughter's "alternative lifestyle." The more the following mother considered her daughter's sexuality, the more agitated she became.

∇   I hate keeping secrets. Yet I don't want her to know my personal stuff because I don't trust her.

She said, "Oh, I already know honey." Which was her way to get back at me for not telling her sooner. "Whatever makes you happy, makes me happy." I thanked her for being so cool, but I had my doubts.

She had not digested it yet. Later she asked, "Did I do something to cause it?" Which implies that something is wrong with me. She is so narcissistic that she thinks everything is caused by her. I wanted to yell, "Get off it! It has nothing to do with you!"

"Did you have negative experiences with boys? Was it because of seeing me and your dad fail?" She feels it's her fault, that she passed it onto me, which is strange given it's Dad's side who has all the gay genes. Yet she was a tomboy and looks very lesbian. I'm sure she has her own doubts about herself. If she had raised me right then she feels I'd be straight.

Today if I bring it up she'll say she can't sleep at night. Hole in her heart and I did it to hurt her. So mean of me, evil, and yet she lets me take care of her.

If current trends persist, most daughters can expect increasingly positive reactions from their mother. It might not occur as quickly as they would like or reach as high a level as they have a right to expect, but it will likely improve nevertheless. One group of daughters who almost always expect to receive positive reactions are those who have mothers with same-sex attractions.

WHEN MOTHERS HAVE SAME-SEX ATTRACTIONS

Perhaps the most supportive mothers, if not initially then certainly eventually, are those who also have same-sex attractions or are avowedly lesbians. Two of the interviewed young women have "out" lesbian mothers, and several more have mothers who appear to be attracted to women. Although the following mothers are supportive of their daughter's sexuality, both young women nevertheless struggled to come out, illustrating the complexity of factors that lead to disclosure. Simply knowing that one will receive a positive response does not preclude youths from grappling with numerous other dynamics.

∇   We've always been bonded very close. She calls me her "amazing daughter." I was upset and shocked when she came out. No suspicions because

I don't think of my parents having sexuality. Here I was this straight person in high school with a lesbian mom. I gave her a hard time, and I regret this.

She was shocked when I told her because she had devoted so much energy to herself. She has lots of internalized homophobia, but she was still bursting with joy. It made it easier to come out to her. I knew her horror stories, and I didn't want others to think she was to blame for me. I guess I wanted to protect her, but maybe I just wanted it to be my own coming out and not hers.

One daughter who has strong suspicions about her mother has not yet disclosed to her.

▽   My parents are happily married, but if not, she would definitely be involved with women. All her friends are lesbians, and she spends lots of time with them.

Growing up she always said it was fine to be lesbian. I'd have no problem telling her, but I'd want to tell both at the same time. She'd be very positive, more happy than if I liked boys. We're very, very close. In fact we look almost exactly the same except for 30 years.

A FINAL WORD

Young women want and receive support from their mother. In large part this is because the relationship girls have with their mothers prior to disclosure is intimate, open, and communicative, enhancing the mother–daughter bond. Most young women disclose because they want to share this most momentous aspect of their identity with the most important woman in their lives. In this regard they do not essentially differ from their heterosexual sisters—who also report greater comfort talking to their mother than their father about personal, emotional matters.[12] Not uncommonly, because of the investment they have in their daughter's life, mothers already know or suspect her unconventional sexuality; they are often the ones to ask or to bring up the subject.

Of course, not all young women and their mother experience this level of warmth and trust. Some youths report being emotionally and physically abused by their mother; this relatively low number feel that they had a distant or nonexistent childhood relationship.

In sharing this aspect of their life with their mother, young women might not use a sexual identity label to express the nature of their sexuality but instead describe their sexual and emotional attractions. They "have a crush on a woman" or "are primarily attracted to women." Identity labels such as *lesbian* and *bisexual* feel too extreme or sexual, or convey the wrong message. They also want to "soften" the message; describing their sexuality in behavioral or attitudinal terms is a more accurate, gentle method of conveying themselves. In some circumstances, a single coming-out event does not occur—disclosure is a series of conversations over a period of years that communicate a daughter's growing understanding of her sexuality.

The need to share "all" with mother is not always realized. Nearly 40% of the young women in this study have not disclosed, and many of these young women expect at least a slightly negative reaction. Mothers, including Wendy's, who are unfamiliar with what it means to be lesbian or bisexual appear to have the most difficulty with the disclosure and tend to embrace stereotypical notions of these concepts, resulting in feelings of shame, guilt, and self-blame. Nancy's mother could not accept her daughter's attractions because her small-town, conservative upbringing precluded exposure to the modern world. To preempt ignorance, some daughters embark on a campaign of education.

▽   All I wanted was to have an open relationship with her, like we used to have, to speak to her about anything on my mind. So, over the last year I began this campaign to prepare, to educate her about gay issues. She had no clue, no idea of what a lesbian woman was; to her a homosexual man was someone who was nonreproductive. She was in the Dark Ages, and I knew that. I didn't want to be embarrassed by her anymore. I wanted what we used to have. God, I was expecting so much!

Research demonstrates that young women are increasingly sharing their sexuality with their mother, while living at home, and through a variety of modalities, whether by a direct telling, not denying a mother's accusations, a telephone call, or an e-mail. Despite this early age of coming out to mother, the temporal rank of this disclosure relative to other identity milestones has not changed over different cohorts. Of 9 such transitions assessed in this project, disclosure to mother ranked 8th—just ahead of disclosure to father—but only a year after the young woman self-labeled and disclosed to a first person. Mothers might be upset, cry, and beg for a recanting, but most eventually accept their daughter. It is important to remember that although some daughters are at risk for rejection—their mother boots them out of the house, severs financial aid, or disowns them—this is a rare occurrence.

Mothers who do not blame themselves for their daughter's nonheterosexuality, who do not have strong conservative religious or political beliefs that peg homosexuality as sinful or wrong, who have been exposed to gay people and gay culture, and who have a trusting relationship with their daughter are those most likely to maintain good relations with this important young woman. Quite often these are young mothers, who were reared at a time (the 1960s) that encouraged exposure and tolerance toward homosexuality. Empirical research has demonstrated that young women who have such a mother are more likely to be satisfied with their relationship, to be out to her, and to have higher levels of self-esteem. Youths who feel acceptance from their mother also feel comfortable with their sexual orientation.[13] It is this mutual interdependence that moves many mothers forward with their daughters to new affiliations and experiences.

ENDNOTES

[1] Elias, M. (1998, December 14). Teen-age girls say mom's become a pal. *USA Today*, pp. 1D, 8D.

[2] Bell, A. P., Weinberg, M. S., & Hammersmith, S. K. (1981). *Sexual preference: Its development in men and women.* Bloomington: Indiana University Press.

[3] D'Augelli, A. R., & Hershberger, S. L. (1993). Lesbian, gay, and bisexual youth in community settings: Personal challenges and mental health problems. *American Journal of Community Psychology, 21,* 421–448; D'Augelli, A. R. (1998, February). *Victimization history and mental health among lesbian, gay, and bisexual youths.* Paper presented at the Society for Research on Adolescence, San Diego, CA; Lever, J. (1995, August 22). Lesbian sex survey. *The Advocate,* 21–30; and Telljohann, S. K., & Price, J. P. (1993). A qualitative examination of adolescent homosexuals' life experiences: Ramifications for secondary school personnel. *Journal of Homosexuality, 26,* 41–56.

[4] In my earlier research, reported in 1990 in *Gay and Lesbian Youth: Expressions of Identity* (Washington, DC: Hemisphere), 59% of female college students had disclosed to their mothers. This is consistent with the 63% of young women who had disclosed to their mothers in Gil Herdt and Andrew Boxer's (1993), *Children of Horizons: How Gay and Lesbian Teens Are Leading a New Way Out of the Closet* (Boston: Beacon).

[5] D'Augelli, A. R., & Hershberger, S. L. (1993). Lesbian, gay, and bisexual youth in community settings: Personal challenges and mental health problems. *American Journal of Community Psychology, 21,* 421–448; and D'Augelli, A. R. (1998, February). *Victimization history and mental health among lesbian, gay, and bisexual youths.* Paper presented at the Society for Research on Adolescence, San Diego, CA.

[6] D'Augelli, A. R., & Hershberger, S. L. (1993). Lesbian, gay, and bisexual youth in community settings: Personal challenges and mental health problems. *American Journal of Community Psychology, 21,* 421–448; D'Augelli, A. R. (1998, February). *Victimization history and mental health among lesbian, gay, and bisexual youths.* Paper presented at the Society for Research on Adolescence, San Diego, CA; and Weinberg, M. S., Williams, C. J., & Pryor, D. W. (1994). *Dual attraction: Understanding bisexuality.* New York: Oxford University Press.

[7] D'Augelli, A. R., Hershberger, S. L., & Pilkington, N. W. (1998). Lesbian, gay, and bisexual youth and their families: Disclosure of sexual orientation and its consequences. *American Journal of Orthopsychiatry, 68,* 361–371. Confirmation of

the second point is in Weinberg, M. S., Williams, C. J., & Pryor, D. W. (1994). *Dual attraction: Understanding bisexuality.* New York: Oxford University Press.

[8] The mean expected reaction was 3.7 on a 1 (*very supportive*) to 7 (*rejection*) scale; for actual, 3.2.

[9] Ben-Ari, A. (1995). The discovery that an offspring is gay: Parents', gay men's, and lesbians' perspectives. *Journal of Homosexuality, 30,* 89–112.

[10] One of my graduate students, Geoffrey L. Ream, is investigating intrinsic and extrinsic religion in the lives of sexual-minority youths by focusing on the former as a source of resiliency for developing a sexual identity.

[11] Page 40 in Espín, O. M. (1987). Issues of identity in the psychology of Latina lesbians. In Boston Lesbian Psychologies Collective (Eds.), *Lesbian psychologies: Explorations and challenges* (pp. 35–55). Urbana: University of Illinois Press.

[12] Collins, W. A., & Russell, G. (1991). Mother–child and father–child relationships in middle adolescence: A developmental analysis. *Developmental Review, 11,* 99–136.

[13] Savin-Williams, R. C. (1990). *Gay and lesbian youth: Expressions of identity.* Washington, DC: Hemisphere.

5

DAUGHTERS AND FATHERS

Peggy

It was going to be real nervous telling Dad because since he remarried he's very upper class now, with the country club, church (he's turned very Catholic, like his new wife), and career advancement with his new investment firm. After he remarried they live on this island, and I now have several stepbrothers and sisters. His life now centers around these things, so I didn't think he'd be happy to hear about me. With this life and new status I figured he'd be quite embarrassed by having this dyke daughter. The court gave him visitation rights every other weekend, but I still never was that close because what he was into didn't interest me. One year I went without seeing him. He's not really the heart-to-heart type of guy.

At Cornell, my sophomore year I decided I wanted to tell him, that now was the time. But the right moment never came up. I was spending time with him and his new wife on the island, and my girlfriend was nearby and I was visiting her all the time. They saw us together, and I guess this was enough to tip them off. I thought we were discreet, but Dad said we were flirting with each other.

The day before I had to go back to school Dad asked me, "Can I ask you a personal question?" We're not real close so I thought it was going to be a simple question, like what my major was or what I was going to do next summer. "Is there a physical relationship between you two?" I said now is the moment, so I said, "Yes." I didn't want to lie to him, but I was holding my breath. I really had no idea how he would react. I knew he'd not disown me, that he'd still love me in his own way, but I didn't know how he'd be beyond okay with it. He was silent for a bit and then said, "It's okay. We love you. Just make sure you take care of yourself because there's lots of people who will try to harm you."

He knew because of the flirting. I was shocked because I thought he had no clue. He never notices personal things like that about me. Then he laughed because he already knew and thought I knew that he knew, which was why he thought we were being so obvious with our flirting, but I didn't know we were that obvious. Overall he was supportive, I guess, but mostly nonreactive.

Since then, he will ask about my girlfriend but won't talk about it a lot. It's just there. Friendly about it but not real supportive. My stepmom knows, but we haven't talked. As a person she likes me and respects me, but she does not ask. Her brother is gay, so I think that helped him be good about it.

My sister called me a week later and said that Dad had figured it out months ago, and he wanted me to know that he knew but couldn't tell me that he knew. He thought I had no clue about what I was, and he wanted to tell me that he thought I was lesbian but didn't know how to tell me. We both had a big laugh over that.

Nan

We're in his car, a rainy night, and he was depressed. He and Mom were having another fight. He was flipping out, crying, so I thought I'd add to his trauma. He flipped, really flipped out. We talk about politics but nothing ever personal stuff. He is not used to hearing about my personal life. So this was a shocker, just to be personal.

He didn't know what to say. Next morning he yelled at me. Said I can't be religious and bisexual. He said he should have known given how close I was to my female friends. He thinks it's the result of my feminism; he is oblivious in general to my life. Said I can't be in his home and bring girls. He thought an older woman had molested me. I guess in a women's studies course.

Until a month ago he never talked about it. He went along, and it never came up. Then had long talk over the phone on all sorts of things, religion, God, slavery, queer women. He was not flipping out but listening. Tolerating it, but he still believes it's wrong, sinful. No real expression since then. He's been civil to my girlfriend. He just doesn't deal with it. No real change over time since that conversation. He loves me because I'm his daughter. He doesn't seem to think he has a choice.

Weaver

We're not very close, and he's very indifferent toward these kinds of things. I never know when or how he is told things about me. No talk between us. He knows everything about me through my mom. Never any personal conversation with him. We don't talk that much, and he knows nothing about me, not even my major.

I haven't told him because we're not on good terms; not on bad terms, just not any terms. I rarely see him, even when living there for a long time, and we rarely talk about anything. I assume he knows, I guess.

It's hard to say how I'd expect him to react. No way would he be negative; maybe neutral. We're not very close, and it will be an awkward conversation, but he will be fine with it. He won't have a strong reaction or freak out. He'd not care so much. He's very laid back, in his own world.

I don't want to bother him with it. Our relationship is just not strong. The only way I'd tell him if I was in a serious relationship and then I feel obligated to tell him. But I don't feel a need to tell him because he's just not a big part of my life. This was never on his agenda or mine. This is not on my list of things to tell him, to share emotional or sexual life.

Although Peggy, Nan, and Weaver have had very different experiences with the decision of whether to tell their father about their same-sex attractions, they share one commonality—each feels that her relationship with her father is impaired, distant, and nonemotional. Indeed, the *lack of a relationship* is the central theme of this chapter. Whether it is less than or varies in degree from the relationship that a young woman without same-sex attractions has with her father is unknown. The nature of the relationship sexual-minority daughters have with their fathers before, during, and after disclosure is explored in this chapter.

THE RELATIONSHIP BEFORE DISCLOSURE

When researchers in the late 1960s compared "homosexual" and heterosexual women, the former "presented a somewhat less-favorable picture of their fathers and of their relationships with them."[1] Compared with heterosexual women, lesbian and bisexual adults were more likely to report having felt anger, fear, and resentment toward their father while growing up and to feel detached from him. To them, he was unfair and rejecting— but not seductive—and did not show favoritism toward another child. They were less likely to identify with him and to describe him as strong, active, and dominant. It should be remembered, however, that many of these women grew up in the 1930s and 1940s, a very different time from the one in which current cohorts of young women were raised. Other than psychoanalytically oriented research studies and clinical case histories, research on the lesbian daughter–father relationship prior to disclosure is scant.

All three women whose stories begin this chapter report distant relationships with their father. Peggy is "not real close" with her father and thus does not know him well. Nan's relationship with her father is so impaired that she had few qualms about adding to his trauma when she came out to him. Weaver and her father communicate so rarely that she feels that he has little knowledge about her. These three youths represent the young women I interviewed. Some have better relations with their father and some much worse, but on average most feel alienated from their father even before they decide to disclose to him. Whether this disconnected father–daughter relationship is particular to this sample or representative of most young women with same-sex attractions cannot be determined by prior empirical research.

Distant Relationships

The vast majority of narratives detailing relations with father reflect neither positive nor negative relations, only nonexistent, distant contact. These narratives are usually short, blunt, and painful, signaling largely non-emotional connections. If involved at all, then the dyadic relationship is usually based on rational discourse. One young woman's father is "intellectual, so we talk about communism and not about sex. He knows less about my personal life; it seems less of his business. We talk about abstract ideas." Thus, the decision to disclose is seldom major or life altering and is determined mostly by convenience or judiciousness. One youth simply said, "We speak only once a year, so his opinion is not that important to me."

Conflictual Relationships

Less commonly, young women recall primarily negative experiences with their father while growing up. These memories include instances not only of neglect but also, occasionally, of physical and emotional abuse.

▽   Because my father was very physically abusive to me and my sister and to the boys, my mom moved herself and my youngest brother out to an apartment to protect him. But she couldn't live there with him because of her job, so I went there to live. Dad flipped out when he found out [about the move]. I got involved with men to protect me from my father and the boys on the street.

▽   He's supposed to be in my life! He's my father damn him! But he's not in my life. He's ignored me as he has his whole family and broke my heart so many times that I don't talk to him now. I never intend to tell him. He's mentally unstable and very negative.
    Give you an idea of how he would respond. When I was 10 he said never bring home any "brownies" as dates. My boyfriend in junior high was Black, so I could never mention him, and he didn't know. I have no memories of him while growing up. He was never around because he was at the office.

Several of the young women interviewed believe that they could have a good relationship with their father were it not for their mother. Despite a history of conflict, one young woman had only respect for her father.

▽   He might be cool about it, but he has been around Mom too long. He is capable of dealing with it. The person is more important than the label, a concept beyond Mom. He is an honest, wonderful person except when around Mom. However, I've lost respect for him because he won't stand up to her. He is a logical person, and I can reason with him. If I told him I know that he'd be disappointed with me, but he would not cut me off. He'd just ignore it.

"Daddy's Little Girl"

Several daughters who felt close to their father while growing up consider themselves to be "daddy's little girl." The warmth and closeness of the relationship sometimes carries through to the present time. The following young woman is one of the relatively few youths who reports such a positive relationship with her father.

∇   I was the classic "daddy's little girl," and I loved it. I and everyone else knew I was his favorite. He told me stories at night and let me come into his shop in the basement, where no one was allowed, and watch him make things. He was the one who talked to me about my body, sex, puberty. He came to all my track meets and got me back in school when I was suspended for smoking.

My freshman year in high school I was listening to the Indigo Girls, and he looked at the CD cover and asked me in a joking way if there was something I wanted to tell him. He's open-minded, and I get lots of attention from him. He'll be the hardest to tell because what he thinks means the most to me.

From these prior relationships, young women must decide whether to come out to their father. Most decide against it, until a later age.

WHETHER FATHERS ARE TOLD

Research has generally acknowledged that the percentage of daughters who have disclosed to their father is considerably less than those who have disclosed to their mother. This discrepancy, however, may be decreasing among recent cohorts of young women. For example, with data collected during the late 1980s, Gil Herdt and Andrew Boxer reported that just over 60% of Chicago lesbian and bisexual teenagers disclosed to their mother, but just over 33% had told their father. During the same time period I distributed an anonymous survey to 103 young women, 60% of whom had disclosed to their mother compared with only 25% to their father. Five years later, Tony D'Augelli reported that 42% of lesbian and bisexual adolescents living with their parents had knowledgeable fathers; this percentage increased to nearly 60% in a second data set collected several years ago.[2]

In the present study, 45% of young women are out to their father, considerably below the 63% who are out to their mother. Although the two do not talk about it, far more daughters believe that their father knows or has strong suspicions about his daughter's sexuality. In similar situations with the mother, the parent and child are likely to talk about the mother's suspicions.

A second point also surfaces from the narratives: A cohort effect appears to cut across sample differences among youths and their fathers. That is, contemporary samples of young women with same-sex attractions are more likely than previous generations to come out to their father. However, the proportion of those who disclose remains considerably smaller than those who come out to their mothers.

Why daughters do not disclose to their father has been a matter of conjecture rather than empirical investigation. The narratives offer several insights regarding the reasons for this withholding.

REASONS NOT TO TELL

Given that half of sexual-minority young women are not out to their father, why have they not disclosed this most vital aspect of their personal life? Of the undisclosed young women I interviewed, nearly one half responded overwhelmingly with a response similar to Weaver, "We're not very close, and he's very indifferent toward these kinds of things." One fifth could not give a reason as to why they have not come out, except to say that they have not gotten around to it. Less frequent, constituting about 10% each of the reasons not to disclose, are it is not the right developmental time, they fear his negative reactions, and they do not want to hurt him.

Not Close

Many of the nondisclosing young women withhold the information because, "It doesn't matter if he knows or not; we're not that close." One youth simply said, "He's not in my life." Not one young woman offered "not close" as the primary reason for not disclosing to her *mother*. Daughters "adapt" to this difficult situation by further emotionally distancing themselves from their father. "Well, he would be very passive. It wouldn't matter to me because he doesn't matter to me. If I did it then it would be by e-mail. I guess he would be disappointed and that would be it."

Many of these fathers are described as "clueless," not only about their daughter's sexuality but also about her life, relationships, and feelings.

▽ He only knows what Mom tells him. He is the scientist type. He has no prejudices. He doesn't care. He would just ignore the subject and wouldn't know how to handle it. Even if I say I like a boy he has no reactions. We talk science and engineering things, and tell bad jokes. We don't talk about anything serious. He'd say, "Go ask your mother."

This famine of intimacy convinces many daughters that it is not particularly important to tell their father. "Our relationship has tempered my desire to tell him. It is not a close relationship anyway. Once before, I told him that I didn't feel close to him and that he didn't know me. So if I told him then that would be something else he would say I didn't share with him. It's not worth it." Some expect negative reactions but most predict no reaction—which is exactly the reason why they choose not to tell him. One youth stated that although she does not know whether others have told him, it is one conversation she would rather not have.

▽ Once he saw me with my woman/woman earrings and says, "Does this mean something?" I said it was just great art. So I denied it because I just didn't want to get into it with him.
    I seldom see him because he travels all the time, but it is purely a practical matter. I'd tell him if I had a female partner and wanted to bring her home. Don't know how he'd respond but probably not be real happy with it. He'd probably ask how I know. I don't want that conversation. We were never that close because of his personality.

Have Not Gotten Around to It

Similar in tone are the young women who have no specific reasons not to come out: They just have not gotten around to it. In most situations, it is apparent that the daughter and father are not intimately connected. The daughter will tell him, probably soon.

▽ We already have the rift that he doesn't know me. To tell him would really tell him he really doesn't know me, or knows me even less than he thinks he does. He doesn't know my friends or my life or the questions I've had, and we've not ever talked about gay issues. I will tell him because I have to, but I don't know when.

Not the Right Developmental Time

For other young women, the best time to come out to their father has not yet arrived. This is often motivated by the desire to avoid pain, for either her or her father, that would inevitably ensue. These 15% of young women require more time before this affront is delivered to their sketchy bond.

▽ He'd say it is not normal, so why put myself through that? There is a big emphasis in his family of being "normal" and marrying. Dad is completely homophobic. He's got no idea of my life or experiences. I can't tell him, not yet. Once I asked him, "What if I said I was gay?" and he said, "You're not gay. Gay people can't get married."

When I was little we had fun times together. As I got older and witnessed the fighting between him and Mom, he became more villainized in my eyes. Since the divorce Mom and my sister say bad things about him, and I agree with them. I've just tried to maintain good relations with him on the surface. We're not ready to do issues with each other. He's 61, and we have got a lot of scars.

What would provoke a disclosure by these daughters? The answer for many is a very serious same-sex romantic relationship that would "prove" to him that they are serious about this "lesbian thing."

▽ He wants me to be more feminine, and he doesn't "get" me. His sister just started dating a woman after three marriages and six kids, and he's been okay with that, but not emotionally supportive. I'm afraid that's the way he'd be with me. Being in love would solve my dilemma. Then I'd have to tell him.

Fear Negative Repercussions

By contrast are the 10% of young women who fear personal and negative repercussions subsequent to a disclosure. These range from losing financial support to foregoing their recently acquired sense of independence and freedom. One daughter considered the possibility that her father might disown her, so she has "no plans to tell him; well, maybe after I graduate when I'm independent of him." Then the unexpected happened.

▽ All my friends said it would be crazy because he would cut my money and kick me out. I was out and active at college, but I couldn't tell my parents. I wanted to complete my degree first, so I decided not to tell them.

  Then he passed away from a heart attack. When my dad was working on the house and needed a helper, then I did that. I liked fixing things like cars, building, aggressive things like haggle at buying things in store, being independent. He liked me when I did these things, although he expected I would marry and stay at home. He could not imagine why I wanted a college degree or to make more money than my husband. He wanted me to be a lady.

An African American young woman has no plans to tell her father because, "He has no need to know. He'd label me for life. He overreacts to everything, like when I dated a White guy. No relationship with him, and I could not have one even if I told him."

Wants Not to Hurt Him

A few daughters choose not to disclose because they do not want to unduly hurt or disappoint their father. Perhaps they have a tentative relationship with him and they do not want to be the "cause" of even slight pain and disappointment.

∇ We don't just "chat" like Mom and I do. Doesn't know the details of my life, which is fine with me, but it does scare me a little. Don't know him as well.

We have such a weird relationship. I mean he's so good to me. He thinks I'm perfect, and I'm afraid it will annoy him if I tell him. I hope he doesn't flip out. He's impressed by the things I do, and he's very happy with me. He would prefer a husband, but he would trust whatever I do.

He's a wild card. He could be very upset. I think he won't be happy but will tell Mom to calm down. He takes the "don't worry, be happy" approach to life. He'll be the hardest. He'll probably make jokes about it and pick on me for a week like he used to do. He picks on me when he's hurt.

He should know, and I have guilt because he deserves to go through the same process I've been through. It's not fair to him. He deserves a mourning period.

Or, a daughter fears that she will hurt her father's status or reputation in the community, especially if she were to come out publicly.

∇ Because of his position as mayor I don't want him to deal with it. Not sure how he'd react, although he is a Democrat! He has no problems with gays in general, but it'd be different for him conceiving it in a positive way and actually experiencing it when it was his daughter. I talk to him about my gay friends, and it is okay with him.

Initially he'd be hurt, and then okay with it. He would accept it though it'd bother him. I'm his baby girl, and I feel it would have hurt him if I told him, that he'd not be elected. He does not believe that it is a choice or abnormal—like a genetic population control. It'd be a struggle because he wants to run for higher office.

I should tell him—and I will, next Break, I promise! Really, though, if I told him he wouldn't say anything but would look grim, go back to reading his newspaper, and later maybe call Mom and ask her to "do" something about it. He needs me and our relationship. If I were in a romantic relationship with a woman I'd have to because I wouldn't do it to her. Maybe he would tell me to think it over—"Is it such a wise choice?" he'd caution me. "Now don't act rashly. Think through the consequences. Be an adult about this. Consider your family." Anyway, that's my guess.

Daughters are often baffled about what to expect from their father if they were to tell him. He is a mystery, and as long as they are unable to predict his reactions they will not come out to him. One youth described her father as "a nut case." She has no plans to disclose, and would only consider it if "I were independent enough and in control of things, then maybe." Many young women long for the time when they can feel more in touch with their father.

The other half of the young women I interviewed disclosed to their father. Their reasons for sharing this information are diverse but for many it is simply the right time, someone else tells him, or it is something "to get over with."

REASONS TO TELL

Although little is known about the reasons daughters do not disclose to their fathers, even less is understood about why others do. Because most relationships youths have with their father prior to disclosure are impaired or, more precisely, nonexistent, daughters are primarily motivated to disclose not to improve their relationship (because they have given up) but to fulfil an obligation. Daughters can be so ambivalent about their impaired or shallow relationship with their father that it seems unimportant to disclose. A variety of other, less frequent, circumstances can also provoke a daughter's coming out to her father.

Right Time and Outed by Another

Nearly three quarters of young women out to their father in the present study report that they cannot specify a precise reason for disclosing to their father, other than vaguely suggesting that "the time was right" or because someone else—almost always their mother—told him. In the former cases, the women decide, usually without emotion, that it is something they have to do—or something their mother asked or demanded of them.

∇ This was a week later, and I felt pressured into it because I had told Mom earlier, and she was so positive about it and proud. She said I had to tell him because it'd be unfair if he didn't know, and he will be so good anyway. I wondered if it wouldn't be different if it's your daughter. But she asked me to do it, so I really had to.

∇ I told him last October because I was going on the internship, and he'd have to know where I was and what I was doing [lesbian-related position]. I don't have a lot of respect for him even though I get a lot from him intellectually. He's not been a great parent, but an adequate one, so it just seemed life would be easier if I told him then.

In the following cases, the young women confirm, usually without offering elaboration, the information because they do not want to lie or they embrace the opportunity "as good of a time as ever."

∇   Either my sister or my mother told him, or he pieced it together some-how. He has met my girlfriends, so it must have been obvious for him, but I never told him directly. Yet one day he asked if I was going with June, and I said that I was. So that was how I knew that he knew about my lifestyle.

∇   Mom told him the next day. I knew she would; she has no secrets from him. He told her that it was my business and not to talk about it. He'd like to sweep it under the rug, he told her. He would not understand such things, and I don't like his view on such things. We can share a lot about careers, ideas, but not about personal things.

Father Asks

Peggy never found the "right" time to disclose to her father; eventually he directly confronted her by asking "the question." A parent initiating the disclosure is far less common among fathers (five times less frequent) than mothers, perhaps because mothers are more in tune with their daughter's life, and fathers do not want to "intrude" into her personal matters. Only about 5% of fathers initiate such a conversation; many more are instructed by their wives to ask their daughter about the nature of her sexual orientation.

Fear of Being Outed

Fear of being outed by others, including newspaper editors, can also be the impetus for disclosure. Apprehension about media exposure is most common among politically active women. One classic example is of a young bisexual woman who is out at college but in the closet in her hometown community.

∇   I was outed by the *Daily Review* [student newspaper] to my family. It is one of my *favorite* coming-out stories because in retrospect I think it is a riot, but it was not fun at the time. My parents had come up for Parents Weekend, and the *Review* took the opportunity to report on student elections. My parents picked up a copy to see my picture with the words "Lesbian, gay, bisexual, and transgender rep" underneath it. They said nothing, but I could feel the tension.
    So we were at lunch, and the Dean of Students stops by and congratu-lates me on my election. So Dad said to me, "So what's this deal with this lesbian gay thing?" and I said, "Oh I identify as bisexual now," and put this huge bite of salad in my mouth hoping I wouldn't have to answer any more questions.

Wants to Hurt Him

Several young women, similar to Nan, decide to punish or traumatize their father by disclosing their sexual attractions. One youth so resented the intellectual, noninvolved relationship she and her father share, that by disclosing this most secretive aspect of her life that she knew would meet with his disapproval, she was hoping to punish him for his prior neglect and to get his attention, to "turn his head."

▽ We have a weird relationship. He's a very nonconfrontational kind of a guy, and his way to solve all problems is to throw money at it. That's his job in the family, the extent of his family obligation. It's him, but it's always bothered me, more now that I'm in college, and I can see that not all fathers have to be that way.

We're not close, so sometimes I've taken to shocking him to get a reaction, or maybe just to get back at him for years of emotional neglect. His voice raised about three octaves. "Are you sure?" Then he went back to his newspaper. I tried.

Wants to Share Her Life

Occasionally, young women disclose to their father because they sincerely want to share this aspect of their life with him. One in 20 young women—as opposed to 1 in 3 with mothers—report that they came out because they desired their father's support and approval, which they usually receive. Despite tremendous pressure not to tell her father, one youth decided that the most important priority was to establish a positive relationship with him.

▽ The question really was why I waited a year after telling Mom. They were getting divorced, and it was a gross divorce. I was being used by both of them, so Mom didn't want me to tell him because he might use it against her in court. It was easy to hide because he lived in New Jersey.

I regretted that so much because it wasn't fair to me. So I finally decided to screw Mom and tell Dad because I wanted a relationship with him. He has to know about me. I told him, and he's been supportive, at least as best as he can.

Because most fathers seemingly do not notice or care about their daughter's sexual orientation, most youths assume that the disclosure is not a very important event to him.

▽ I told my friends and most of the people at college. Dad was fourth in the family, after my second sister, mother, and oldest sister. It was most important to tell them, but I knew one more and I'd be finished. It was my mission to get it all over with by the beginning of the summer. That only left Dad.

This "only leaving Dad" usually ends when his daughter comes out to him under orders of her mother. As is apparent in the next section, quite often the mother has already disclosed her daughter's sexuality to her husband.

WHEN AND HOW FATHERS ARE TOLD

Few research studies document the average age at which daughters disclose to their father, because the investigator did not ask, did not differentiate father from mother ("parents"), or grouped sexual-minority young women with young men. One exception is a study that reported an average disclosure age of 17.2 years among support group youths,[3] more than a year younger than the young women I interviewed (18.5 years). The latter timing corresponds to freshman year Thanksgiving Break for those in college. The range is from 15 to 25 years, although some of the older youths have not yet disclosed and have no plans to do so.

Similar to the research of others, none of the young women disclosed to their father before anyone else. Father as an object of first disclosure has varied from 0% to 3% in other studies.[4] Seldom, but occasionally, daughters disclose to their father before they disclose to their mother—four young women in the present sample did so. Eight young women disclosed to both parents at the same time.

Direct Disclosure

The majority of daughters who come out do so directly, if they can find an appropriate context in which to have a private conversation with their father. This is not always easy. She often has to corral her father while he is watching television or in a car, or otherwise attempt to manipulate the situation such that he is a captive audience.

▽   So when he picked me up at the end of my first semester and we were driving home I told him. Mom wasn't there, which was important because I wanted just us, and we are almost never alone. I had this all planned out and even told Mom not to come because I wanted some time alone with Dad. Of course she knew why and warned me to be careful, but I knew he could not get away or ignore me in the car. That was important because that defines our relationship—he ignores me and my issues.

The daughter might also exert control by assembling a family meeting.

▽   I told Mom and Dad together, 10 days after I came out to myself. I was so happy with my discovery that I wanted to share it. I had been questioning my sexuality and had been miserable, depressed, hated school, and they were worried about me. They sent me to a psychiatrist to help me feel better, but I couldn't tell him or my parents. I just wanted them not to worry anymore. I was 18 at the time, and they were surprised. I thought they knew, like I thought I had given so many clues, but they hadn't picked up any.

One daughter intended to tell both parents together, but her plan was foiled when at the last minute her father decided to turn in for the night. She told him later, "in passing, no big deal. That's how we are as a family." Another youth knew she had to tell her parents together, because if she did not, "he'd know within two to three seconds because Mom would tell him. No secrets in our family!"

Indirect Disclosure

When a daughter does not disclose directly to her father, 40% of the time it is because her mother beat her to it. This does not always please the young woman.

▽ She wanted me to tell him, and so the next day I did. But she had already told him. I told her not to tell him, but she did anyway. I wanted to tell him. I was really furious with her.

Even if the youth's mother does not tell her husband, the disclosure situation is as likely to be instigated by the mother as by the daughter. The mother might arrange a "family meeting" in which the information is divulged by the daughter or drawn out by the mother. It is almost as if the father is a bystander. When one daughter was 16 years old, her mother pulled her aside while she was washing dishes and said, " 'We need to talk to you about something.' Dad was watching TV. 'We think you're having problems with your sexuality. Do you want to share it with us?' Dad was not getting involved in this, but he was hearing."

Although daughters usually disclose to their father through direct means, many prefer to avoid the awkward or unpleasant situation and are thus perfectly satisfied to hand off responsibility to their mother—who indeed is likely to share the information with her husband. Daughters can, however, count on one thing—fathers almost never ask directly about the nature of their daughter's sexual attractions.

In indirect situations, a youth seldom knows how her father reacted because she was not present at the disclosing moment—although she may receive reports from her mother about his reactions. Alternatively, the father discovers the news on his own and acts as if he knows, even though the daughter never had the "real" conversation with him.

∇   I never actually sat down to tell him, like in a direct way. I don't feel comfortable talking about my sexuality with him. Never said the words like you're supposed to. It would like have been awkward for both of us.

Whether the manner in which disclosure takes place reflects the nature of the mother–father or the daughter–father relationship is not always clear from the narratives.

FATHERS' INITIAL REACTIONS

When reading the research literature, it is often difficult to disentangle reports of a father's initial from his current reactions. Empirical investigations frequently ask, "How has each of the following persons reacted to your disclosure?" Unclear, however, is whether youths are reporting the current state of parent–youth relations or how their parents initially reacted to the news. In one study, by a 2-to-1 margin, fathers were perceived to be more accepting than rejecting.[5] Fathers most frequently reacted in another study (sex of child unspecified) with shock, shame, and acknowledgment and rarely with rejection or anger.[6]

Once Peggy "confessed" her same-sex attractions, her father completely accepted her. This is in marked contrast to Nan's father, who first screamed at her and then asserted that she had either been molested by an older woman or converted through the many women's studies courses she has been attending. Because this range of reactions characterizes fathers, any generalizations about the content and emotional tone of their initial reactions must be suspect.

Expected Versus Actual Reactions

One stereotype is that fathers react in a very negative way, and this expectation prevents daughters from disclosing. However, as noted earlier, young women do not disclose to their father not because they expect him to be negative, but because they are not close to him. Indeed, youths who have not disclosed expect a reaction midway between "neutral" and "slightly negative."[7] This is nearly identical to the reaction actually received by young women who have come out to their father. Similar to the mother's initial reaction, daughters recount that the most common response from their father was "slightly positive" (1 in 3), followed by "slightly negative" (1 in 4), and then "neutral" (1 in 7). One in 15 was either extremely positive or negative.

Perhaps fathers most likely to react negatively to the disclosure are not told precisely because of this expected reaction. Countering this argument, however, is evidence that those who have not come out to their father report nearly the same level of negativity as that received from those who have disclosed. As noted throughout this chapter, the most likely reason daughters do not disclose to their father is because he is not a particularly important person in their lives.

Positive Initial Reactions

Despite less than ringing endorsements of their daughter's sexuality, some fathers respond positively, even with support, to having a daughter with same-sex attractions. Peggy's father should not be considered the exception. One father thought it was "no big deal" and readily approved the woman his daughter was dating: "He's gone out to dinner with me and my girlfriend. They hit it right off." In fact, some father–daughter dyads discover that they share a common desire for women: "With him we can watch movies and comment on the good-looking women. If Melissa Etheridge is on TV he'll call me. I like her music; he doesn't, but we both like her body." Another father told his daughter that he was proud that she had the courage and conviction "to follow your feelings. Whatever makes you happy makes me happy." Other fathers experience general parental concerns, such as whether their daughter will be safe in a homophobic world.

∇   We're pretty good friends. He travels a lot, so I don't see him a lot. Not as close to him as Mom. But we get along fabulously well. He's more politically conservative and very logical. He was not as much concerned either way, which is normal for him. He'd say, "Okay, do your own thing, whatever makes you happy." He would not care. He was most concerned for my safety because he knows what kind of world is out there. But he would not judge me badly.

The relationship might actually improve following disclosure. In the following father–daughter dyad, the historically awkward, emotionally vacant relationship did not bode well for a positive response to the information.

∇   Our time was always very awkward, as it is for many Chinese daughters and their father. I visited him once with my girlfriend, and I had to edit what I said and did, and this really bummed me out. How could I look her in the face and say we had an honest relationship? I kept putting it off, but I knew I had to.
     I finally told him over the phone. He was fine, and this shocked me. He knew about the genetics and that you can't control it. His support was strong, but I knew that he had problems because he is a very traditional Chinese man. But he wants to be PC and modern, and it is hard to get around this.
     He was supportive, but this is a facet of my life, my sexuality, that we don't talk about. He is not happy with my being attracted to women, and this comes out in different ways, like arguments over money. It is

still an issue with him and source of some friction. Now we talk more and are getting close for the first time. Maybe he sees his chance to be a parent, since my mom is not doing well with it. This is his chance, maybe his last, to relate to me.

Neutral Initial Reactions

A significant number of fathers is neither positive nor negative in their initial reactions because they frequently depend on their wife for appropriate directives regarding how to react during family calamities. In her absence, they are at a loss for how to react. Thus, they may provide little indication to their daughter about how they actually feel about her same-sex attractions. One father who simply took his wife's lead to find out how he ought to react perpetuated the weak ties in the father–daugher relationship. The crisis, which severed family relationships for months, might have been averted if he had sided with his daughter and tempered his wife's outrageously negative reactions to the disclosure.

∇   He is very submissive and passive to Mom. He's afraid of her, so when she yelled at me to "get into the fucking van," he thought it was directed at him, and he got in real quickly! He doesn't stand up a lot to her or anyone else. I want to share things with him, but he feels he has to be equally accepting or rejecting as Mom. I can't speak about it with him because I don't want to get him into trouble with her. If she were to find out that he knows something she doesn't then all hell breaks loose. He can't know anything. I'm mad at him for being so nelly in front of her.

On their own, fathers often demonstrate their uncertainty and, from the perspective of their daughter, incompetence in reacting to their coming out. One father said that it is not what he would "choose for her." "He only said this because he did not know what else to say, and this seemed like a safe thing to say, like he had read it in a book that this was what you were supposed to say." Quite often this "will always love you" response rings a little hollow for the daughter.

∇   Dad said he'd love me no matter what—but he said that just because it's what he thought he should say. He hugged me and said he loved me. He was "not happy" with it and said I'd not be kicked out—probably because then the family friends and his parents would know something was wrong, and he'd have to tell them. But it shocked me to think that he'd even consider kicking me out!

Another youth theorized that her father's response appeared less than sincere because, as the city's attorney, he was more concerned with protecting his reputation than entering the emotional life of his daughter. She sarcastically reported, "He didn't want to be embarrassed by public displays of unconventionality, especially by members of his *first family*." Now that he is safely married to a more "respectable" woman than his daughter's mother, he wants to keep intact his reputation as a "family man with family values."

∇   He nodded along at first, blowing me off by saying trite kinds of crap. This is what he's been like most of my life, only this was worse. It had some shock value on him, mixed in with other things I never expected to hear from him—like we're all born bisexual. I've never even heard him say that word before! It was his way of saying, "nothing special" and "get over it."

Then he said "make no public announcements about it" and "don't go marching in any parades." I think he was afraid for his reputation in this small town. He feared for his image and what my outing would be like for his new family and children.

As noted earlier, in reality many young women do not know the first reactions of their father because they are not present for the disclosure. Their mother tells him and then sometimes reports his reactions. Or, the father makes an opaque reference to knowing but does not reveal how he feels at the time. Not infrequently, daughters assume one response from their father and then later discover that he had reacted in a quite different manner.

∇   I'm 16 and we're talking about it, and I asked him how he would deal if he had a lesbian daughter, and he said he already knew he had one— so I guess Mom told him. I told him I was going out with a girl, and he said, "Yeah, okay, whatever makes you happy." He said it didn't change anything, he still loves me, and they'd never kick me out. He just did not want me to talk about it, wanted to avoid the whole topic. I've never had real good communication with him, and I've found out that e-mail is the best way to communicate with him. He can type his emotions better than he can say them.

I thought everything was basically okay, and then Mom tells me that he was disappointed about it, feels it's a rejection of their lives and the way they live. He sees it as a choice because I could have been with a man. It is hard to know about him because he's so nonexpressive. He said this was not what he would choose for me, but he has not mentioned it since. He doesn't want me to tell anyone.

Negative Initial Reactions

Fathers also respond as adversely as do their wives. Exemplary dyads include the mother and father who attempted to "steal" their daughter from her "lesbian-oriented" college to save her from herself, as well as the religious parents whose daughter disclosed only after a "friend" threatened to tell them. These disclosures ended utopian years for the adolescent girls. Unquestionably, the daughter in the second scenario reported the most negative reaction from a father.

∇   I was a tomboy, and I'd attach onto Dad and watch him work and become his little boy. I identified with him. Once I heard my parents argue, and Dad said, "You know she's a lesbian," and Mom said, "I know." Not sure they were talking about me, but it shook me up. This was when I was 14 and showing no signs of attractions to boys, as opposed to my sisters, who were boy crazy. The defining moment came when I was 15. I had been good friends with Jessica, and Dad took me into the garage for one of his long boring talks. I zoned out until he said, "You know, lesbians aren't as happy as they look."

After I told him his first reaction was, "I knew it! But I didn't think this soon." I said, "Why didn't you do anything to prevent it? You should have stopped me." I felt very guilty, on my own, no support or help, that this was one of the worst things in my life. He was really angry, so furious. He yelled at me, "What are you going to do about it?" and he said I had to change if I ever wanted to be a part of the family. He kicked me out, and I had to live with my grandmother.

Of course, a father's response can also be the more reactive of the pair. In the following narrative, although the young woman's mother is not particularly accepting of her daughter's sexual status, she at least acknowledges and supports her daughter's sexuality.

∇   He was a lot worse because he's more conservative. He's a big Rush Limbaugh fan, can you believe it? Newt Gingrich is his hero. It's not because he thinks it's a sin because he's an atheist, a scientist, and a physicist, so he does not believe in sin. He has more problems with it than he'd like to admit. He knows he should be liberal about it, being an academic and a scientist, but he really isn't. Dad had actually seen something between me and my girlfriend that made him suspicious. He told Mom to find out what was going on. I don't think he like really wanted to know.

I'm like him in temperament so initially we had serious, even violent, arguments, and so we've learned to avoid controversial issues. He wanted me to tell no one at his work or any of his relatives. We never talk about it, so I don't know what's going on. He's still half in denial. He thinks I'll marry a man, so he holds onto the bi thing.

Is the continuation of a father's initial paternalistic behavior toward his daughter's same-sex attractions the last word on the subject? The essential question is, does the disclosure improve their relationship? Does it mark the onset of increasingly bad relations, or does it have minimal effects?

As noted in the mother–daughter chapter, the very limited research literature suggests that parent–child relations generally improve after the initial disclosure. Unfortunately, sex of parent and sex of child are seldom separated. Thus, whether relations between father and daughter actually recuperate, deteriorate, or remain the same is unknown. Data from the present study convey a mixed outcome. Although father–daughter relationships seldom worsen after disclosure, they also seldom improve, which is quite distressing for young women who had hoped against great odds that the net upshot of the risk they undertook to come out to their father would be the establishment of a real relationship. However, few are that surprised, primarily because they had so little real communication with their father before disclosure that they have little reason to imagine a better situation. This alone might be their last chance to connect with their father. The vast majority would be disappointed.

The Relationship Continues

Peggy's father initially responded positively to the confirmation of his suspicions that he had a "dyke daughter"—and during the intervening years he has not wavered from that support. So too, Nan's father has remained steadfast in his negativity toward his daughter and her sexuality. Both daughter–father relationships reflect the predominant pattern among such dyads—relatively little movement in degree of support and acceptance months and years after the disclosure. In the present study, 85% of the young women report "no change" in the relationship they have with their father after disclosure. Four relationships were enhanced after the initial disclosure, and one declined.

Most typical are situations in which daughter-tells-dad-who-is-tolerant-but-not-happy-and-they-avoid-the-topic-thereafter.

▽   I'm not sure of his support. We've had huge fights about it—he claiming that I'm so selfish to be bi, that it is affecting the family financially, making everyone angry. I don't know how my bisexuality is costing them money! Dad accepts me only because I'm his daughter, but what does that mean? That he'd not accept me if I weren't his daughter? And what is his acceptance worth? He won't let me bring a female home. He calls me here at college and asks how things are going, real generic. He can't talk about it, so we don't.

   He said things like, "I support you." "Life is too short." "Hope you find someone to love." But there's no follow-up, no sincerity. He tends to hide his feelings anyway. He's not much involved in my life, but he's never been before. He said things like, "I know you can handle it." "You'll do just fine." What does all that crap really mean? He doesn't bring it up, and won't.

∇   I think he had sensed something was wrong because I was going out with women so much. I wasn't dating men, and he couldn't figure out why, not that we talked about such things. He also knew that I had gone to a student group meeting of queers, but I officially came out to him a year ago when he helped me move to graduate school. It opened up a dialogue with him. He was sad because I was involved with a woman. He's in his late 60s, and I don't expect him to understand. He loves me, won't kick me out, but is still uncomfortable with it. We don't talk about it, then or now.

    I'm better off than most because I'm accepted, but no real change. He fears that I won't be accepted, and that is very important to him. He came to see me recently, and he'll say nothing although I'm there with all my lesbian books and posters. Or, when I try to talk to him he'll say we'll talk another time.

Several young women believe that their father could have progressed toward greater understanding and eventual acceptance save for one factor—this shift would negatively impact the tentative relationship he has with his wife. That is, several fathers sacrifice the relationship they have with their daughter in order to "keep peace in the family." Their daughters understand, but do not like it.

∇   After I left the letter and the book for Dad he tried to talk to me, but he is such a sweet man, and he just doesn't get it. He never tried to talk me out of it, but he does wish I not be gay because it upsets Mother. He believes it is a choice, and he doesn't understand why I would ever chose it. But he is not allowed to respond when Mother is present. He can't support me if she disagrees with me.

    I'll give you an example. Dad was fine with my girlfriend being over but that was because Mother wasn't here. I thought he was coming around last year. I was dating a Roman Catholic guy, and both thought I should not be dating someone who was not Jewish. We had this huge fight. I was shaking with anger at what my parents were saying. My dad then says, "We rather you dated a Jewish girl than a non-Jewish man." I thought that was a really big step forward, but once Mother gave him "that look" he quickly had to take it back.

    I used to hate him because Mother told me he was an evil man, but then I began to see him in a new way, as totally under Mother's thumb. He is getting better, but our relationship is not wonderful. He still doesn't understand a lot, especially about my life, and he is always afraid of Mother. Like he can't know something officially without telling her or else he'll get in trouble. So he'll "know" about my girlfriend, but we won't talk about it.

Another example of a stifled relationship—this a negative one that stayed bad—is the rather dramatic story of a young woman whose father threatened her with expulsion from the family when she was 17 unless she altered her sexual orientation.

∇   Dad never changed. He yelled at me for 2 years and kicked me out when I went to his mother's house to live to go to college. He told me he never wanted to speak to me again, and this was a relief because it meant no screaming.

The next 2 years we didn't see each other except at family functions. No speaking, no communication. As if we didn't know each other. I could tell Mom was upset by this. She had to agree with Dad, but she didn't like his intensity or him pushing me away.

Two years ago I started working on the relationship. We had lunch, and I discovered that I had not forgiven him and I wanted to patch it up. Like taking a live-and-let-live approach. This Christmas Jessica and I went back, and he was very irate. He felt she was replacing him in the family. He just screamed, and we vowed never to see each other again. There's been no contact, and I think this time it is permanent. He blames me for their divorce, but I know there were other problems before me.

The Relationship Improves

Several narratives reflect more optimistic outcomes—the possibility that over time fathers change for the better, however gradually. Frequently this process underscores the reality that the daughter's sexuality is not the true issue with which the father is confronting. Entangled and conflated with other unrelated problems at the fore of her father's life, one daughter's sexuality became a misguided focus of their problematic relationship.

∇   I told him I was in love with a woman, and he thought it was because of the divorce, which he blames on everything in order to blame my mother for his unhappiness.

He had not brought it up since then, so I checked in with him several months later and told him that I was going to a gay bar in order to be honest with him and to have a conversation. He then asks me how gay am I, which was a start.

We've lost touch with each other lately, and I feel it is because of this. He used to call me twice a week and then it became twice in 2 months. He said he was just busy. I don't have the energy to confront him. A month ago he asked about my life and we talked some—more progress. This was when I started going with someone, and he started to take me more seriously. When I said this he was silent for 2 minutes, and I was not about to break it. He said it was such a burden and why bring it on myself. I told him I'm okay and happy. I can't talk to him a lot about this, like all other issues between us. He connected with me because he knows what it's like to be in love with someone who is not in love with you.

Someday I'd like to talk with him much more. I told him eventually we'll talk, and he said that he won't let me down. He then admitted that he was so out of touch with me. He'll be okay with it eventually. He views everything as related to the divorce—like how I viewed him while growing up. He'll ask my sisters if they really think I'm gay, and my oldest says, "Yes, duh!" His sense of being a worthwhile man was challenged by the divorce. It was a surprise to all, though later we found out he was depressed, and they'd been in counseling.

Young women all too often dismiss the possibility of change. Some fathers adapt, perhaps because they perceive they have no other choice if they are to maintain their status as father. Despite great discomfort with the "family secret" that he prefers not to face, the following father eventually came to the realization that his daughter is too important to lose.

▽   Mom was the one who knew everything about me, although I was considered "Daddy's little girl." He was shocked and upset; it was foreign to him. He was upset that I had not come to him to tell him.

We didn't talk about it at first because he hates talking about emotional issues. He is a more even-handed, organized guy. Since, he's done research on the topic and reads. He talked to my therapist, and this was helpful to calm him down. He never reacts explosively but avoids conflicts at all costs, but he was very upset. He thinks it's disgusting, but he still can't deal directly with it, so he asks me while he was watching TV, "So I hear you're a lesbian," in an off-handed joking way. I told him this was no way to talk about it.

For him I'm still his daughter, and he still loves me and won't cut me off. He's more cool about it now, and we can talk about gay issues. It's not yet "okay," but he can hear the words, and I can talk about my girlfriends. He was the one who encouraged Mom to go to the Pride March. He is quiet about it and is still weirded out about the public thing. His brother gets manicures, is very effeminate, married four times with no children, but I can never talk to my dad about it because it would offend him. I don't think he's dealt with having a gay brother.

The majority of relationships between daughters and their father remain the same over time—deviating little from their original negative, positive, or distant trajectory. One daughter reflected that her father asked few questions about her current romantic relationship, then offered the resigned recognition, "Well, I guess he asks about her the same amount as he did about my other romantic relationships with guys, which wasn't much really."

WHEN FATHERS HAVE SAME-SEX ATTRACTIONS

Four daughters believe that they were almost guaranteed a positive reaction from their father because of *his* same-sex attractions. Among these daughters, two fathers appeared surprised but pleased, and one had very mixed reactions; one daughter is not out to her sexual-minority father. One young woman's father came out to his wife 8 years earlier.

∇   He had no clue. He said he loved me, but we didn't talk much. He was extremely happy that I had gone through the psychological turmoil and was now happy and secure in my identity. I had no clue about him.

   I later found out that my parents had struggled with his gayness, and he even went to conversion therapy for awhile. They decided to stay together, and he had no male lovers while they were together. But he was so depressed because of it and not being able to change and on every kind of medication you can think of. He needed to be a gay man. So he understood about me, although I think it was easier for me than for him.

However, having a sexual-minority father does not guarantee solely positive reactions. One youth did not receive the expected positive reaction from her father because of his fears that he caused her lesbianism.

∇   He came out to me a week before I did to him. His coming out told me he'd be good about me, but I was wrong. They were '70s progressives, so I had high expectations of both.

   So the next week after an 8-hour conversation I told him, "I'm dating a woman now." Well I lost all respect for him because he advised me to act straight around straights and gay only around gays. I try to be myself all the time, but he does not want me to get hurt. He stills juvenilizes me and thinks I'm 15.

   Maybe because my father was bisexual I expected him to be better than my mother, but he was more upset, upset that maybe I did it because he had come out to me, which is absurd and an insult. I didn't do it earlier because I thought he might freak out, so now I thought he wouldn't. I could just as easily blame his mother, who I wonder about because she is so independent and masculine, but in that generation no one said anything about it. I don't like to answer the question of why or whether it's his fault. It's not important, and I can't tell you in any case. I grew up in a gender nonbiased environment, and so I didn't have any rules on how I had to act. For him to think it's his fault is just crazy.

A young woman who is not out to her sexual-minority father experienced one of the most unusual circumstances among the interviewed participants. Her father is a male-to-female transsexual who divorced the daughter's mother to legally marry a man, a man who does not know about his "wife's" former life or that "she" has a daughter. In addition, the daughter believes that her mother is a lesbian; she is fairly certain her uncle is a cross-dressing married-to-a-woman gay man and that she has an unknown number of first cousins who are lesbian or gay. "I had no choice in being a lesbian!" She is not sure what her father thinks of her sexual status because following his sex operation he severed all ties with her. Although he is not an important person in her life, she believes that if he knew he would likely be supportive. Her coming-of-age as a sexual minority was relatively easy because, "He raised me to be open minded and never said anything negative about gays and lesbians, but I don't know if he'd blame himself."

A FINAL WORD

Similar to their heterosexual sisters,[8] many young women with same-sex attractions have poor to nonexistent relations with their father, often characterized by lack of mutual knowledge and by emotional emptiness. More than sons, daughters are disappointed with the "emotional unexpressiveness" of fathers[9]—especially given their momentous decision to come out to him. Young women often want more from their father but despair of ever receiving the closeness they desire. Thus, they seldom confide in him—and he almost never spontaneously queries about their failure to date boys or their "special" friends—and not infrequently they let his wife tell him the news.

Daughters choose not to come out to their father because he is not central to their life or they have not gotten around to it yet. One father–daughter dyad shared many things, including knowledge about her same-sex attractions; however, discussion about her emotional, intimate life was not one of them.

∇   The other day Dad asked me why I wasn't wearing dresses, yet he raised me "never to depend on a man." I like power tools, carpentry, mechanics, and doing things with him. People always said I was the spittin' image of him. I worked with him while my brother stayed in the house and did artwork with Mom. He's not gay, however.

His work has him working a lot with gay people, but that is work and this is family. If I told him tomorrow he would not believe it or say why am I doing this to him. I think he would blame himself for spending so much time with me. Once Dad asked me when I was in the ninth grade if I was gay, and I said no—I just wasn't ready then. But clearly he has his suspicions. He seemed very glad I said no, but I still thinks he really knows.

Even when the relationship is positive and long-standing, fathers often choose to avoid the obvious—that their daughter is not the same as other girls. If she chooses to come out to him, she does so because the time is right. This knowledge might lead, at best, to sporadic discussion—a continuation of the relationship that existed prior to the disclosure.

After learning about her same-sex attractions, a father's initial reactions are not usually horrified but oriented toward the positive or neutral; when negative, they are usually milder than his wife's response. One daughter reported, "He's okay with it I guess, and if not, then he wouldn't tell me. Same reactions to me now as he's always had. He does not bring it up." She admitted that she had adjusted to not having a "story-book father." "We speak only occasionally, so his opinion is not that important to me. We are so alienated it could have been done at a bus stop when I told him, and I would have gotten the same response." His primary concern is that his daughter's sexuality not embarrass him in front of his family or work colleagues.

Of course, not all fathers are so callous. Similar to all parent–child dyads, father–daughter couplings vary considerably regarding whether and how daughters disclose to their fathers and their reasons for telling and not telling. Fathers react with support and expulsion; most appear to react with little affect. Some dyads improve over time, but most remain as they were initially, whether with positive, neutral, or negative regard. Again, however, this is not always the case.

One young woman followed a unique pathway in coming out to her father. She did her homework, asking her grandmother how she thought her son would react to having a bisexual daughter. The outcome, not initially positive, strengthened their relationship.

∇   I thought that since he was associated with Broadway he would be real cool. But my grandmother told me he had a hard time dealing with the gay community and had lost out on some commissions because he's not gay. Plus some think he has AIDS. So she said, "Not good."

   This seemed confirmed when he made some homophobic comments about how lucky he was not having a gay child after I read him a coming-out story in the newspaper. After I came out to him, he apologized for this when I reminded him about it. He basically said, "Gee, okay. As long as you're happy."

   Since then Dad has been more willing to talk. He is willing to discuss lots of things, and I really enjoy this. He's got all these great Broadway stories about who is gay and not gay.

In the sequence of developmental milestones, many daughters disclose to their fathers as their last transition from a heterosexual identity—after developing a romantic relationship and a positive sense of self as lesbian, bisexual, unlabeled, or questioning. This should not imply, however, that fathers are always unimportant to their daughters. One study found that if father and daughter have a satisfying relationship with each other, then she is likely to be out to him. Feeling acceptance from her father predicted a young woman's self-esteem level only if she also reported that he is important for her sense of self-worth.[10] The challenge is how to encourage these close, intimate father–daughter relationships.

ENDNOTES

[1] Page 133 in Bell, A. P., Weinberg, M. S., & Hammersmith, S. K. (1981). *Sexual preference: Its development in men and women.* Bloomington: Indiana University Press.

[2] Herdt, G., & Boxer, A. (1993). *Children of Horizons: How gay and lesbian teens are leading a new way out of the closet.* Boston: Beacon Press; D'Augelli, A. R., Hershberger, S. L., & Pilkington, N. W. (1998). Lesbian, gay, and bisexual youth and their families: Disclosure of sexual orientation and its consequences. *American Journal of Orthopsychiatry,* 68, 361–371; D'Augelli, A. R. (1998, February). *Victimization history and mental health among lesbian, gay, and bisexual youths.* Paper presented at the Society for Research on Adolescence, San Diego, CA; and Savin-Williams, R. C. (1990). *Gay and lesbian youth: Expressions of identity.* Washington, DC: Hemisphere.

[3] D'Augelli, A. R. (1998, February). *Victimization history and mental health among lesbian, gay, and bisexual youths.* Paper presented at the Society for Research on Adolescence, San Diego, CA.

[4] D'Augelli, A. R., Hershberger, S. L., & Pilkington, N. W. (1998). Lesbian, gay, and bisexual youth and their families: Disclosure of sexual orientation and its consequences. *American Journal of Orthopsychiatry,* 68, 361–371; D'Augelli, A. R. (1998, February). *Victimization history and mental health among lesbian, gay, and bisexual youths.* Paper presented at the Society for Research on Adolescence, San Diego, CA; and Weinberg, M. S., Williams, C. J., & Pryor, D. W. (1994). *Dual attraction: Understanding bisexuality.* New York: Oxford University Press.

[5] D'Augelli, A. R. (1998, February). *Victimization history and mental health among lesbian, gay, and bisexual youths.* Paper presented at the Society for Research on Adolescence, San Diego, CA.

[6] Ben-Ari, A. (1995). The discovery that an offspring is gay: Parents', gay men's, and lesbians' perspectives. *Journal of Homosexuality,* 30, 89–112.

[7] 3.6 on a 1 (*very positive*) to 7 (*very negative*) point scale.

[8] Larson, R., & Richards, M. (1994). *Divergent realities: The emotional lives of mothers, fathers, and adolescents.* New York: Basic Books.

[9] Youniss, J., & Ketterlinus, L. (1987). Communication and connectedness in mother– and father–adolescent relationships. *Journal of Youth and Adolescence,* 16, 265–292.

[10] Savin-Williams, R. C. (1990). *Gay and lesbian youth: Expressions of identity.* Washington, DC: Hemisphere.

6

SONS AND MOTHERS

Paul

The first time I can recall the subject coming up was talking to my mom and my sister at the kitchen table about something, about not understanding homosexual stuff. So my mom was explaining what it meant, and I remember saying "oh" and "yuck," and my mom defended homosexuality. She said we were both just being silly. I don't really remember how the whole topic came up, but I know this was just before junior high. Shortly after this for some reason she asked if I was gay and, mortified, I quickly yelled, "No!"

About a year later, when I was 12, I told my mom, "I think I might be gay," and she asked me, "How can you tell?" She was the first that I told about these feelings—but she just seemed to dismiss it as something normal for boys coming into the physical changes of life. I had had sex with several of my friends, and I knew that I liked it, wanted more, and wondered what it all meant. Well, a year later my mom found my gay porn magazines, but she didn't say anything at all about it. It really got me mad that she was going through my stuff. My lesbian aunt also suspected it as well, but no one ever said anything. We have a very open family, so there's no sense that anyone would ever confront me about it. If she would say, "When you are ready to talk about it," then I would talk about it. My mom would love me no matter what, and everything I did would be certainly forgivable because she loves me for who I am and not what she wants me to be. I guess actually I just didn't know how to bring up the subject, the magazines. She, I guess found them accidentally, but I also played with Barbie dolls when I was young, and my parents bought them for me. They thought maybe this was a little bit odd, but they certainly never tried to stop it. They saw I had lots of friends, was polite and bright. They noticed I didn't like sports, but that was okay, and they noticed that I was rather flamboyant and that I took piano lessons. All of this, of course, was okay with them.

So I told my mom I was "very likely gay," and about a month later I thought I was gay, and she was very supportive. She asked me if I wanted to talk to someone about it, not to get me to change, but just to feel more comfortable with it. I did speak to a psychiatrist who was a real moron, and he gave me even more reason to sort of stay in the closet because he said I couldn't be sure about it until I was 21. So after he said that, well, otherwise I would have come out probably very much more publicly by the age of 15.

Finally, I said to my mom that I knew absolutely sure I was gay 2 years ago at age 15. So I knew it'd be okay to tell her. She at first was upset because of the difficult life I'd have; she's really into her kids, but homosexuality doesn't particularly bother her. Whether or not I'm married isn't all that important, but the fact that I would not be having kids and having AIDS and people hating me, that's what she was most upset by. A few days later my mom was much better about it. My mom said then that she thought that perhaps I might be gay because I was just way too sensitive and flamboyant in my mannerisms. One of my problems is that I've always felt that coming out as gay would definitely affect my mom in a very negative way, her job and status in our town, where everyone knows everyone else.

But I also think that my mom really did not believe or maybe entertained some hope that I'm not gay because she saw me dating girls. We just really don't speak of it these days; she knows of my gay friends, including my relationship with my boyfriend, but once again, she just doesn't deal with it. I think she just calls us best friends. So last weekend we talked about it again, and she was much better able to deal with it.

I am very close to my mom, really close, and maybe that's it, or maybe that is a consequence of me being gay—that I'm close to her because we like the same kinds of things, like decorating. I think it's probably both genetic and environment. I was raised by a close mom and a distant father. In first grade I picked every flower in the yard and decorated my room with flowers, and my mom was a little bit upset by that but thought I did a good job.

Nick

Well she knew when I was 14. She found out because my friend wrote this very explicit letter to me telling me how big he is and how much he wanted me and what he'd do to me—because he had a really big crush on me, and she found the letter and figured it all out. I guess it really wasn't that hard! She really flipped out; she really went like really crazy. She blamed it on "those guys"—which ones I've never figured out and one of these days I'm going to ask—and she kept saying, "Oh my, what did I do wrong?" and saying that I'd better grow out of it. She wouldn't talk to me, not a word and just look the other way when I came near her for a couple of weeks.

I then began throwing comments here and there a couple of years later, but I decided I didn't want to tell her any more because I feared that she would cut me out and not let me come to Albany. But I was really hinting over Christmas break, and I sort of planted the idea. She would ask, "How are the women at Albany?" She would say, "Why don't you date girls?" and I'd say because I was too busy. Little did she know I was too busy dating guys! It's like she totally forgot about the letter.

One night I was really giving her attitude, and I was very quiet. She came into my room because she was concerned with what was wrong with me because I wasn't talking with anyone, and I seemed very depressed. I told her at that time that the reason why was because I was gay. She acted in the typical way, really freaking out. She said, "How can you do this to me? How can you do this to us! How can I deal with it with my friends?" She thought I was just confused, the result of being at Albany, and that everything could be fixed up. She said to me, and I quote her here, "I'm not going to pay for a faggot to go to Albany."

So this whole thing lasted 4 or 5 hours. Finally she tried to get me to go see a therapist to get me changed. I agreed that I would go to her counselor, but only if in fact she would go as well for help. So we went 2 days later. During this time we just never talked about the issue, even though I wouldn't let it die because I kept bringing it up and kept mentioning gay issues. She didn't like this, but she knew she had no choice.

Well, we went to the therapist, and the therapist was a real cool guy, and he was totally on my side. I told him what I felt, and then he said that what I felt was valid. She was rather shocked. He then turned to her and said that she was the one who needed to deal with it and that this was not a phase, that this was not a choice, and that things would only get better after she learned how to deal with it and that at that point things would be able to be worked out. Well, we went home, and she was in shock but from then on out she treated me much better, and since that time she has begun to deal with it. I'll know a lot more when I go home next time.

I guess now she accepts it, though she's not real supportive except in her own way, like buying me condoms. She'd rather just sort of keep everything quiet and not talk about it. We've got a really big family with scores of cousins, aunts, and all, and she doesn't want them to know.

Walt

I haven't told anyone in my family yet, in large part because my education is not yet paid for, and I don't know how they would react. When I was very young, my mother went through this very fundamentalist Christian phase, and she let it be known that homosexuality was a very, very bad thing. Somehow I felt that it was connected to me, that it made sense. My mother said that gay people ran around in dresses, and they loved each other like mommy and daddy did and that they would all go to Hell. I thought to myself, "Well, I like to wear dresses, so maybe?"

My mother always blames herself for not being a good enough mother. She always says that it's her fault that I'm not more mature or that I'm not more well planned. She also blames herself for letting me play with Barbie dolls when I was young and for letting me play with cousins who dressed me up like a girl. Maybe she would think that she should have allowed me to play more with boys in the neighborhood. It's just that I wouldn't feel comfortable when I visited them if I knew that she knew. It would just complicate my life, and there's just too much else to do. But I always have this feeling that my mother must eventually know.

My mother would not react positively. When I was about a sophomore in my high school my mother and I were watching *60 Minutes*, and this episode on homosexuality came up, and she went on and on about how she didn't agree with it, about the lifestyle and what it was all about, but that she didn't feel like she could pass judgment. It felt like she was just talking directly to me. I didn't say anything except just to nod agreement or that I was listening to her. My mother essentially raised me and my sister, so whatever we are she feels responsible for and my father would chastise her if he found out that I was gay. When I was in my junior year of my high school I overheard a conversation that my grandfather had with my mother and he told her, apparently, to be careful about me going to prep school because I might turn out badly. With a shaky voice she shouted, "Are you saying that he's gay?" They haven't talked since.

Since then I've dropped hints, and I can't decide when I want to tell. My mother has constantly made comments that she knows. One major time was when we were watching at home the movie *Four Weddings and a Funeral*, and I just said offhandedly, "Wow! Look at Hugh Grant's ass!" My mother looked at me rather strangely and sadly, and I quickly changed the subject.

She has to know! As a child I've played with Barbie dolls, Strawberry Shortcake, a lot of dressing up. Everything feminine was me, because after all I did have four sisters. Mother was a pacifist, and so she didn't allow guns or anything masculine like that in the house, but I did have my Matchbox cars that I played with. As an adolescent I was into drama, I really got into it, directing and choreographing. Lord, Mother many times said that I was "doing that voice," which was a very feminine high voice that she hates. She says that I do this even today. She was so concerned because of my fascination with the fact that I kept crossing my arms, and my mother said, "Only girls do that!"

Slightly more is known about the mother–son relationship than other parent–child pairings discussed in this book, largely because more research is conducted with sexual-minority males than females and because mothers are more likely than fathers to volunteer for research studies. Many gay and bisexual young men perceive that they have a unique relationship with their mother, and thus her reaction to their sexual identity is considered by most sons to be a critical component of how their life has gone or will go. If he is out to only one parent, it is nearly certain that the parent is a mother. As will be apparent in this chapter, the reactions of mothers are often more animated than those of fathers. For many young men, to be "out" to their mother is truly to be OUT.

THE RELATIONSHIP BEFORE DISCLOSURE

Psychoanalytic writers are fond of portraying the mother–gay son relationship as one of enmeshment, overdependency, and seduction, implying that this causes homosexuality in the youth. Most analytically oriented studies lent support to this characterization. A large-scale empirical study during the late 1960s confirmed this depiction but found no evidence that it was instrumental in causing a nonheterosexual orientation. Researchers Alan Bell, Martin Weinberg, and Sue Hammersmith reported that homosexual adult men were more likely than their heterosexual counterparts to report feeling particularly close and communicative with their mother while growing up. Although mothers might have been somewhat overprotective of their son, they were not perceived to be seductive. Many men described their mother as a strong individual who was responsible for most child-rearing decisions. No evidence was found to support the view that homosexual sons were more likely than heterosexual ones to identify with their mother.[1]

By contrast, contemporary empirical studies have generally ignored the dynamics of the mother–gay son relationship prior to adolescence, thus providing no viable alternative to psychoanalytic theory to help us understand this very important relationship. Data from the interviews included in this book indicate, despite some variability, that the vast majority of gay and bisexual sons indeed had an emotional, intimate relationship with their mother while growing up; psychoanalysts might call this *enmeshment*. For example, Paul noted that his mother is "really into her kids" and that "my mom would love me no matter what." Although the relationship Nick has with his mother is less obviously positive, ultimately it is supportive. Notwithstanding her threats to limit his educational plans and her name-calling ("faggot"), when Nick was despondent, she came to his aid. So, too, Walt and his mother share an intimacy that is not apparent in his relationship with his father.

When discussing their mother, sons repeatedly raise two issues. One, both mother and son frequently "blame" the son's same-sex attractions on the intensity and closeness of their relationship. This reflects the degree to which empirically unsubstantiated psychoanalytic theory has permeated Western culture and molded the values and beliefs of family members.[2] Two, mothers have "known" for a long time that their son is gay—because of his sex-atypical mannerisms and interests. These two themes cut across the nature of the mother–son relationship developed during the youth's childhood.

Supportive Relationships

Although the nature of the mother–son relationship before disclosure varies, as do all such relationships, the vast majority is characterized by sons as warm, caring, and intimate. The mother's knowledge of her son is usually so complete that relatively few are totally surprised by his nonheterosexuality. Mothers often "suspect" based on stereotypic notions that feminine behavior in boys equals homosexuality or on "mother's intuition." Some feign shock, but it is apparent to their sons that they knew but did not want to know. One son declared, "We've been so close during the last decade, how could she not help but know! She knows me so thoroughly!" Another youth reflected on the quality of the relationship he has with his mother.

∇ She thought she had the perfect mother–son relationship. Maybe I was just a little too withdrawn, obsessed with soap operas, and I couldn't distinguish between reality and my imagination. This meant that we got along great because she was the same way. We were always a team, and this bothered the rest of the family. When she missed *The Young and the Restless*, [TV soap opera] I filled her in; when she was bored with housework, we did creative artsy stuff together. I never caused fights like Robert [brother]. I was the perfect child, so of course she'd liked me best.

So, too, Paul's mother thought her son was overly sensitive and "flamboyant," but rather than punish or discourage his behavior, she accepted it. Mothers are usually tolerant because they benefit from their son's unmasculine ways.

∇ She let me play with dolls and hair styling very early on. I liked to cross-dress. Looking back now at pictures of me, I can't believe she didn't figure it out because I was really into dolls and feminine kinds of things. It seems to me that she encouraged me in this. She never said I had to go out and play with the neighborhood boys or really go heavily into sports. Like I'd do her make-up and tell her how to dress. She asked me to come along when she picked out wallpaper color or things like that. Very stereotypic things. I always had to be different, always bringing something different, not boring, into the family when I was young.

Some mothers have little intent or desire to change the feminine behavior of their sons—even if they could—because of their political ideology. Not uncommonly, they have gay friends and have been exposed to sexual-minority issues.

▽   She frequently had over her lesbian friends when I was small, and it seemed that homosexuality was in the air from the first. Actually in church there were these two men, very friendly men, sort of older that everybody really loved, and they taught Sunday school classes. So one day I asked if these two guys were married, and my mother said that they were gay.

   When I was small I liked playing with dolls, and at first she said "guys don't do that," but it was clear her heart wasn't into it. Like she did not get angry with me about it.

Mothers may take this closeness to heart and blame themselves and the relationship they have with their son for causing him to be gay. This is the first theme noted earlier: At some point in the son's childhood, mother and son entertain the possibility, consistent with traditional psychoanalytic notions of enmeshment and overdependency, that binding mothers are the cause of male homosexuality. Their close relationship has made the youth unmasculine and gay. The following narrative is a classic psychoanalytic wet dream.

▽   I was tracked into it [being gay] because she protected me so much that the masculine side of me never really developed or the side that was not aggressive or "all American" or just like all of the other guys. Maybe she protected me because I was so hyperactive, or she felt like she had to do something and that something was to protect me too much. I had a physically absent father, and I was raised by a mother that was repulsed by male hierarchy and power. All my role models were female— teachers, mother, grandmother, older sisters.

   She also always seemed sort of jealous whenever I went out with girls, and she always seemed to sabotage my dating. She told me they were only after one thing—to get me married. She wanted me to do music, dance, and gymnastics, and she signed me up for drama, and this undermined my masculinity, like I would always be her little cute, darling boy. She let me dress in heels and dresses and carry purses, and this really pissed off my father.

   So then she would say I wasn't manly enough for any girl, and I think she blamed herself because she sort of henpecked me. She said I didn't stand up straight, that I slumped. I also sucked my fingers and, of course, there was the whole issue of bedwetting that I did off and on until junior high. She cleaned the sheets and said how much work I caused her.

"Blaming mother" was also Paul's initial take on why he is gay, but he also entertains the possibility that they are close *because* he is gay. After all, they both like decorating. Another youth considered several possible causes of his homosexuality, including the consequences of having six over-involved women in his life: a mother, a grandmother, and four sisters.

∇   I used to think I was gay because I was only around women. I never
       really had a strong father. Now, however, I discount that theory. I think
       maybe it's totally genetic. I know I would eventually have come out,
       that I would have identified myself as gay. Maybe it was just because I
       felt at ease around girls, maybe it had something to do with that, but
       not so much that it caused me to be gay, just feeling good about being
       gay. I think my upbringing may have had a little bit to do with me
       being gay, but all of my gay feelings are very natural.

Conflictual Relationships

Some mothers, however, are not appreciative of the sex-atypical behavior of their child. It causes conflict in their relationship, but they feel
relatively powerless to change it. When her son was an early adolescent,
one mother wanted to halt his "childish" ways.

∇   Mom expressed her concern about me not doing things that typical
       boys did when I was young. I remember her making contemptuous
       comments about my mannerisms, the way I sat with my legs crossed,
       the way I talked, and the toys I played with. She even tried to correct
       me by telling me to hold my wrist more firm and enrolled me in speech
       therapy, with a really handsome guy. I would have played with dolls,
       but it was not a possibility because she would not buy me any. She
       thought I was a little "femmy" and told this to her friends.
         In junior high she worried because I was too sensitive and had no
       real positive male role models. Like I was always trying to make myself
       prettier and look androgynous. I wore make-up, especially eyeliner, tight
       leather pants that gave shape to my new developments, and blouses. I
       did this because I liked it. Like I remember one time she really got
       upset because I dressed up like a woman, and I was really proud of how
       good I looked. She wanted me to be outside more with other kids and
       to be more active. I really didn't care, and I really did nothing at all
       about it.

Mothers in some ethnic-minority homes also share these concerns. In
sex-segregated cultures, it is particularly noteworthy when a male does not
pursue a traditional masculine pathway. One youth noted that his mother
constantly chastised him because he did not display traditional behavior
expected of Puerto Rican males.

∇   This is as early as kindergarten when I told my mother boys were cute,
       and she wasn't very happy with that. Well my mother always said I
       had "an attitude." Like I would say, "Oh, please," or I would give a
       motion with my hands. She called this pouffy, too effeminate. My
       mother would tell me to calm down, don't laugh the way I laugh, close
       your hands, don't move your hips. Then she'd do everything she told
       me not to do.

Exasperated because she could do little to change his behavior, she gave up and placed him in dancing classes. If he was going to act feminine then he might as well find an "acceptable" outlet.

Whether mothers liked them or not, they nearly always recognize the sex-atypical interests and mannerisms of their son. Both frequently believe that they have meaning for his sexuality—at least once he has come out to her. Most mothers, however, do not allow these characteristics to interfere with the close, intimate relationship they have with their son. They usually express considerably less concern than their husband about their son's femininity and lack of masculinity, often concluding that this relationship is easier to "manage" than the ones they have with their masculine sons. Of course, the son's failure to be more masculine can also cause conflict, as is evident in several of the narratives in this section.

Glaringly apparent from the young men's narratives is that no youth described his relationship with his mother as distant or noninvolved. Sons usually and eventually assume that this intimacy means primarily one thing—to be out they must come out to their mother. Youths seldom decide not to disclose to their mother, although they might decide to postpone it until such time that they feel safe. These exceptions will be evident in a later section of this chapter that details the expected and actual initial maternal reactions to the disclosure.

WHETHER MOTHERS ARE TOLD

Although mothers are seldom the first person to whom a young man discloses his same-sex attractions, if a parent is told first, it is almost always a mother.[3] In the present study, youths were eight times more likely to tell their mother before their father. This may be a matter of moments or years, but many consider it more important, or perhaps safer, to tell their mother. Investigators have seldom asked why this is true.

In terms of how many youths disclose to their mother, the percentage varies depending on the age of the respondents and the year data are collected. Among 2,500 gay and bisexual male adult readers of the gay–lesbian newsmagazine The Advocate, 64% reported that they had specifically told their mother about their same-sex attractions, usually during their late teens or early 20s.[4] Many nondisclosers felt that their mothers knew from other sources or would not be surprised if they were to find out. A review of the published data during the past decade with gay and bisexual male youths reveals that the proportion of sons who disclosed to their mother ranges from 40% to 70%.[5] Isolating those who lived at home, Tony D'Augelli reported that only 7% of mothers did not know or suspect.[6] In the present study, 65% of youths report that they told their mother, with many others believing that she knows or suspects—but the words have not been spoken. These high percentages reflect a cohort effect: Contemporary youths are disclosing to their mother, often while still living at home and, as will be noted later, at increasingly earlier ages.

If approximately two thirds of sons have explicitly shared with their mother the nature of their sexuality, then it is important to understand their reasons for disclosing this "secret" when others have not. First, I turn to motivations given by gay and bisexual sons for not telling their mother.

REASONS NOT TO TELL

Sons may decide it is best to withhold disclosure until "later" or, for some, until "hell freezes over." The complexity of reasons for this procrastination has seldom been investigated, although popular literature has not neglected the topic. It cites as the primary reason for not coming out to mother the fear of the "bad things" she would do to her son if she knew. This reason, however, represents only one of many explanations offered by the young men I interviewed.

Walt is concerned that his born-again Christian mother would disapprove of his sexuality and react with great hostility, but it is also evident that Walt desires not to hurt or disappoint his mother, who is burdened with considerable guilt raising her children alone. The time is just not right. Walt is the "universal nondiscloser," articulating four of the following five most common reasons the interviewed youths gave for not coming out to their mother: not the right time, fear of her reactions, have not gotten around to it, desire not to disappoint or hurt her, and her moral disapproval of his sexuality.

Not the Right Developmental Time

The belief that the "right" time to disclose has not yet arrived was articulated by 30% of sons. Disclosure is thus delayed until a youth feels that he has progressed sufficiently in his own identity development. To tell mother before he feels secure with his sexuality is too risky, especially in the initial phases of his development.

▽   I'm not comfortable talking with her about my sexuality. We're a close family, but we really never talk to each other about these kinds of things. I think what I need to do is establish myself really first, to feel very good about myself as gay. I just came out a month ago, and I've got so much internal work to do. I'm just out to a few. I'm barely here today. I'm working on myself first, and after that I'm telling her.

Despite negative views held by his mother, a bisexual son feels confident that he will not be rejected if he were to tell his mother. However, he is waiting for the right circumstance and opportunity in order to repair their relationship—but he still has many questions.

▽ I'd rather tell her when I'm actually living with them rather than just telling her that I'm leaving to live with Will. I know she won't embrace the idea, but I also know for sure that she won't reject me. Black mothers don't throw their Black boys away. She is kind of closed-minded and very homophobic, but I feel by not telling her we're growing more distant. Always before we've been very close. So this is really kind of a painful thing between us.

Fear of Negative Repercussions

One of four gay and bisexual sons elects not to disclose because he knows his mother does not have positive images of gay people and that she would thus react in a negative way if she were to know. In part, this is Walt's fear. Not all damaging reactions, however, are based on evangelical religiosity or conservative politics. Some mothers accept perceptions about homosexuality that were prevalent during their growing up years.

▽ The first memory I have of the word *homosexual* was when I heard it as a warning from my mother—a very horrible sick person who was perverted, a child molester, subhuman. But, on the other hand, they had sex with males, which was exactly what I wanted, but I knew I wasn't the other things. This is when I was in the fifth grade.
   I always knew I was interested in sex with other boys, but how could I tell her if she believed all of these other things? Once she gave me a book, I think it was called *Growing Up Straight* or something like that by Reckers, Reekers, or whatever, and it was a ghoulish, horrible presentation. The main word was "perversion," the word I saw most in that book. Maybe this was her way of warning me not to tell her, but I was angry at her for shutting off communication and making me feel horrible, sick, perverted. I think she still thinks that book is the last word on the subject.

Mothers need not be perceived as homophobic for youths to fear disclosing to her. In one particular poignant example, a mother is liberal regarding sexuality issues in general and even has positive views about gay people, but this flexibility would not be extended to her son's sexuality. Her son speaks sarcastically of his mother's political correctness, which does not diffuse into his life.

▽ My mother is very accepting of all sorts of sexualities, sort of in a very general way and civil rights for all. She has read gay books, is very tolerant and very accepting, has gay friends, but I don't think she would ever accept me.

You'd think she was Ms. Gay Lady USA! Worked for Blacks, for women, for displaced dishwashers, for green grass, for everyone but me. My mother, Ms. Flaming Liberal, but she's made it clear that I'm not to be gay. I started to tell her, but she wouldn't let me. She can have gay friends but not a gay son; her gay friends are cool and so she is cool, but my gay friends are fruity, dregs, fags. Her best friend is a lesbian, but my lesbian friend is weird.

Youths also decide not to come out for practical considerations, such as the fear that they might lose support for their college education. One stated, "I'd like first to graduate and then be independent before I told her." Another replied matter-of-factly, "I want her support for my educational funding, so to do that it's best to not tell her directly." This need for independence is more financial than emotional.

▽ I don't know if my mother knows, but I certainly have not told her. Everyone thinks she knows, but I haven't told her yet because I'm afraid it would do me more harm than good. She controls the money and has warned me before not to take for granted their support. She wants me to go to Montclair State where it's cheaper. So I have to be careful what, when, and why I tell her.

Another thing, her sister, I think, is lesbian, but she's not very open about it, and my mother is not very happy about it. So I'm waiting until I'm in a better position. On my own, educated, then I feel like she'd be more likely to support me when I'm on my own. I want her to know eventually. Yet, it feels like it might be a problem, and I just don't want to deal with it. But I hate lying to her about who Ted is, although she must know.

I'm not sure what to do. I want her acceptance, and she will accept me, but she's been so damn homophobic ever since I can remember. Is it worth telling her? Maybe we could talk more like we used to but did we really talk? It's going to take the right time.

Wants Not to Hurt Her

Closely associated with the "inappropriate time" argument is a youth's stated desire not to experience or cause his mother's hurt and disappointment. Slightly over 10% of nondisclosing youths recognize that eventually they must come out, but they delay telling because they believe it will cause irreparable damage to the mother–son relationship. To hurt his mother is to cause pain to the most beloved person in the son's life. One youth from a particularly close family elegantly expressed what many other youths feel— the desire to delay the inevitable "scene" they know will disrupt their family.

▽ My family is very WASPy, very upper class, very well educated, very homogeneous. My dad is *the* lawyer in town, and my mother is *the* queen of charities. I almost told the queen this summer but then thought better. Maybe I'll tell her at Christmas, toward the end before coming back, or maybe over spring break, just before coming back.

My mother, I don't want to hurt her, and it would hurt her a lot. It's hard for me to deal with her mourning the loss of her son. She is so attached to all of us and has the ideal perfections for us. She's really looking forward to grandchildren, and my feminist sister is not really into having them. My mother would look bad in the community, and that would hurt to know I caused this embarrassment. Among her friends she is tops, and she'd lose this if I told her.

Youths want to avoid repeating a family pattern of always being the one to hurt Mom.

∇   I don't want to disappoint her; she has lots of misinformation. She treats me like I disappoint her a lot, like in terms of grades, not going out for sports, not being popular with the girls, not helping out Dad, and not making enough money.

Of all family members, what he does appears to have the most impact on the mother's well-being. This power as an emotional anchor is as much given by the mother as taken by the youth.

This is often quite apparent in Asian American homes. Young adult Asian males who have not disclosed to their mother often express the explicit desire not to be in a situation in which they would have to bring "bad news." "Her hopes are on me. I've got to make it. She has told me this a thousand times. She has stayed home; she has sacrificed." They recognize the cultural prescription of fulfilling family responsibilities, which includes not bringing pain or discomfort to parents. To disclose means wounding their mother very deeply, something few wish to do. They know they will not be rejected or discarded, but the guilt associated with being the primary agent of maternal pain is too overwhelming for many of them.

∇   Mothers know everything! I'd love to tell her, but there's too much baggage. I probably won't unless I am with someone very special. I know she's going to be very hurt. Maybe she'd blow up and cry because of social attitudes, shame, and our Korean culture—but mostly because I'm her hope.

Not Close

Another reason not to disclose, commonly articulated by sons about their father, was given by a less than 10% of young men about their mother.

Because they do not feel close to her, they see little need to share this information with her: "Not sure my life would be any different if I told her." Dubious about their relationship, one youth does not trust his mother with any intimate details about his life. He is holding back, in part to punish her for past grievances.

▽   I act flaming, and this aggravates her because I knew it irritated her. Like once I volunteered to play a girl in a school play. In front of all her friends I did this play, dancing, singing, swishing all about. I'd have guys over and lock my door, and we'd have wild sex in the basement. This was junior high.
      I don't expect her support. She knows but isn't ready for it. She is pushing the female question, asking me if I'm dating. She is very percep-tive, very evil woman. She knows too much, but I'll not tell her. She knows this indirectly. It's her chromosomes—her sisters, her aunt, her cousins, her fault.

More self-identified gay and bisexual youths disclose to their mother than do not, at least among those I interviewed and as reported in previous research studies. Perhaps youths who do not volunteer for interviews chose not to because they fear being known as gay, including to their mother. Although it is important to understand their reservations about disclosing, we do not. Would they agree with the interviewed young men, that they desire not to hurt or disappoint their mother, perceive their mother as too homophobic to tell, fear losing particular privileges such as financial support, have just not gotten around to it yet, or do not feel close enough to share this intimate information about their lives? Is it simply not the right time in their life or hers? What is known in greater detail are the reasons their peers who volunteered to participate in this research project gave for coming out to their mother.

REASONS TO TELL

More often than not, contemporary youths who identify as gay or bisexual are out to their mother about their same-sex attractions. They do so for a multitude of reasons, some of which vary from the reasons given by young women. Paul lives in an open family; he began the process of telling his mother in junior high school because in his family, members talk with each other in an open and honest manner. Nick disclosed by confirming his mother's suspicions after he became despondent.

Nearly 60% of the youths report that the primary reason they came out to their mother was because she asked or they volunteered the information in order to share their life with her. Otherwise, external circumstances can dictate the timing of disclosure.

Mother Asks

The primary reason the interviewed youths give as to why they disclose to their mother—endorsed by over one third—is not because they take the initiative but because she asks. She frequently asks, as noted in the last section, because she suspects he is gay given his sex-atypical behavior or her intimate knowledge about him. One youth reached a point in his life at which he had begun to feel positive about himself. "I didn't really want to pretend any more that I was something that I wasn't." In response to his mother's question, he shared his lifetime secret. "It was sort of a test pattern. She didn't really expect me to say 'Yes!' but I decided I wasn't going to lie." Another youth faced a similar situation after graduation when he decided to devote his life to gay-related causes.

∇   I decided to go to Washington to work on AIDS, and she objected. She said I couldn't. We argued back and forth, and it seemed to have no end. It wasn't really the AIDS thing, since she always wanted me to do medicine. I knew what it was all about. After a long pause she asked in desperation if I was homosexual. *That* was the issue, and I knew it. I've never lied to my family, so I said "Yes."

Suspicious mothers who ask "the question" represent all ethnicities, social classes, and geographic localities, as the narratives from an urban Korean American and a rural White youth attest. The clues most indicative of their son's nonheterosexuality are the same as for other mothers.

∇   My mother said she knew since high school when I began to act kind of freaky and hanging around weird people. There is very little discussion of premarital sexuality in general in Korean families, so it was never brought up as a topic, even of dating females. In high school, however, it is more common to discuss sexuality. So, she asked me about dating females, and because I wasn't, she had begun to suspect. I always remained silent whenever she asked about my girlfriends. Also, I think she suspected because I've been an AIDS activist since my junior year in high school and she was always very concerned with this.

∇   It happened on the farm one morning when I was helping her with the milking. I had promised myself if she asked I would tell. Asked if there was any woman in my life, and I told her no, and as a joke she said, "Any men?" I said, "Maybe." She took awhile to respond, finished milking, but said she suspected because of an earring I wore and also that I didn't spend much time and money on girls.

Wants to Share Life

The second most common reason, characterizing 2 in 10 youths, is to end pretensions. Sons want to reclaim closeness in the mother–son relationship, and disclosing is an obvious means to this end given the nature of their preexisting relationship. It is an attempt by some youths to recapture a former affinity that has become frayed, in part because their secret has been withheld.

∇   I got back from a visit with my boyfriend, and I felt relatively guilty because my parents had paid for this vacation, but they didn't know why I was going. It felt like my relationship with my mother had drifted after being very close and I wanted, especially with this relationship, to tell her and share what was going on. We used to share everything. I told her about my dates and what we did. I told her about my first sex with a girl; she gave me a condom, actually several since it was my first time, and arranged for her and Dad to be gone that evening. Yeah, she figured the first time we'd do it several times—or maybe that I'd break one or wouldn't get it on right.

She kept badgering me when I got back, "What's wrong?" I kept acting so distant so to build up our relationship again, that night I told her I'm gay. I felt so much relief that we could be close again.

The relationship sons have with their mother is such that they "must" tell her everything about their life. They often feel guilty about not coming out to her *earlier*. One college freshman took the first opportunity he had to tell his mother face to face what he had learned during his orientation week.

∇   During Fall Break I had to talk about it because I was so excited about my new understanding and what now suddenly made sense, all the fantasies I had of guys and all the infatuations with guys since junior high. And we talked for hours! We talk a lot, several times a week, over the phone. I wanted to share with her the gay things in my life, the politics, the beautiful guys. The only thing that kept me from telling her before was not knowing what the fantasies meant and wanting to share with her in person this new adventure in my life.

This close-knit mother–son relationship is commonly reported by Latino youths I interviewed. Many feel a special bond with their mother, the person closest to them. They cannot truly be out and gay until they share this aspect of their life.

∇   Oh god! I had wanted to tell her earlier, but I just couldn't. I've been very, very close to her all my life, and it's hard to keep secrets from her, but I don't want to hurt her. I had hinted to her about people, my views, activities, and things of that sort. It's very radical in Puerto Rico to say you have gay friends, and yet I told her that I did. I knew what I was doing, to tell her gently, to test the grounds, to desensitize her. I told her I was going to a gay bar. Then I said I was going to be seeing a "him." That's how I told her. She understood. We had communicated.

To Elicit Support and Outed by Another

External circumstances also arise that oblige youths—nearly 3 in 10 among the interviewed young men—to disclose their sexual identity. Two of these are being in a situation that necessitates eliciting parental support and being publicly "outed" by others. Coping with the vicissitudes of falling in love is a common example of the former.

▽   In adolescence I once tried to tell her that I wasn't normal like other boys because I couldn't feel attracted to girls. But she just said, "Oh, you're just very studious. Your brother is the romantic one. Your time will come." My senior year in high school she knew I was upset, and this is because I had a crush on a straight guy, so I told her that I *might* be gay in order to leave myself an out.

    In college I had been visiting home every 2 weeks, and I came to a point in my relationship with Dan that I felt terrible that I was lying, so I just felt like I had to tell her.

Another youth felt strong familial ties to his Jewish family and yet was conflicted regarding where his family loyalties resided during holidays—with his new *created* family. This internal struggle reached a climax when he had to decide between spending the holidays with his family of origin and spending it with his boyfriend.

▽   She kept pushing, pushing—when was I coming home for Passover and when was I arriving and why hadn't I told her before this. I wanted to bring Jason along but if this was going to be a problem, well, I wanted for us to celebrate our first Passover together. So I told her about Jason.

Family "outing" can also be provoked by another—a boyfriend, another family member, the press. In most circumstances, a youth realizes in advance that in the near future he will be publicly known as gay without having had disclosed this information to his mother. He might be grateful that someone else will do his work, thus forestalling or avoiding embarrassing or very awkward moments.

▽   I was seeing Brian, who was this very militant gay who believed that everyone ought to be out and proud, marching in the streets, and rallying at the state capitol. He was on my case all the time for not telling my parents. How could I march and not tell my parents? So he told my parents, for political reasons, as he had threatened me when we had arguments. So it was for the best for us.

Another youth, who was out to his father, arranged for him to tell his mother just before he, the son, was quoted in the local newspaper. The editor called his parents for comment, and his mother was gone at the time. "But I knew next time she might not be, and my dad couldn't handle everything."

Sons tire of lying to their mother about their attractions and their romantic, social, and political life. They long for personal integration, honesty, a sense of genuineness and, in some cases, a return to a previous relationship that was more open and honest. Or, a mother suspects something is amiss, and she reaches a point at which she confronts her son. Most sons reveal the truth. Circumstances can also dictate a disclosure, either because a youth has begun to establish a new "family" and wants his mother's support or because he will be "outed" by another.

WHEN AND HOW MOTHERS ARE TOLD

Researchers seldom inquire as to when or how youths first disclose to their mother. The average age varies in several recent studies from 18 to 20 years among support group and college-age youths.[7] In nearly all cases, adolescent males first disclose to someone else, usually a friend. Among the youths in the present study, the average age of disclosure to their mother is 19.2 years, which is over a decade after they first feel attracted to other boys, over 2 years after they label themselves, and over a year after they first disclose to someone else.

The average age of disclosure, however, is less instructive than the range of ages over which sons disclose to their mother. Paul told his mother when he was 13 that he "might be" gay; at 14, he was "likely" gay; and at 15, he was "absolutely sure." Nick knew that his mother knew when he was 14, but he did not confirm it until he was 19. Although Walt's mother "has to know," at age 20 he has not yet come out to her. Among those who have not yet "officially" disclosed, most feel fairly certain that their mother already knows, probably from the time he was quite young, because of his sex atypicality or because of her intimate knowledge about him.

Direct Disclosure

Research has generally supported the view that mothers more than fathers are directly rather than indirectly told. Approximately three quarters of youths in a Chicago support agency told their mother directly; a greater willingness to discuss their sexual orientation with their mother than father was reported by youths in other urban support groups as well. One explanation frequently offered is that youths more often fear the reactions of father than mother and thus refrain from telling him in a manner that would encourage a confrontation. Another is that sons simply feel a closer affinity to their mother.[8]

Among the interviewed youths, sons are as likely to directly disclose to their mother as to their father. Although a direct disclosure is the norm, youths are also exposed because someone else outs him, he is outed by accident, or some other indirect means occurs.

Indirect Disclosure

Indirect disclosures are often quite subtle, such as a youth leaving "hints" around the house or his mother discovering the information by accident or through the assistance of a third party. The task of revealing a youth's sexuality may be delegated to a sibling, a friend, or circumstances. In many cases these are not pleasant occasions.

One youth decided he would wait until he was financially independent before telling his parents. However, he broke up with his "roommate" and in retribution the ex sent an exposure letter to the youth's parents detailing their "secretive, sordid affair."

∇   They confronted me, asked if I was gay, and if I was going to keep seeing my gay friends. They gave me a week to decide. I wrote a letter to them in which I said I loved them and that I'll always be gay.

Another youth's mother caught him "fooling around with my cousin and a love letter I wrote him because he had cut me off just as we were developing something." One youth went to a march for gay rights and while he was gone he received a flyer about the march that was opened by his mother. "What was I going to do? If she was going to open my mail, then I was going to admit to it."

Many sons, perhaps a majority, implicitly or explicitly leave hints or traces of their unconventional sexuality prior to or instead of a full verbal disclosure. Thus, many mothers already suspect or perhaps know by the time their son "gets around" to telling them. In the following dyad, the "clues" have become so plentiful that the mother can complete the puzzle, if she wants.

∇   We both know that she knows. I think there was just some sort of implicit understanding that she knew. She never actually accused me, but for the last couple of years she said my friends are all gaylike and why am I attracted to them. She thought my haircut [braids] might cause others to think I am gay. She thought I was just doing it because that was the thing to do, but she also thought I didn't realize that people would think I was gay because of the way I am. She won't accuse me of being gay even though I say, "Even if they think I'm gay, so be it."

Twice she caught me screwing around with guys, once when I was a kid with my cousin when we were giving each other blow jobs in the furnace room and a year ago when she came in on me and Carlos screwing in the shower. But even after that she "didn't know" officially.

Of course she had to know but she never really probed the issue. At the Christmas table she said it was important in life to feel fulfilled. I joked, "Well then I should go to a male prostitute!" But she really didn't get it. She'll ask about my love life, and I'll say there isn't any woman I'm interested in. She's caught me looking at men. She slowly shakes her head and gets this look of fright or disgust. She's asked me if Carlos is gay because his voice sounds lispy.

Growing up I played with Barbie more than my sister, who was taking ballet, and I wanted to but Mother acted as if I had asked to be a girl. She asked if I liked girls at all sexually and asked why I didn't have a girlfriend during junior and senior high school. She has always pushed me toward developing girlfriends, and she complained that I stayed in the house a lot, maybe too much, and drew a lot. She kept telling me to go outside. "To do what?!" She'd say, "To be a boy"—which was weird. Boys have to go outside to be boys? She thought I was a snob because I had an attitude of superiority.

It bothers me that she keeps pestering me with all of these questions about my sexual attractions, nonstop! She's never confronted me directly, but there's this time she and my second oldest sister were in a fight and my sister says, "You always stick up for your faggot son" and then something like, "You always ask me if he is blank, blank, blank." I didn't hear what she said, but I've always wondered if she said "gay." This was when I was 15. She's always had her suspicions but never really said anything. Except once she says to my aunt, "Well maybe I'm a gay mother," and this was 4 years ago.

Sometimes hints are transparent, without the explicit words ever being spoken. What seems to matter most is that everyone knows about "it" but no one, especially not the mother, wants the words to be uttered. In the following two narratives, mothers skirt the real issue. They are "liberal" women, but this does not appear to ease the transition to a gay identity for their sons. These narratives illustrate that factors other than sex atypicality can cue suspicions in mothers.

∇   She supposedly doesn't know but, well, once a guy came to sleep over with me, and we slept in the same bed the first time. Mom said nothing. The second time she said, "Are you very good friends with him now? Others say it's not good for him to come over. It's not a good sight." I think this is because he looked gay. He was just a friend; we weren't doing anything.

She then said to me a couple of days later, "You know you've been acting kind of fruity lately, but I don't want to know anything." And, before going to Italy my mother said to me, "Now, don't be gay; life will be too hard for you." She just gave this as a snippet of advice. I just said, "Whatever."

I just want to yell it in her ear. She was raised in San Francisco, so she's not naive about things, except when she wants to be stupid, like with my life.

▽ Thinking back, my mother had questioned my sexual identity. Maybe it was just the way that she talked about the issue. "We brought you up liberal, to love everyone," and I wondered at that point whether she was trying to imply whether or not I loved males in a particular way. I would always debate with her issues about homosexuality, especially when I did my project in college, when I shared with her all of the new information that I had. Maybe I had some hope that she would pick up on this and want to talk to me about this issue.

There's no indication that there's anything about the way I acted or behaved that would imply to her that I might be other than heterosexual, although she expressed some concern regarding the fact that I was on the phone too much and not studying enough. She was also bothered by my hot temper and that I was not showing enough respect. Also, I wasn't practicing the piano enough. There was some sense too that she was somewhat bothered that I let others push me around, but this bothered her because she was concerned that I might not be fighting my own battles. She said that I talked way too much because I apparently talked all the time.

Other youths have no idea how their mother found out—whether it was their clues, someone else told her, or she just "always" knew. One youth was surprised on his 21st birthday when he received a very explicit card from his mother with two nude males holding each other. "So I never actually told her, which is too bad because she wouldn't actually have cared in the end if I had."

Mother Asks Based on Suspicions

Most commonly, as noted earlier in this chapter, a mother suspects because her son displays sex-atypical behavior, is not athletic or lacks other forms of masculinity, does not seem interested in girls, or has gay-appearing friends. In these situations she is as likely to ask as the son is to volunteer the information. When asked, most youths confirm their same-sex attractions or sexual identity.

▽ Everyone always said I was the sissy in the family, and I guess I was. In the second grade I was always hanging around girls, and Mom thought at first it was so cute. But she must have wondered about me because I remember her saying at some point, almost pleading with me, "Don't be gay." Those were her exact words! I didn't feel at the time it applied to me because I just thought of myself as being asexual.

Well, she must have suspected it later because all my friends were still girls, and I wasn't getting into sports but into acting and art. She never really said anything officially when I was in junior high, but I think she really knew. One time in seventh grade when I was running

I held my arm in a particular way, and she said not to hold my arm that way. She didn't say that it was gaylike, but I could tell it was negative.

Finally, Mom asked my junior year after she found out one of my best friends was gay. Maybe it was all too much for her. Well this was certainly no big leap of logic for her.

One youth was friends with a feminist, which was interpreted by his mother as "some sort of a statement." After he supported gay rights in front of her, called her on her gay jokes, and reported that he wanted to live in San Francisco, she asked him, "Are you trying to tell me you're gay?" A bisexual youth's mother feared that her son's gay political activities implied more than the liberal philosophy that characterizes everyone in the family.

∇   I was talking with her one night with the lights off, like we did a lot, and she seemed to be making assumptions about my heterosexuality. She almost seemed to be baiting me by asking if I had ever done anything with a male, and I finally said at one point that I had. I told her my experiences with guys were not enjoyable in order to give her hope that I would eventually marry and have children.

Association with "suspicious" friends also prompts mothers to conjecture the possibility that they have a gay child. One mother wondered about her son's sexuality for three reasons: First he joined a theater group, then befriended a gay couple, and finally entertained "faggy Tony" in the home. On Christmas Eve, she finally asked "the question." " 'Is Tony gay? Is there something I should know?' I told her I was bisexual but not that Tony was more than a friend."

Some youths have accepting parents who encourage them to explore all sexual options. Although rare, such parents ease the transition from being in to out of the closet, in part by asking directly about their son's sexual attractions. In high school one youth dated a woman for 2 years, but at Disneyland he had a new experience.

∇   I really hadn't dated anyone else, even though I was popular in high school. When I was 16 we were at Disneyland, and I met someone, the man of my dreams, and I told her that I met someone. She asked if I was attracted more to guys than to girls, and I denied this because there were all sorts of people around. Five days later I told her that she had been right. "I always had an idea you were headed in that direction." I got a little angry, because I didn't know why she'd say that. I mean I dated one girl for 2 years! She had just noticed that I looked a lot at guys, which surprised me then because I didn't know that I did.

Once mothers know or strongly suspect, they react with a variety of responses—from a calm acknowledgment and acceptance to an emotionally violent response.

MOTHERS' INITIAL REACTIONS

Because most gay and bisexual sons tend to feel close to their mother and are more comfortable discussing their personal life with her than with their father, investigators often assume that once they are told mothers are less likely than fathers to respond with anger, verbal threats, or physical abuse. Although sons are more likely to report feeling "protected" and supported by their mother than their father—over two times as many in one study—that mothers actually respond with less negativity is an unsubstantiated claim. Tony D'Augelli and colleagues reported significant differences in how parents currently respond, with mothers perceived as more supportive. Others agree with these findings.[9] However, the question of how mother initially reacts remains unsettled.

Expected and Actual Reactions

In the present sample of sexual-minority youths, the initial reactions of mothers are slightly more negative than those received from fathers, averaging "slightly negative."[10] The range, however, is wide, from mothers who are extremely supportive to those who react with screams and threats to abandon their son. Indeed, in no other parent–child dyad does the average initial reaction register so strongly in a negative direction.

In addition, the relatively few young men who have not come out to their mothers do not expect her to respond positively. When compared with the expected reactions of all other parent–child combinations, the level of anticipated anguish in mother–son dyads is exceptionally high. No undisclosed youth expects his mother to be supportive, or even neutral, and several anticipate that she will threaten to cut off emotional and financial aid and will mandate conversion therapy. Potential reasons for this overly negative response to her son's same-sex attractions have not been investigated, but likely are connected with the importance he has in her life. She might be reacting to the guilt she feels that their historically intimate relationship has made him gay and that she has "failed" as a parent (that it is indeed *her* fault), to the perception that he will now have a very thorny and complicated life, or to her realization that this favorite child of hers will not be producing grandchildren or a socially "respectable" life.

The range in mothers' reactions is reflected in the three narratives that begin this chapter. After initially dismissing Paul's early adolescent questioning, his mother was subsequently supportive several years later when he finally asserted, "I'm gay." Partially aiding her acceptance were "hints" of his earlier questioning, her discovery of his gay porn magazines, and the observations of his sex-atypical behaviors. Her primary concern, according to Paul, was with the difficult life that he would have once he was generally known as gay. Her reaction is in marked contrast to Nick's mother, who "really flipped out." She blamed his friends and, ultimately, herself. This silenced Nick for several years, until he came out to her a second time during his freshman year of college. Again, she freaked and became self-absorbed: "How can you do this to me?" She demanded that he seek psychological help that would convert him to heterosexuality, but refused to talk openly about his sexuality after her initial outburst of panic. Walt is fairly convinced that once he discloses his mother will blame herself and argue that it is a sinful lifestyle, unless he wants to go to hell.

Negative Initial Reactions

Few mothers respond as negatively as Nick's. The most common reactions are "slightly negative"—constituting denial, negative comments, and discouragement. Together these characterizations represent nearly one half of all mothers who know about the nonheterosexuality of their son. Extreme hysterical and angry maternal reactions are relatively rare, but they do occur—in 4% of the present sample of male youths. Overall, no dyadic interaction is as negative as the mother's response to her son coming out.

The most damaging reaction to her son was elicited by a mother who "freaked out" and was rushed in an ambulance, at her demand, to the hospital with severely elevated blood pressure. She thought she was having a stroke. After returning later that night, "She wanted to kill me. Totally unaccepting. She called the cops and had me arrested for trespassing because I was not 'her son' anymore."

∇ This was my junior year of high school. She was very distressed for days. She cried, she really lost it. For several days she'd just begin screaming, and I'd scream right back at her and then she sort of came to her senses. Then she denied it all and said I wasn't gay, and then she started saying, "What will everyone think? What will the church think?" She's afraid that her social life, her social world will be destroyed. She is very selfish about it actually, afraid what will become of the family name, that she'll have no grandkids, what will my father say, and how do I know anyways because it's usually just a phase. Then she tried to say that maybe I'm just bisexual, can get married, ignore this, have children, and be normal.

Though this mother had always professed deep love for her son, her affection could not overcome her paralyzing fears, shame, and unrelenting concern about the integrity of her own social status and well-being.

Also extreme is a mother who instigated a family crisis that transpired into an overnight calamity, with first one family member and then another reacting to the disclosure. The worst was the youth's mother.

▽ My mother burst into tears. She had a really red face, sort of a completely blubbering reaction that was very horrible. She just kept saying, "I can't believe it! I can't believe it!" But why couldn't she believe it? She's known for a long time, but she thinks just because I'm 15 I can't know.

This started a family crisis that lasted the whole night. This should not have shaken her up like it did. Said it was a bad thing and did all this stereotyping about I would never be happy, her dreams were shattered with having grandchildren, and I was going to get AIDS. Yeah, right! She was only concerned with her own skin, her own reputation, her own dreams. She told me not to tell anyone, and she wouldn't let me touch her or anyone else in the family.

This is by far the biggest crisis I've ever faced on earth. Sooner or later maybe she'll catch up with the modern era. I had always thought she'd be there for me, but I was wrong, wrong, wrong, and I wish now that I had never told her. My friends are now my family.

More typical are reactions that, although negative, do not threaten the mother–son relationship. Several disclosing youths were fairly certain their mother would not respond in a positive way because of her religious beliefs or ethnicity, or because there is little evidence of her giving emotional support in their past. Despite these barriers, she is told.

▽ I told her 3 weeks ago. She didn't cry, but she did seem really angry. She has a hard time expressing emotions, and she has a really hard time with my being gay because of her religion, which she pulls out whenever handy. It's really her problem and not mine. She wants me to try a relationship with a girl again, one last time. She feels like it's a sin to be with a man.

She has always taken my father's side in our many violent arguments, even though she never called me names as he did. Once after a TV show she asked if I knew what homosexuality was. I knew what it was but I said I didn't because I wanted to hear about it. She believed me and explained what it was and how evil it was from a biblical point of view. This was after she caught me having oral sex with a boy in my bedroom when I was 12. She told me it was wrong and unclean and so on. But I think she just put it out of her mind because she didn't want to believe it.

Other youths are taken aback by the extent of their mother's tirade— they expected and wanted better of her. She might even embark on what appears to be a rational, intellectual course of action—to change her son's sexual orientation. She will "handle" the situation once she has better control over her son.

▽ I told her over the phone, and she then began screaming, which is very unlike her traditional Chinese demeanor. Then she called back a few minutes later and apologized profusely. In a very even tone she asked that I keep my mind open, "Don't do anything!" She clearly didn't like it, but in the call back she was very nonemotional and intellectual about it. She was relatively calm, which is usual for her. She said she wanted me to come home after graduation. "Don't make any major life decisions."

I asked her why, and she said so she could change my sexual identity! You see, she's got all these lesbian friends and is president of the local NOW chapter, so she has to pretend to be liberal. But when it comes to her own son, she can't like handle it down deep. She told me she thought and hoped I would grow out of being gay and just to leave my options open. To be a responsible mother she had to encourage me to hold off on my final decision.

The mother–son relationship is particularly prone to volatility if a mother is surprised or shocked by the disclosure—which appears to be the norm when her son is masculine and not sex atypical in behavior or mannerisms. According to one youth, "My mom was shocked. She always assumed I was straight. I was just simply a slow bloomer with the girls."

Positive Initial Reactions

Few sons can expect as positive of a response as that which Paul received. Slightly over 1 in 10 youths report that their mother gave unqualified support. Her primary concern is usually the well-being and safety of her son. "She said she wasn't surprised, but she cried rather softly. We talked. I gave her stuff to read. I thought it went very well. She says she loves me, always will no matter what, but is concerned for the hard life I'll have. But she said she'd be there for me to overcome whatever came my way."

Two in 10 mothers are more "guarded" in their positive reactions. These are often women who struggle to understand and reconcile the knowledge that they have a gay or bisexual son, yet they love their son and want to maintain good relations with him. For example, one youth grew up in a working-class trailer park home; his mother was 16 years old and with one of her many boyfriends when she gave birth to him.

∇   I don't remember any particular time when she questioned my sexual orientation. She raised me and her boyfriends were really rotten to me. They really knocked me around, so maybe I just tried to emulate her.

I turned masculine and began dating when I was 17. I reacted in a fairly negative way to her questioning, but I can't recall that she ever directly confronted me. I know that I can only fall in love with men. My mom's brother is bisexual, but she never talked about it. I think maybe she worried about my sexuality but couldn't bring herself to accuse me directly.

So she didn't take it so well, but then not badly either. She's just not comfortable with it, not happy. But on the other hand, she says she loves me because I'm her son. She was not surprised and had wondered about it but never gave any hints that she knew.

Other youths are reasonably certain that they will receive a positive response, primarily because of the history of their relationship with their mother. They know her views about alternative forms of sexuality, and she has apparently anticipated the news, come to terms with it, and is waiting for the youth to find the right moment to come out.

∇   At the time I was being told about the birds and the bees she told me that if I was gay my lover would be accepted into the home as if he was my girlfriend. I didn't realize my mom's open mindedness at the time, but later when I was 14 when I told her I was bi I guess I knew she would understand.

She was comfortable with me being bi, but she wanted me to lead a straight lifestyle because it'd be easier for me. It's not that she's homophobic, but she suggested that I talk to someone, not to change but to feel more comfortable with who I am. She said it was not the biggest shock in her life. She seemed very unaffected by it and said didn't I think she knew this already. She said she was quite a tomboy when she grew up but that did not make her a lesbian, so I guess that reflects some homophobia.

When I reminded her a year later I was bi she reacted extremely well, asked me to be safe, and asked me if I wanted to marry a girl and have kids. I said that was my goal to give her some hope and that I would be happy doing this, although at some level I knew that this might not be completely true. She assumed I would be following this path.

Although mothers' initial reactions vary from outright rejection to full acceptance, most rare are neutral reactions to the disclosure. Silence or a stance of neutrality occurs in all other parent–child dyads. The normative response, counter to popular literature, is to express mild forms of grief and then quickly move to acknowledgment and acceptance. If a favorable reception is not immediate, it usually follows fairly quickly. What happens after this initial reaction is a variety of "long-term" solutions to the mother–son relationship.

RELATIONSHIPS AFTER DISCLOSURE

During his early adolescent years Paul disclosed with ever-increasing clarity that he has strong same-sex attractions that could only mean that he is gay. His mother was at all times tentatively supportive, although Paul feels that she held out hope for his heterosexuality. It is not that she openly opposed his lifestyle but rather that she avoided talking about it. Unhappy with this resolution, Paul initiated a campaign of discussing his attractions and sexual identity, with a corresponding movement on the part of his mother toward greater comfort with her son's sexuality. Progress toward acceptance for Nick's mother has been slow and difficult. She blamed herself and sought conversion therapy for him. Only recently has she begun to "deal with it" by squelching her disappointment and buying him condoms.

Unfortunately, previous research cannot assist our understanding of how the mother–son relationship evolves following disclosure because few if any investigators have asked the question, "How has your relationship changed in the intervening years?" Among the youths I interviewed, 50% report that matters have improved after disclosure, 40% believe that little has changed, and 10% say that a decline in their relationship with their mother has occurred. This overall optimistic report should not imply that progress is inevitable or that change always results in a positive outcome—some dyads move from a situation that is horrible to one that is simply bad, but still not positive.

The Relationship Improves

Many mothers learn to accept their altered reality that they have a gay or bisexual son relatively quickly after disclosure. Because most mothers have a historically special relationship with their son, they want to be supportive; the son may even demand enthusiasm as well as her acceptance for his discovery. He is excited about his new and honest life and would like her to share in it. Although relatively few mothers initially give full endorsement, many try to recuperate after the initial setback. One religious mother found a way to do this through her church.

∇   Out of desperation she tried to get me to see a priest, but he turned out to be gay. When I told him I was gay he said, "Fine." That was all there was to it. Once my mother found out it was okay with him she gave up her objections. She won't do nothing to either help or hinder the development of my homosexuality. She has always defended the positions of the Catholic church, so it's important never to mention the word because even though she's supportive of me, she has to be against homosexuality, at least when we use those words.

It was hard for her because of the five of us I've been the model son, and I'm my mother's favorite. So now she's much more comfortable about it, although she always worries about the AIDS issue. She made me keep my promise not to tell my father. They themselves are having some problems. My mother assured me that they would continue paying for college.

Another group of mothers initially responds poorly and then recovers their bearings to offer at least acknowledgment and sometimes acceptance. One mother initially threatened to sever all financial ties, "but she didn't.

She wasn't happy with it, but she learned how to deal with it." The youth understands that his mother's "bigoted" background makes it difficult for her to accept his sexuality, "but she is trying, although deep down I can tell that it's really bothering her." As his sexuality is "normalized" and he openly talks about it, and as his mother finds other mothers who have the same "problem," he believes she will continue to increase her support, although perhaps never advancing to the point of being a political ally. Another youth knows that his mother's full acceptance will take time: "She certainly has reservations about my homosexuality because of her religion. She worries about my spirituality and whether or not this will keep me from going to heaven." Most of the time, however, the two ignore his sexuality and their relationship has become increasingly intimate, warm, and gratifying.

The mothers of bisexual youths frequently have a particularly difficult hurdle to overcome: If their son is attracted to girls, then why not "choose" to pursue the socially acceptable route? Even mothers who accept their son's bisexuality and have a reasonably good relationship with him might still be perplexed with his decision to be with a man.

∇   She wasn't all that surprised even though she said she hadn't thought about it. After a calm, "Well, that's okay," she didn't mention it. I brought it up again a week later, and she said she thought it was a phase and that I'd go the straight route. She's much more excited if I'm dating a female than if I say something to her about a guy. It's easier for her to accept the bisexual element because she assumes I will do the Jewish thing and develop a straight relationship and have kids. This would make her happy, and I've always tried to make her happy. So things are okay as long as I don't push the gay envelope too much.

Let me give you an example. I was getting interested in this guy, and this freaked her out, so at this wedding she made sure I sat with Sarah and her parents and that we danced. She never mentions my boyfriend and ignores my comments when I do. But she'll ask me, "How is Sarah doing?" or "Isn't Sarah's hair so beautiful?" The other day she even said she traced the Bernstein's family line, and there was no history of mental illness or retardation!

Mothers usually want what is best for their son, and they *know* that means choosing a girl. One youth's mother told him to "be pragmatic. 'Your life will be much easier with a girl.'" Mothers worry about their son being beaten up, losing his professional life, or being infected with HIV. Being with another man only complicates life.

Protectionism permeates many of the "second responses" a mother has to her son after the initial disclosure. Whether the potential protagonist is her husband, the external world, or AIDS, she wants, perhaps feels an obligation, to protect her son. Even if her initial reactions are harsh and incredulous, on many occasions this can be traced to her desire to shield her son against the evils of the world and a perceived difficult life. She *is* responsible for him!

Nonetheless, many mothers mellow and become increasingly accepting once they realize that the possible consequence of their continued objections is that they will lose their son and their ability to protect him. One mother asked questions "about my dates with guys, and she'll actually ask about what we do and don't do. She wants me to meet boyfriends." Initially hesitant to tell his mother, once one youth came out to her she became "respectful of what I did. We're good friends now. It was very liberating." Mothers may also realize new benefits from having a gay son—they get "the daughter" they always wanted. "I'll talk and help her out in the kitchen, fix meals, while my brothers just say to her to fuck off, and watch TV."

The Relationship Continues

Four in 10 mother–son relationships do not improve or worsen after the initial disclosure but remain essentially the same. Indeed, the most common maternal reaction after the initial response to the disclosure is to "not talk about it." Without discussion, little opportunity exists for initial reactions to evolve. Continuation could entail an initially negative response staying bad, a positive one staying positive, or a neutral response staying neutral.

Many youths agree with the following teenager who received a relatively neutral, silent reaction from his mother: "She tries still to deny that part of my life and at this point, this is simply a topic we don't talk about. So while she is not rejecting of me, neither is she willing to deal with this issue at this time." A mother may place prohibitions on her gay son, demanding that he not act on it or talk about it with anyone, especially "your dad because he just wouldn't understand." She thus reduces the spectrum of negative ramifications that the news will have on herself and perhaps her son, diminishes the visibility of her son's homosexuality to the point that she can place it out of her consciousness, or pretends it just does not exist. If he does not "act on it," then his same-sex attractions will seem less real to her and, hopefully, to him, thus increasing the probability in her eyes that he will "choose" heterosexuality. The son may have planted the seed, but the mother will not nourish it, with the hope that it will die. This stance may last for days, months, or years.

In the following dyad the topic of homosexuality has not reemerged for 5 years since the initial disclosure. Consequently, a bad reaction has remained bad. The son takes a dim view of his mother's ability to handle difficult information. This was true when her oldest son disclosed his homosexuality to her and appears to also characterize her reaction now that her youngest son has "rocked her world yet again."

∇ My mother knows but is stupid and doesn't want to talk about it. Basically I think it's denial in certain terms. She denied that my brother's relationship with his boyfriend existed, as if they are best friends who live together in a one-bedroom apartment. My mother hasn't talked about it, not once since I told her. Topic not brought up ever by her. She's set in her stupid ways.

I guess since she's known it's changed our relationship, and we pretend a lot and don't talk about anything like we used to. So it doesn't exist. It's the trump card she holds over me. I'm being mentally and physically abused by her, so I guess I'm on my own.

Mothers who initially acknowledge their son's same-sex attractions with acceptance often move no further toward fully embracing their gay or bisexual son. Sons complain, as one youth stated it, that, "Nothing else happened. It was like she had done her loving, motherly thing. I would have liked more." When asked what else she should have done, youths often want political action, active discussions on gay topics, and invitations for boyfriends to spend a weekend or holiday. For example, a mother might agree to let her son's boyfriend come for dinner, but most requests have to be initiated by her son. "Why couldn't she think of it? She's always inviting my sister's husband to come over."

The Relationship Deteriorates

Not all mothers, however, progress in a positive or neutral manner. One in 10 mother–son relationships worsen over time, with very little evidence of positive developments. "She sent me to the shrink a week later and made me tell my sisters as a way to punish me—to embarrass me and make me out the fool. I'm afraid she'll use it against me sometime." Another youth faced an even harsher judgment and consequence. "She freaked out and never really mentioned it after that until a month later. Then she really started to harass me, said it was a phase and that I could change. At the time I discovered I was HIV positive, but I couldn't tell her. Now I'm uninsured because she's taken me off her policy, saying I'm no child of hers."

Mothers who respond positively and then become increasingly negative evince a relatively rare pattern. In most cases this is the result of independent changes occurring in their life—usually they become "more religious."

∇ I dated this guy, and he stayed with us and she became quite fond of him, let us sleep in the same bed and considered him part of the family— the man of the house. He was 21, 6 years older than me. I didn't think we had an ideal relationship, but after we broke up she became more negative. She's become much more spiritual, sort of New Age with crystals and palm reading, and she sees homosexuality as part of the materialism or jet age image.

She has actually very few controls over me at this point. I see her very little now. I say to her, "Let me use my own judgment." She'll cringe and say I'm still like a boy and I'm trying to get out of self-responsibility and that's why I'm gay.

For most sons, maternal tolerance, if not acceptance, emerges either immediately after they come out to their mother or soon thereafter. Few mothers want their son to be gay or bi, but once they know he is serious in his proclamations, they revert to their protective position that he is, after all, their son and they must be there as his parent. The two now have a new bond, one of mutual understanding and support.

WHEN MOTHERS HAVE SAME-SEX ATTRACTIONS

The majority of mother–son relationships become ever more positive over time, although at differing rates and to varying degrees. Although it is difficult to predict which relationships will become most positive in the shortest period of time, one characteristic that is a usually good sign is having a mother who has significant same-sex attractions herself. One youth recalls a long history of positive gay images in his family.

∇   My mother had this great love of Liberace, and on TV I once saw Elton John with the long dangling earrings. At the time I remember her saying, "Well, it's his business, whatever he is." But I also remember media figures like David Bowie who was supposedly gay. The positive part was not so much that these people were there but that my mother's reaction to them was positive. "They have a right to it."
     Me and my brother just went, "Ugh!" One time I protested, and she reminded me of several of her friends, this lesbian couple in church I like a lot.
     There's lots of homosexuality in our family as it is. Two sisters who are bisexual. One has come out to me, and the other hasn't, maybe even to herself, but several of her [female] friends told me they've had sex with her. I have a cousin on my mother's side, and he is gay, but my grandparents have really deserted him. Then there's a cousin on my father's side, but we never see him. I even think my mother went through an experimental stage in the '60s. She was this real beatnik kind of a person, and I sort of think she experimented sexually with women.

Indeed, just under 5% of the youths I interviewed believe that they have a mother who either had at one time significant same-sex attractions or are currently lesbian or bisexual.

∇   More and more she has said she has these significant attractions, and she leans more that way, toward lesbian. She shouldn't be surprised because her brother is gay and her sister I suspect is lesbian because she's never married and she keeps hanging out with this one female friend for many, many years.

A FINAL WORD

Most gay and bisexual sons disclose to their mother before disclosing to their father. It is as if it is most important to come out to her first, perhaps because she is their emotional center, the one who nurtured them through their childhood and adolescence, the one who taught them values and self-respect, and the one they most want and need to know supports and accepts them. Indeed, one empirical study demonstrated that youths who were out to their mother or who had a satisfying relationship with their mother had the highest levels of self-esteem.[11]

When a mother fails to provide this support, youths may feel betrayed, perhaps question the sincerity of her past love, and note that the mother–son relationship deteriorates. Fortunately, when faced with the prospects of losing their son, most mothers relent and accept him in a more holistic fashion—still their child, but now with a same-sex orientation. Those who reach this position are most likely to have had previous contact with sexual-minority people or a history of nonheterosexuality in the family; have a warm, open relationship with their son; or share his same-sex attractions. Some cannot offer unconditional love—perhaps the result of selfish self-interest but often because they want nothing more than to continue what they have been doing since his conception: protect him from the hardships of life. To acknowledge his sexuality is to condone, perhaps even encourage, a life they believe will only harm their child.

No youth reported that his mother responded neutrally to his coming out. She reacted! Some respond negatively to discovering that they have a gay or bisexual son and remain negative. More start positively and stay positive. Only the rare ones begin positively and become negative. The vast majority originate from a slightly negative position and become at least tolerant or extremely supportive over time. At the time of my interview, most youths reported that they now have a positive relationship with their mother, and they expect this to continue. This portrait, strikingly at variance with stereotypic images of family calamities and chaos, is part of the new face of being young and gay in America.

ENDNOTES

[1] Bell, A. P., Weinberg, M. S., & Hammersmith, S. K. (1981). *Sexual preference: Its development in men and women*. Bloomington: Indiana University Press.

[2] Despite widespread scientific evidence that sexual orientation likely has a substantial genetic base, only 32% of the American public believe that homosexuality is genetic. The rest attribute some aspect to learning or the environment, including parenting. See Reuters (2000, February 8). *Most in U.S. favor laws barring gay discrimination.* Distributed via e-mail list server Channel Q News (list server@channelq.com), managed by Doug Case (Doug.Case@sdsu.edu).

[3] Although the percentage is usually under 10%. See D'Augelli, A. R., & Hershberger, S. L. (1993). Lesbian, gay, and bisexual youth in community settings: Personal challenges and mental health problems. *American Journal of Community Psychology, 21,* 421–448; D'Augelli, A. R. (1998, February). *Victimization history and mental health among lesbian, gay, and bisexual youths.* Paper presented at the Society for Research on Adolescence, San Diego, CA; Herdt, G., & Boxer, A. (1993). *Children of Horizons: How gay and lesbian teens are leading a new way out of the closet.* Boston: Beacon Press; and Weinberg, M. S., Williams, C. J., & Pryor, D. W. (1994). *Dual attraction: Understanding bisexuality.* New York: Oxford University Press.

[4] Lever, J. (1994, August 23). Sexual revelations. *The Advocate,* pp. 17–24.

[5] Savin-Williams, R. C. (1998). The disclosure to their families of same-sex attractions by lesbian, gay, and bisexual youths. *Journal of Research on Adolescence, 8,* 49–68.

[6] D'Augelli, A. R., Hershberger, S. L., & Pilkington, N. W. (1998). Lesbian, gay, and bisexual youth and their families: Disclosure of sexual orientation and its consequences. *American Journal of Orthopsychiatry, 68,* 361–371.

[7] D'Augelli, A. R., & Hershberger, S. L. (1993). Lesbian, gay, and bisexual youth in community settings: Personal challenges and mental health problems. *American Journal of Community Psychology, 21,* 421–448; D'Augelli, A. R. (1998, February). *Victimization history and mental health among lesbian, gay, and bisexual youths.* Paper presented at the Society for Research on Adolescence, San Diego, CA; and Sears, J. T. (1991). *Growing up gay in the South: Race, gender, and journeys of the spirit.* New York: Harrington Park Press.

[8] D'Augelli, A. R. (1991). Gay men in college: Identity processes and adaptations. *Journal of College Student Development, 32,* 140–146; D'Augelli, A. R., & Hershberger, S. L. (1993). Lesbian, gay, and bisexual youth in community settings: Personal challenges and mental health problems. *American Journal of Community Psychology, 21,* 421–448; D'Augelli, A. R., Hershberger, S. L., & Pilkington, N. W. (1998). Lesbian, gay, and bisexual youth and their families: Disclosure of sexual orientation and its consequences. *American Journal of Orthopsychiatry, 68,* 361–371; Cramer, D. W., & Roach, A. J. (1988). Coming out to mom and dad: A study of gay males and their relationships with their parents. *Journal of Homosexuality, 15,* 79–91; Herdt, G., & Boxer, A. (1993). *Children of Horizons: How gay and lesbian teens are leading a new way out of the closet.* Boston: Beacon Press; and Savin-Williams, R. C. (1990). *Gay and lesbian youths: Expressions of identity.* Washington, DC: Hemisphere.

[9] The following research studies address the issue of relative parental reactions once disclosure has occurred: Cramer, D. W., & Roach, A. J. (1988). Coming out to mom and dad: A study of gay males and their relationships with their parents.

Journal of Homosexuality, 15, 79–91; D'Augelli, A. R. (1991). Gay men in college: Identity processes and adaptations. *Journal of College Student Development*, 32, 140–146; D'Augelli, A. R., & Hershberger, S. L. (1993). Lesbian, gay, and bisexual youth in community settings: Personal challenges and mental health problems. *American Journal of Community Psychology*, 21, 421–448; D'Augelli, A. R., Hershberger, S. L., & Pilkington, N. W. (1998). Lesbian, gay, and bisexual youth and their families: Disclosure of sexual orientation and its consequences. *American Journal of Orthopsychiatry*, 68, 361–371; Pilkington, N. W., & D'Augelli, A. R. (1995). Victimization of lesbian, gay, and bisexual youth in community settings. *Journal of Community Psychology*, 23, 34–56; Rotheram-Borus, M. J., Rosario, M., & Koopman, C. (1991). Minority youths at high risk: Gay males and runaways. In M. E. Colten & S. Gore (Eds.), *Adolescent stress: Causes and consequences* (pp. 181–200). New York: Aldine de Gruyter; and Savin-Williams, R. C. (1990). *Gay and lesbian youth: Expressions of identity*. Washington, DC: Hemisphere.

[10] Actual reactions averaged 3.9 on a scale from 1 (*very supportive*) to 7 (*rejection*); expected reactions averaged 5.1.

[11] Savin-Williams, R. C. (1990). *Gay and lesbain youth: Expressions of identity*. Washington, DC: Hemisphere.

7

SONS AND FATHERS

Pete

When I was 17, two of my best school friends, two girls, told my parents out of their concern for me that I "needed help." When my dad confronted me about what I needed help about, well, I had to be honest, because we've always as a family stressed honesty with each other.

As expected, he was supportive, especially so it seemed, probably because my dad's boss is gay, and my dad is very liberal, so in our house we talked very openly about homosexuality. Because of his boss being gay, my dad said that it was okay to be gay. He said he knew and he had no problem, except he thought it was his fault, and I reassured him that it wasn't. This was uncomfortable for me, but then he had been always supportive. He just wants me to be successful. He has always been great, never saying anything negative about homosexuality. At least we talked about it, all night in fact. He thought originally when I was a kid, he later told me, that this would be just another phase of my very difficult life—life has not been easy for me because of illnesses, asthma, medication addiction—but over time he maintained support.

He always knew, and I didn't know! He would just joke about homosexuality and was very comfortable with the topic—not sure why it took me so long to tell him. I have a lesbian sister and a brother who is bisexual, so maybe he's used to it. Then an uncle who is a priest I think is gay and avoiding it. Once Dad was bothered when he caught me playing with a doll. He said this was sissy without much emotion—like he was resigned to it.

Everybody has always thought I was a clone of Dad, from the day I was born, I've been told. As a child I had a great affection for clothing, and he thought I was too concerned with this, although he was always a sharp dresser himself. I don't think he necessarily associated it with being gay. He was just concerned with anything that was feminine or might look gay. Because I was into clothing he thought that was a feminine thing, but really I wasn't unmasculine. But I do wonder about my dad—his hyper concern with not appearing feminine, his sharp dressing, his love of the theater, and his many very attractive male friends.

Nolan

My junior year in college over Thanksgiving I told him after my mother told me I had to. I didn't want to talk about it, but he confronted me and thought that it was best for me to start talking about it. My father is Italian and of a different era. He sort of is out of this modern life, essentially. He never sees my point of view. He started going crazy, cursing at me. He then pulled down his pants and said, holding his penis, "Is this what you want?!" He physically attacked me, tried to strangle me, and hit me. I ran out of the house and went to my best friend's house.

It was a terrible weekend that Thanksgiving and then again at Christmas. He kept talking to me; he kept me inside the house and wouldn't let me go out unless I was accompanied by a member of the family. He wouldn't let me talk to any of my friends. He kept trying to talk me out of being gay.

Father said I could stay at college only if I were to see a psychologist. He made me move out of the dorm and moved me off campus, and my family basically started living with me. They wanted me to continue my education, but they couldn't trust me with any other gay person. I went back to college to lead a straight lifestyle.

I went to see a psychologist who was actually a chaplain. He said to my parents that they had a problem and not me. He never said that he was going to try to change me, but he was willing to talk to me about my family problems. He's been very decent.

My father feels that if he supports me then he ends up supporting homosexuality. He must have had suspicions about me when I was younger because I had these erotic posters of male rock stars in my bedroom. My father said that I was into effeminate men, and he's always tried to discourage anything gay, such as my involvement in music or dramatics. They're both in liberal professions, and I've always had good grades and I've done things to make them proud, but in the gay things, such as singing and musicals and acting in high school, they've never really liked.

William

I ask myself, why should I tell him? Perhaps only if I am in a real serious relationship and I didn't want to try to explain who this particular man was, then I might tell him. Or it may be a problem at graduation here [in my dorm], that is, because I have a lot of magazines and novels and art and if you look real careful you can tell that I'm gay. If he were to come up here then I would have this big decision about whether or not to de-gay my apartment. If he really wanted to know, then certainly there would be enough evidence.

Yet it feels like it's a rite of passage to tell, and I suspect eventually I've got to do it. I wouldn't expect my father to be particularly terribly negative about it. Basically, it seems that he has ignored the issue; even though I've never dated, he really never asked or pushed me to go out with women. I figured that he just figured it out a long time ago, and he basically decided that whatever I do is my own business, although at times he really pushed me to be more sportslike, but I really was not very interested. In sixth grade he made me join the football team, but this was just awful. I had no concept of what it was all about. In junior high school he made me join the soccer team, and that was more awful. In senior high he made me join the swim team, and that wasn't awful. Even though I did not excel, I was at least okay at it.

Why tell? We're not like real close or anything, but I guess I should, out of respect.

Pete, Nolan, and William made different decisions about whether, when, and how to tell their father about their sexuality. Although it is unfair to label their experiences as normative or typical of young men with same-sex attractions, to some extent they represent three facets of the relationships gay and bisexual youths have with their fathers. They also illustrate the diversity that is apparent among youths who must decide whether they want to share this knowledge with an individual who may have been, at least at some point, the most important man in their lives.

THE RELATIONSHIP BEFORE DISCLOSURE

Among gay and bisexual male adults interviewed in San Francisco in the late 1960s, a majority reported that they did not feel close to their father while growing up. He was not warm or intimate, and they had little admiration or respect for him. Knowing that they were not their father's favorite child, they felt detached from him. They perceived themselves as unlike their father in his masculinity, activities, and independence, and they had little desire to grow up to be the kind of person he is. Almost three quarters reported that they were more similar to their mother than their father.[1]

Many of the gay and bisexual youths I interviewed express similar sentiments. Although few experienced such battles with their father, as did Nolan, that their interactions erupt in violence and outright rejection, nearly half of the youths report conflictual relations with their father. The clash usually centers on the youth's child and adolescent sex-atypical mannerisms and behaviors. Equally typical are the narratives of Pete and William—distant but compatible relationships with their father. Their greatest "sin" is not being sufficiently masculine. A few had good childhood relationships with their fathers, only occasionally punctuated by bickering and squabbles over "hot" issues.

Conflictual Relationships

Many horror stories, recited in coming-out books, chat groups, and on-line magazines, are of real-life father–son encounters in which fathers will not or cannot tolerate a "faggy" son. Youths who recall such discord in the father–son relationship frequently attribute the friction not to concern with the direction of the youth's sexuality but with his displays of sex-atypical behavior. Pete's father did not appreciate his son playing with dolls or his interest in clothing; Nolan's father objected to his son's involvement in singing and acting.

From an early age, several youths I interviewed faced nearly daily recriminations because of their sex-atypical behavior. One father was, according to his son, "Really burned up because of the way I walk, the way I talk, the way I carry myself. He always tagged me as a pansy, like a fruitcake." Another youth feels that he is a failure in his father's eyes. If he comes out to his father, he fears that he will displease him yet once again. Thus, this most important aspect about himself is known by his mother, friends, academic advisor, collegiate gay community, minister, doctor— everyone but his father. Coming out to his father will be his final exit from the closet.

∇ He has always questioned my behavior. When I was young, from 4 years old, he wanted me to play baseball because it was so important to him, and I just wasn't into it. I was terrible at it, and he was always yelling at me and calling me a sissy because I threw like a girl. He would say when I cried to act like a man. He worried about my posture and thought I was too smart. He didn't like my dancing, my listening to Big Bands, or my humor or my cooking. He didn't want me to wear faggy clothes.

I was teased heavily, and I was very sensitive to it. Some said I was a little girl because I couldn't play baseball. This occurred basically by everyone, but I was actually teased more by my father than by anyone else, and this is what really hurt. I would turn real red or try to escape or deny that I was a girl. Maybe it was because I was so sensitive that I would get teased. I was known as the smart kid, but this was not good enough for him. I actually had few friends because I was quiet and avoided people. My father and I fought a lot because he thought I was too smart, too domestic.

I had to participate in some sports just to please him. So in high school I did soccer, track and field, and long-distance running until I broke my leg. I was the fastest runner in school but was terrible and horrible at basketball and baseball. Guys always laughed at me, except my father, who'd see red; it only made him mad to see me flail about.

I think I'm gay because of my self-image and my father's name calling, and eventually I came to believe him. But then maybe it was my sex play, or maybe it only reinforced what already was. I know that I've been gay for a long time, probably I was born with it.

Fathers can also become frustrated with their son if he is not following in their footsteps—not "replicating the old man," as one youth describes it. A former world-class athlete, one father made his son try out for Little League baseball, despite the son's protest. "What Jew does baseball?!" He tried out, made the team (as did everyone who tried out), and became a fixture in right field who consistently batted last; his father was the coach. Their relationship became somewhat less conflictual when the son made the wrestling team. This sport was more to his liking because of its unique benefits.

∇   My father wanted me to join all-male activities. You know, sports teams and things like that to prove my masculinity. I loved wrestling. Can you imagine rolling around on the floor with a muscular guy in tights! Stealing a grab or pressing my crotch against his ass. Sometimes I would prolong the match just to spend more time with an attractive guy and get a hard-on. My father loved that I loved wrestling—and so did I!

A more common response of fathers to their son's sex atypicality is to note it, to occasionally express misgivings or displeasure, but to refrain from systematically harassing him about it. By contrast to the preceding father, one youth knows that his father still loves and values him as a member of the family.

∇   He certainly noticed that I was more feminine than most boys. Not directly, of course, because that's not him, but way back when I was 5 years old he caught me playing with a lipstick case. I wasn't trying to put it on or anything, but he seemed very concerned that I might be. And when I look back actually at family pictures I can always tell that I am really flaming. My hips are out, my hands are out—this was true even at age 5! I just thought it was because I was a big ham.
     At age 7 he said to me sort of randomly that all males have problems changing clothes in locker rooms and that I should not be ashamed to change my clothes. When I put chalk on my fingernails, Dad sort of had a hissy fit about it. He didn't like my knitting, and he failed to understand the injustice he was causing me. But he wouldn't talk about it, just say that I was overdoing it, trying to look good. He also said that I looked very limp-wristed, so eventually I did do tennis, swimming, golf, and run some.

Distant Relationships

Not all sexual-minority sons are sex atypical in their activities or interests. At least an equal number are not particularly feminine, but neither are they masculine—youths I label "unmasculine."[2] In families with such sons, a father is not so much impressed by his son's feminine behavior as he is disappointed with his son's failure to engage in classic masculine behavior and to become involved with male peers, especially in athletic activities. Fathers want their son to participate in competitive team sports, and when he does not, they are disappointed. William was badgered by his father, not because of his femininity but because he was not sufficiently masculine, not suitably absorbed by sports. The effect on the father–son relationship is to negate it; they have so little in common that they disengage from each other.

In the following dyad, although the father appreciates his son's accomplishments, he clearly would have been happier with a success or two in masculine pursuits. The net effect is that a potentially positive relationship did not develop.

▽ As a kid I was really very much a loner, and I would do sort of unboyish things like read rather than doing sports. I was a very good student, and I loved playing the violin and reading. I received a lot of praise from my father about these things.

  Eventually he sort of had problems with me being a loner, and he persuaded me not to read as much. He never pressured me not to read, but he was concerned I wasn't involved enough in athletics. He kept emphasizing it was the healthy thing, that I needed to run more, exercise. He pressured me because he wanted me to be strong and "be like a man." He kept pushing me into sports, but I was always sort of the last chosen for about every sport there is on this planet. I knew I was clumsy, and he knew this. Though he didn't ridicule me for it, he made disparaging remarks about it.

Fathers across all social classes and ethnic groups can withdraw from their son's life because he does not live up to masculine standards of behavior. One Hispanic youth remembers that from an early age he frequently disappointed his father; now they seldom interact.

▽ When I was 8 years old I was really not very masculine by Mexican standards. I've memories of my father saying during arguments in Spanish, this word for *faggot*, and he basically said to quit acting like one. He didn't say I was one—just said quit acting like one. I hated PE classes. It was the bane of my existence! I hated football, hated hockey, hated basketball.

A self-described "working-class poor" youth recalled that he and his father did not have a particularly close relationship. Despite the father's general lack of connection to his child, he frequently disparaged his son for not being sufficiently masculine, beginning when the son was 5 years old.

▽ I was playing with the neighborhood kids in the trailer park, sort of just the normal sex play—and there was lots of it. I remember Dad was making sort of a big deal because he caught us boys doing it. But actually, at the time I did it with both sexes, but he taught me that it was more naughty to do it with boys than with girls.

He's always considered me a "weirdo" anyway because I didn't do all the male-type crap, like guns and sports. I read and went to concerts with my grandma. I used to make beads and jewelry, and Dad always commented about it because he didn't like it. I stayed indoors too much, like that means something about my sexuality! He called me a "faggot," but then Dad calls all his friends faggots, like he calls people "niggers." It's just sort of shop-talk to him, part of having a blue collar.

So, in one last desperate attempt to make me heterosexual Dad subscribed to the Playboy channel. Well it just so happened that the first time I watched it was a male strip show, which I liked a lot. But the second time I watched it was sort of soft heterosexual porn, and I told him it was naughty.

Supportive Relationships

Occasionally fathers and their sons have an excellent relationship that is manifest in mutual respect and support. Harassment in these dyads is rare, and the father accepts his son as is. About 10% of the father–son relationships are of this nature. For example, after school one day a fifth grader approached his father for support because classmates were calling him "fag" and "gay-boy." "So in tears I went to my father, who had always told me to defend myself. I wanted to know what it meant, and he sort of nervously said it meant nothing important." A year later this same father learned that his other son was gay and his daughter was lesbian. "So gay and lesbian issues were very much within my family, but he still seemed to love us just as much." In junior high school, the younger son overheard his father telling his mother that he wondered if the family was "three for three."

∇   I didn't seem to have any girlfriends or posters of girls up in my room. I drank bottled water, and my male friends who came over insisted on doing the dishes. He questioned if my friend was just a friend or a boyfriend. He was always very curious about my very close relationship with my friend, like one time he was walking past my room and looking in when he was over.

He encourages me to meet more "people," which I assume he means girls. However, he did say "people." I should be picking up girls right now, but I never have, and he's not saying anything. I guess his deepest concern is that I do well in school, and so he never pressures me to date. He only worries that I spend so much time alone. He wants me to get out more with friends. I am sort of the best little boy in the world.

This range in the ways "pregay" sons and fathers relate, from physical and emotional harassment, to disregard and discount, and to understanding and support, is seldom recognized or acknowledged. The horror stories are plentiful, leading some to wonder why any son would risk disclosing to his father. Yet, many do and do so during their adolescent and young adult years.

WHETHER FATHERS ARE TOLD

A survey of 2,500 readers of the gay and lesbian news magazine *The Advocate* found that just under one half of gay and bisexual men had explicitly disclosed to their father, most typically between the ages of 18 and 22 years.[3] Many who had not come out believed their father had "figured it out" in the absence of a direct disclosure. In research published since the late 1980s, from 25% to nearly 60% of gay and bisexual youths had disclosed to their father.[4] This percentage is largest in data collected within the last 3 years, reflecting a growing tendency for sons to disclose to their father during their adolescent or young adult years, often while living at home.

The present study conforms to this pattern; 48% disclosed to their father prior to being interviewed. In large part, this low percentage reflects the nature of the relationship that young men have with their fathers prior to coming out to them. One student leader who has been out for years, has appeared in television documentaries, and was interviewed by the national press finally came out to his divorced father, whom he rarely sees, because, "I was so politically involved, I felt like a hypocrite if he didn't know. I felt like he should know from me."

REASONS NOT TO TELL

Previous empirical research offers little to help us understand why youths do or do not come out to their father. Popular literature suggests that youths do not tell their father because they fear his negative reactions. So, too, Nolan feared his father's reactions—a man from the "old school" in terms of cultural definitions of masculinity and family obligations—and would not have disclosed had his mother not issued an ultimatum.

Although fear is a major reason for not disclosing in the present study, endorsed by 1 in 4 youths, it is only one of the three primary reasons. In addition, youths do not come out to their father simply because they do not feel close to him. William has not disclosed to his father because they share little in common; he is not an important person in William's life. A third major reason for withholding information is the feeling that the present time is not the right developmental time in their relationship for him to come out. Together, these three reasons account for 80% of all motives youths give for not coming out.

Not Close

Nearly 3 in 10 youths delay coming out to their father because, similar to William, they simply do not feel particularly close to him and thus have little motivation to divulge this personal aspect of themselves. One youth believes he might do so in the future, even though his father's coldness does not inspire him to share his life with him.

▽ He's made his homophobic views clear. He's not in my life. No way. Never has been. You know, he's the classic business-oriented, wealthy dad. I don't care if he knows. Not worth the effort. I was a nerd, a geek, not athletic. We had nothing in common, ever. No sex talk, no sports games. Nothing. He would make very rude comments to me or say, "I don't want to know." He really wasn't much involved in my life. His approval just wouldn't be there. He's the only one who doesn't know.

Not uncommonly, the father's status as removed from the daily activities of the family is also perceived by other family members. One mother attempted to convince her son to share with his father this critical aspect about himself but the son refused, much to his mother's dismay.

▽ I'm not really close to my dad, and I just don't tell him personal things in general. Actually, all of us kids felt distant from him, and this was hard on Mom, so she kept her promise not to tell. I just never really discuss sex with him at all. I never really want to have that kind of a discussion with him.

Mom assured me they would pay for college and that she would see to it that I was not kicked out of the house. I saw a counselor with her my senior year in high school. I can remember my brother asking my parents what was wrong with me. My dad is a very important person in the community, and he never has time for my problems.

He never suspected, even after I broke up with my girlfriend. He decided I wasn't one [gay] because I had been with her for so long. He never really caught on to Tom or that I lived with lesbians my sophomore year.

Sexual-minority sons often feel that they have been deprived of a loving, supportive father. They desire intimacy and are saddened that they do not have it. Perhaps fathers do not know about the longings of their sons or perhaps they are simply unable or unwilling to provide intimacy. Conversations with fathers would clarify their motivations and behaviors. The following youth became teary-eyed when he spoke about his anger toward his father; he also blames his father for making him gay.

▽ If he doesn't know, then he's just stupid. He's just very blue collar. My dad has always been very macho. He struts, he yells, he belches, he farts. He keeps asking me all the time if I'm dating or if I've been to a whore. When he demanded that I date more, I ignored him; when he told me to play more sports, I ignored him. I just felt like I was letting him down, always. There's no avenue for dialogue.

I've thought maybe I'm gay because I was never given a positive male role model. My dad wasn't around physically, emotionally, and I never admired him as a decent human person. Maybe there's some genetic predisposition and circumstances that could do it to you early, like having a nothing for a dad.

Despite this son's animosity toward his father, it is also clear that he wants more than he is receiving—greater acceptance, more support, and less abuse. These desires reflect the feelings of many other sexual-minority youths who fear the outcome of telling their father about their sexuality. In particular, youths worry that by telling him they are gay, they will once again be letting him down, thereby destroying any chance of establishing a future relationship with him.

Not the Right Developmental Time

Belief that the present is not the most opportune time to disclose was articulated by 1 in 4 youths. Often this is rooted in the trepidation that the development of the father–son relationship would be irrevocably impaired with a disclosure. Not uncommonly such youths have grown up in very religious homes. Issues of moral condemnation and eternal damnation are linked with homosexuality. One youth remembers an incident a decade earlier that continues to haunt him, serving as a reminder of why he cannot tell his dad about his same-sex attractions.

∇   When I was 9, the family was watching a TV movie with two guys and a homosexual scene, and Dad ordered me to leave the room. I wanted to stay, begged to stay and watch. I was more than curious. He called me into his room later that night and asked me if I knew why it was wrong to be homosexual. He emphasized that he was not suggesting that I was. He sat me down and asked me this question. I quoted the Bible and said, "Because the anus was made for exit and not for entrance," sort of as a joke, but he didn't laugh. He found this acceptable, and that was that.

How could he not know! I just can't tell him. He's Catholic, and my family just never talked about sex. I know how he'd react: "It's abnormal." It's a very controlling family. He wouldn't understand. I'd want to make sure he'd accept me before I tell him.

Ethnic-minority youths often cite "not the right developmental time" as a primary reason for failing to come out to their father. They want to share this aspect of their life, but it would be difficult because their father's generation is deeply rooted in a native, traditional culture in which homosexuality and same-sex attractions are viewed as Western or White "degeneracy." They believe time will soften this view; youths also believe that once they are financially independent of the family they will have more leeway to conduct their own lifestyle. When a Chinese American youth was asked if he had disclosed to his father, he practically shouted his answer.

∇ Hell, no! I'll never tell him unless he asks. But I won't lie to him— but he has to ask. My dad is a very traditional, conservative Chinese man. He doesn't like my long hair, my earrings, or my pierced eyebrow. He doesn't understand being gay except that it's American and would disgrace the family.

Although ethnic-minority sons often experience intense anxiety when they disappoint their father, many believe that they will not be ousted from the family. The family is of such paramount importance in many minority homes that parents will do nearly anything to maintain its integrity. Indeed, research indicates that although an ethnic-minority youth is less likely to come out to his father than is a White youth, very few fear that once they come out they will be rejected.[5] Fathers might be disappointed and chastise their son, but they will not throw him out of the home.

∇ He's Spanish, and his family is very important to him, so I know he wouldn't reject me. He's very career and money oriented, and I think he would feel like this was a detriment to getting ahead. My need for approval from my father, it's a very strong need right now. I would like to free myself by saying to him, "I'm gay." But another part of me doesn't want to sort of push the issue right now. I think I might like to tell him over the phone, probably at the same time as Mom, though I think I have slight preference to tell him first, but definitely tell them both on the same day.

Fear of Negative Repercussions

Embedded in many of the narratives is a youth's uncertainty of how his father will react to his disclosure. Many do not feel that they know him sufficiently to risk coming out, but their primary fear is that his reaction will be, however mildly, negative. One convincing reason not to come out is the anticipation, articulated by 25% of the youths, that they would face negative repercussions. One critical concern is financial stability, especially important for those dependent on family money for their college education. Because college education is a luxury that parents are not obligated to fund, some youths fear monetary support can be too easily revoked.

∇ Once I got in college there was a fear that he would financially cut me off, and I couldn't pay for college. I don't want to take them for a ride, but I need their support, so I don't tell him. My father is not open to sexuality. It's a real hard dilemma for me. He asks me about women, and I tell him that school and a career are priorities. I use that as an excuse for why I'm not seeing girls. I've been the model son, so he's not suspected. I'd like first to graduate and then be independent before I tell.

Three youths express a realistic fear that if they were to disclose to their father they would face extreme conflict, verbal abuse, and perhaps physical violence or rejection. These infrequent reactions receive the most media and research attention and thus are often erroneously assumed to characterize the relations most gay sons have with their father.

▽   I almost told him once, but he's very homophobic, and he actually believes gays are members of a secret society that recruits people. I'd always sort of challenge him when he'd say those idiotic things, and at one point I asked him how he would feel if I told him I was gay. He raised his fists, got red in the face, and sputtered some nonsense.
       After that Mom forbade me to tell him. Once he said in a joke that if he ever found out I was gay he would shoot me. He's a firm believer in hell and eternal damnation. I actually agreed in not telling him. It's very difficult to argue with my father because he can get so unpredictable. He uses "faggot" in every other sentence. He uses it especially to mean anything that is slightly effeminate. I remember once he was enraged, violently angry when he caught me doing sexual things with a boy. He's very concerned with "inappropriate" behavior.

Although one youth knows his father will not hit him, he does not want to create the scene that will likely follow a disclosure.

▽   He would throw a fit. He would break chairs and everything. He's in very big denial. This is a very big Korean thing to do if you are a man. There's very little communication between us. We don't talk about personal issues, only financial ones.

A youth might desire not to hurt or disappoint his father or believe that their relationship cannot tolerate the information. These could be connected with a fear of his reactions or a conviction that now is not the most appropriate time to come out. Many narratives are complex, offering numerous reasons why a youth has not yet disclosed.

▽   I know that if I told him it would break his heart. Telling him would destroy our relationship, or he would look at me differently, more from a distance—he would distance himself from me. I would have the worst feeling in my stomach, that I had let him down.

An equal number of gay and bisexual sons have come out to their father. The following section focuses on what motivates youths to share their sexual identity with their father.

REASONS TO TELL

Interviewed youths seldom provide elaborate explanations for revealing their sexuality to their father. In many circumstances the disclosure appears to be poorly planned or occurs "by accident." Two reasons for coming out are commonly given, constituting nearly 60% of the total:

- To garner support or to establish a more intimate relationship: "I was having a rough time in school, and I wanted the kind of close relationship I've always dreamed of having with him."
- In response to being forced into disclosure by someone else or circumstances: "Mom said she'd tell him if I didn't." "He found my porn, and so I had to tell him the truth."

Perhaps equally noteworthy is the absence from this list of the major reason youths give for disclosing to their mother: She asks because she suspects from their sex-atypical mannerisms and interests. Although a father may notice the same behaviors, either he seldom draws the link between them and his son's same-sex identity or he does but chooses not to confront his son with their meaning. In either case, this omitted confrontation likely reflects the poor prior relationship the two shared during the son's childhood and adolescence.

To Elicit Support

Consistent with the most popular reason for disclosing to a father, Pete wants a confidante, someone with whom he can share his distress and concerns and receive the understanding and support he needs. Thus, once he had conclusively decided that he was gay, he shared it with his father, with assistance from two friends. Another youth sought relief from depression by disclosing to his father. He recalls a time when they were closer and hopes that renewed intimacy will buoy him.

∇   I wanted his support and to tell him what was going on, especially after my boyfriend and me broke up. He kept badgering me about what was wrong, what was the problem. So I decided to tell him to build up our relationship again. I hate keeping secrets from him, and I wanted to feel close to him. I felt we were drifting apart since I had gone away to college.

Some sons believe that their father already knows but, as distinct from their mother who is likely to ask "the question," the father has not yet broached the subject. He might be embarrassed, not know how to talk about it, or believe it is none of his business. Or, the unstated but speculated "issue" might need the right impetus to push it into explicitness. Often it is the son's personal development, including his need for advice about a budding same-sex romantic relationship, that is the catalyst for disclosure.

∇   My father had actually been waiting for me to tell for quite awhile. He was clinging to every aspect of women I might bring up. He hung on every word, and when I talked about a girl he would ask if she was "special" to me. I played along, talking with him about women. He also went out with women and talked about it incessantly to me. It was like a male bonding thing, I guess, some heterosexual thing. Then it came to a point in my relationship with my boyfriend that I needed some help, and I felt terrible about lying. So I just told him.

Outed by Another

By contrast, Nolan represents the second most common reason. He had no desire to disclose to his father but was forced by circumstances to reveal the nature of his sexual desires. So, too, if William's father is ever told it will be by accident or because William no longer cares what his father thinks or how he will react. Frequently, it is the boy's mother who "forces" the issue.

∇   If it had been my choice, I wouldn't never have told him. But Mom, she wasn't happy having me keep this secret from him. She said it placed her in a half-ass backward position and that I'd have to or she would. That would have been okay with me, but she said I had to do it. So I did. And that was that, and it kept peace in the family.

In contrast to the primary reasons young men come out to their mother—because they seek authenticity within themselves and in the relationship they share with her and because she beats them to the point, asking about their sexuality before they offer the information—few youths note either of these dynamics as motivation for disclosing to their father. It is as if a son has given up hope of ever establishing an honest relationship with his father. It would be a worthy goal, but in the meantime he pursues a more limited and practical objective—to garner a modicum of support—or he has no choice because his mother has already told his father.

WHEN AND HOW FATHERS ARE TOLD

Investigations of sexual-minority male youths have generally found that most disclose to their father after their mother. This may be minutes or years later. In one study of support group adolescents, over 60% first told their mother; another 25% told their parents together, leaving about 10% who told their father before their mother.[6] Percentages in the present study are remarkably similar: 62% of male youths first disclose to their mother, 26% tell their parents together, and 12% come out to their father before their mother.

The most frequently articulated reason for this maternal preference is the closer relationship sons have with their mother. They thus believe that her reactions will be more moderate than their father's response and that he will be less likely to understand their life circumstances. Additionally, it should not be surprising that in relatively few cases is a father the first person to whom a youth discloses his sexual orientation. In the present investigation, no youth disclosed to his father before friends.

A question not always posed in empirical investigations is the age at which a youth comes out to his father. Several recent studies report that the age averages between 17 and 20 years, considerably younger than previous cohorts of youths but months to years after a young man discloses to his first person, usually a best friend. This may be because sexual-minority youths expect their friends to be more supportive than their father.[7]

The young men I interviewed disclosed, on average, just after their 19th birthday. More meaningful than this group average is the wide range of ages at which disclosure occurs, illustrating one diversity aspect of the coming-out process. For example, Pete was 17 and Nolan was 20, but William, age 22, had not yet disclosed. One youth told his father at the beginning of junior high school; another youth, age 25, had not disclosed at the time of the interview—and had no plans to do so any time soon. "I'm not so sure I'll ever tell him. He's very old, and he's gotten very morbid about his upcoming death, so why make it worse!" Some of the youths I interviewed may never come out to their father.

Direct Disclosure

Disclosure can occur through a direct statement initiated by a son or a confirmation of a question posed by a father or by numerous indirect means. Many fathers in one study learned about their son's sexuality only after their wife informed them.[8] In general, fathers are more frequently indirectly than directly informed, perhaps because many fathers and sons rarely discuss personal issues of any nature. For example, youths attending an urban support group were less likely to openly discuss their sexual orientation with their father (44%) than with their mother (68%), a finding consistent with earlier studies.[9]

Of interviewed youths out to their father, the majority disclose directly, either at their initiative or in response to a direct question from him. In many face-to-face disclosures, the son is fairly confident in advance that his father will be supportive—perhaps even fairly certain that his father already knows. Otherwise, he would have taken a different tactic.

∇   My father's brother was gay and died of AIDS 3 years ago. My father
    was always accepting of him and never rejecting. He was an artist and
    lived in Florida. He stayed with us for awhile while he was sick.

        So it was inevitable that I was going to tell him after this. During
    the month after he died I wrote the secret letter to my brother telling
    him why I was so depressed. My father kept asking me what was wrong,
    what was in the letter, and didn't I have something to tell him. So I
    told him during supper that I'm bisexual. He was not surprised, but I
    broke down in tears, like I was confessing. I wish I had been stronger.

Although rare, several fathers, similar to their wives, became aware
of their son's sexuality during his adolescent years and asked him "the
question." One high school student directly replied affirmatively to his
father, who seemed surprised by his own question.

∇   In terms of my stepfather, it got to the point when I stayed with them
    on college breaks that I would go into town and not go back to the
    house on the weekend. He began to wonder what I was doing, so I told
    him that I was at a bar, which was not a lie, and he asked me, "So
    does that mean you're gay?" I said I had tried both ways, but think I'm
    gay. So when he brought up homosexuality and I confirmed it, well he
    wasn't really prepared and became flustered. I had no real intent on
    talking about it, but he brought it up.

Indirect Disclosure

Nearly all indirect disclosures are instances in which someone else
told the youth's father. Usually this is the youth's mother, often without
the youth's consent or knowledge. Nolan told his mother, who then, against
his will, shared this information with his father. Others, such as Pete, who
had the "assistance" of friends, are outed by friends, siblings, or ex-boyfriends.
Although Pete's friends had his best interests in mind when they approached
his parents to express their apprehensions about his mental health, indirect
methods often have potential negative repercussions.

For example, when a son discovers, as some inevitably do, that his
father has known for years but has never broached the issue with him, the
relief he feels of not having to say the words directly to his father can be
overridden by feelings of frustration and anger. The following adolescent
was angry at his father for not telling him that he already knew about the
son's same-sex attractions.

∇   I had always wondered if he knew or suspected. Like one time when I
    was 8 or 9 I overheard him saying to his father, my grandfather, that
    he thought I might grow up to be gay. So he really already knew,
    because Mom told him; he just chose to pretend not to know. It makes

me angry because then I would not have agonized so terribly long about the decision of whether to tell him.

Finally, a son might be uncertain whether he ever *really* disclosed to his father. He speaks about other issues that lead to an inference about his sexual orientation, or he speciously assumes that the words have been spoken or implied and that his father knows, whereas in fact the youth is simply speaking or acting in ways that do everything but say the words, "Hey Dad, I'm gay!"

∇   I was feeling really anxious about getting AIDS because I had let this guy penetrate me without a condom, and I was feeling really scared and guilty because I knew better than to be sexually active. I tested negative, and I was so relieved that I had to tell somebody, and so I told Father I was HIV negative. He then concluded, later I found out, that I was gay, though he actually never directly asked about it, and I never really told him. But after that point everyone just assumed he knew, including me.

∇   He has to know! My gay friends were over at Thanksgiving when we had partied, and he must have suspected it because several were really camping it up. I collect gay porn, and my father saw it at one point when I was 16.

    I've never really talked with him about sex, but over Spring Break last year we did, and he asked me about my friends last Thanksgiving. I said that about 90% of them are into gay sex, so I guess he got the hint! We never spoke about it other than that, but he told me not to tell my mother "anything" about myself until after my brother's wedding.

Youths who have not disclosed often develop contingency plans for outing themselves or with coping with their father's reactions if the topic ever comes up. If William decides to come out to his father, then his strategy is to simply allow him to figure it out from the evidence in his "gay-friendly" apartment, with gay-oriented posters, magazines, and pins. Not uncommonly, if their father asks, they will tell him directly, as do most gay and bisexual youths.

∇   My father lives in Brazil and never married my mother. His sisters know because I told them. So, I assume in some ways that he knows. We talk every 2 weeks on the phone about business. If he asks me, then I'll tell him, but he never brings up the topic of my girlfriends or even his girlfriends.

Accidental Means

Another means of disclosure are "accidental" events in which a youth does not intend to disclose, but does. One youth was sharing his story with his mother, with the intent of telling his father at a later point, when his father unexpectedly walked into the kitchen and overheard the conversation. Another youth was planning with a lesbian friend over the telephone that they would take each other "to do this prom thing," and then split afterward to be with their same-sex dates. His father picked up the extension and understood the implications of their plan. "He told me at that point to hang up because he didn't want to hear this. I almost ran away from home while walking the dog that night while he was asleep."

Although it is conceivable that fathers "know" by intuition their son's homoeroticism but never speak directly to him about it, this number is likely to be small because so few fathers have such intimate knowledge of their son. Facts about their son likely originate from their wife or the association they make with the son's femininity or lack of standard masculine behaviors.

When and how gay and bisexual sons disclose depends to a large degree on the reaction they expect from their father. Sons hold stereotypes about what will befall them if they were to disclose to the "master of the house," as one youth phrased it.

FATHERS' INITIAL REACTIONS

Several research studies suggest sons believe that their father will be less supportive of their homosexuality than will be their friends, siblings, or mother.[10] However, it is not clear whether fathers necessarily respond with more negative fervor and abuse than do mothers. Indeed, sons' fears about coming out may be overgeneralized from stereotypes they hold, although relatively little is known because few research studies explicitly assess initial reactions to disclosure. One small sample of young adults and parents (not of the young adults) reported mixed findings regarding which parent reacted the worst. Fathers were more likely than mothers to initially deny their child's same-sex attractions and to reject their child as a result; however, they were less likely to respond with anger and guilt and were equally likely as mothers to report feeling shame and to eventually acknowledge the child's sexual status.[11]

Of 105 fathers who belonged to a P-FLAG group, the most common initial reaction to their child (sex of child unspecified), endorsed by two thirds of the fathers, was "afraid for child," followed by "sorry" and "sad." Relatively rare feelings were "glad," "sick about it," "angry to be told," and "did not matter."[12] Several research studies have shown that youths who have not disclosed their sexual identity to their father expect a more negative reaction than that received by those who have disclosed. In one, nearly two thirds of nondisclosers expected their father to be intolerant or rejecting, which is considerably higher than the generally neutral reactions of fathers who were told. Relatively few youths, around 5%, expressed fear that they would suffer physical harm from their father or would be thrown out of the home if they were to be more open about their sexuality.[13]

Expected and Actual Reactions

Youths in the present sample expected a more negative reaction if they were to disclose to their father than that received by those who had come out. Though this may reflect fears of those who have yet to disclose their scariest secret, it might also characterize a nonrepresentative subset of youths coping with an unfortunate reality—an uncompromising father who will not respond well to the disclosure. The mean expectation is between "he could deal with it" and "he would make negative comments, saying it was just a phase." The range is wide, from a projected full support to one youth who cannot imagine disclosing to his fundamentalist father, "He can't even say the word!" The son dreads a tumultuous reaction, "He'd blame himself, and then I'd feel guilty."

William believes his father would simply ignore the issue or react calmly to the revelation. Similarly, other youths anticipate a mild reaction. One youth plans to tell his open-minded father within the next couple of years.

∇ I'm not sure what he knows about gay people, though. I don't expect him to give me much support, nor do I think he will overreact because he knows me well enough to know that I would not do anything corrupt or horrible. He'd just be silent and then we'd never talk about it again— which is fine with me.

Of course sons can also incorrectly predict how their father will react. This misattribution can be in either direction—anticipating a father to react better or worse than he really would. My sense is that this is far more common in the relations sons have with their fathers than with their mothers, largely because youths have relatively little knowledge about what their father knows or feels about homosexuality. He is a mystery to them, and quite often they project their own internalized homophobia onto their father—or they are familiar with the dreadful stories recounted in the popular coming-out literature and assume they will be one of the "statistics."

Alternatively, youths might feel so positively about their total coming-out process, receiving support and exclamations of joy from friends (and perhaps even their mother), that they mistakenly believe their father will share in the ecstasy of their discovery. The following youth had not initially anticipated that his father would react in a negative, stereotypic manner. His father, who apparently did not have the long-standing "suspicions" that all other family members had, was shocked by the news and underwent a period of denial, believing his son was only going through a phase or was merely experimenting. The son *knew* his father would be accepting and was thus surprised when he abruptly said, "I'll put your mother on [the phone] now."

▽   I didn't really understand his punt at first, and then later he kept
    trying to talk me out of it. He felt very uncomfortable with it and felt
    uncomfortable with hugging me. He sort of tried to brush it off; dismissed
    it by simply saying I was experimenting.
        Later that night he argued that he thought I was only making a
    choice. That I was choosing this gay life, and he couldn't understand
    why I would choose a life that would be more difficult for me. I just
    kept telling him that this was not a choice. He still feels I'm straight
    and that this was just a one-time occasion.

Much to the surprise of many sexual-minority youths, fathers react in a less negative manner than do mothers. The most common reaction (40% of all fathers who know) is of support; two thirds respond in the "supportive" to "slightly negative" range. Many youths agree with a youth who stated, "Their reactions were the opposite of what I expected. My father was very good about it. He's not given me any shit over it. Mom went ballistic!" His father, trying to hold the family together, "calmed Mom down and was supportive in his own way, although to this day he has not talked about his feelings."

Positive Initial Reactions

Although most fathers prefer heterosexual sons, the vast majority appear willing to parent a gay or bisexual son. For example, prior to his son's disclosure, Pete's father long suspected he had a gay child. Once this was acknowledged by his son, he calmly accepted this fact and engaged his son in an all-night conversation. His greatest fear was that he might have been responsible for creating his son's same-sex attractions.

Indeed, what might appear to be an initially negative reaction may reflect a father's struggle to process his disappointment and lost dreams for his child. Or, he may blame himself for not being a better masculine or heterosexual role model. For these fathers, a self-centered emotional state conflicts with how they know they should behave if they truly love their son. Two weeks after telling his best friend, one youth decided it was time to come out to his father. Although this was devastating news to him, the father was committed to maintaining their good relationship.

▽   He had his face in his hands and was silent. He seems to keep a lot
    inside. He said he knew something was going on, but he didn't know

what it was. The fact of my being gay had crossed his mind, but he was hoping that was not it. He was supportive, as he always has been, even though he had all the stereotypes. He said it's okay with him, and he would support me. He swallowed hard—he knew this to be the truth.

Initially he was not willing to discuss my homosexuality, and he certainly has not been willing to inquire about anything. I bought him [the book] *Now That You Know*. Actually, he has started going to P-FLAG. He was most uncomfortable with the sexual aspect of it.

Negative Initial Reactions

These positive reactions are in marked contrast to Nolan's father's response who, in a state of extreme agitation, reacted in a reckless, violent fashion. This is the only father among the youths I interviewed who reacted with rejection or physical attack. No youth was evicted from the home, although Nolan's father physically assaulted him. Fewer than 15% of fathers responded in a manner approaching the negative, punishing behavior of Nolan's father.

Although few could rival Nolan's father in terms of emotionality, some fathers are quite shocked by the knowledge that they have a gay son. One in five asserts that his son is just playing a game and can be made straight. One son reports that he received an emotional lecture from his father regarding how "unnatural" homosexuality is to God, the family, and society.

∇ My dad's face turned white. He was shocked. His eyes were wide open, and he took a very patronizing approach. I said it is just a part of me, a long-standing aspect that I can't change. To that he said, "God created AIDS and homosexuals to prove that homosexuality was wrong" and then he gave Liberace as an example. He said it was wrong and how could I do this to him. He refused to talk to me and told me to get out of his sight. He went into a state of depression, and so did I.

He just can't cope with me not following in his footsteps. He's a medical doctor, and yet all this is very much an emotional reaction, not a professional one. A week later he tried to start another discussion, but I refused to stay around for this kind of lecture, so we haven't talked about it since.

Horror stories aside, fathers generally do not react with violence or abuse. Far more fathers than not respond positively, or at least tolerate their son's sexual status. Few want to lose their son, although many do not know what to say or how to offer support. Their stories are seldom heard or recognized in the literature.

However, many youths also express ambivalence about whether they want to talk about their sexuality and sexual identity with their father. So few have a history of intimate, sexual discussions with him that, although they prefer acknowledgment and acceptance, they do not wish to engage their father in an in-depth exploration of their sexuality. They are not quite sure that they sufficiently trust him with this most personal information.

RELATIONSHIPS AFTER DISCLOSURE

Other than the current state of the relationship and perhaps the father's initial reaction to the disclosure, empirical information about the father–sexual-minority son relationship virtually ends here. Among the interviewed youths, the relationship fathers and sons have after disclosure ranges from complete alienation and ongoing conflict to emotional and verbal support. Pete felt sustained by his father after their confrontation, and they have continued to talk about Pete's same-sex attractions, identity, experiences, and loves over the past several years. This level of interest and support is rare, but their story does confirm its occurrence. Even more exceptional are cases in which fathers engage in political activities to better the social conditions that sexual minorities encounter in Western culture. Equally singular are the reactions of Nolan's father, who essentially placed his son under house arrest and threatened him with physical harm and conversion. Their relationship has improved slightly but may never fully recover from things said during the tumultuous period following Nolan's disclosure.

The Relationship Continues

The most common consequence of coming out is simply the continuation of the relationship the father and son previously shared, essentially ignoring the "gay issue" whenever possible. Forty percent of all dyadic relationships are unchanged following the initial disclosure. One youth, who represents many others, reports that his father responded by "loving me no matter what because I was his son. But that was the last word ever spoken about it. He really just didn't want to deal with it." He was initially more optimistic because his father had responded so well, but over time he has had to face the reality of his father's seeming indifference.

▽ Now that I'm dating this one guy you'd think he'd have to face the issue a little bit more forcefully than ever before. Well, he just ignores everything and treats my boyfriend like he was a casual friend. I can't see that anything is that different from a year ago.

The Relationship Improves

Nearly as common as the "no effect" outcome is improved communication in the father–son dyad. Among these pairings, disclosure initiates increased expressions of interest and an overall deepening of the relationship. This is the state most youths hope will occur and a substantial number, nearly 4 in 10, are not disappointed. The following youth exemplifies this progression.

▽ Realistically, compared to other fathers I've heard about, it's been good. I feel like we have greater depth in our relationship. I gave him a book to read, talked about the Bible and so forth, and communicated real well. He was very rational, not at all emotional, and very scientific about it. Eventually he seemed very calm about it and then very supportive. As long as I loved God and God loved me then it was okay. We can now talk about it, and he is much more accepting these days, and I feel I have a much stronger bond with him than with my mother. He allows me to show affection to my male friends, and we can also talk about it. He's dealt with it sensibly.

Even at times when a son expects his father to explode in anger and reject him, the coming-out process can be educative and transforming of the relationship. A Puerto Rican father had stereotypic notions of "homosexuals" and had routinely labeled them as perverts. Once he discovered that his son was one of these "depraved debauchees," the outcome was quite disparate from the son's expectations.

▽ He had lots of stereotypes, like it's okay to fuck a guy but don't get fucked, and I don't get fucked! At first he thought I wanted to be like a woman, and he did not raise a son to be a daughter. He also believes that a homosexual is a female in a male's body, but actually the talk brought us closer together. He's been, however, disappointed in me because I'm not into sports, tools-and-die, and everything, but I know he loves me and he says it.

This enhancement of their relationship can result from a father's misperception about the son's future sexuality. In particular, bisexual sons frequently face a unique dilemma, especially if they express any interest in women. Their father may only initially support the relationships the son develops with women and ignore or discourage the son's homoeroticism. Believing that bisexuals can choose to be straight, he does not want to "give up" on his son or his potential to become "heterosexual-like." This heterosexist belief—that heterosexuality is better, more natural, safer, more desirable than homosexuality—permeates their interactions, often causing stress until the son unambiguously clarifies his sexuality. After disclosing his bisexuality to his father, one youth feels that his father does not really believe the extent to which he is attracted to males.

▽ In college I dated a female for two and a half years, so he now thinks I'm straight. But I wonder since he's rather a smart man. He loved Christie and was always talking about her and asking how things were going. Of course he'd back off if I challenged him on what he was doing. He'd never ask about my gay side or guys I liked. Maybe he'd acknowledge them and then not follow up.

When another bisexual youth dated a female classmate, his father concluded that his son was heterosexual again—that "it was all a big phase." He was especially jubilant when his son's new roommate was a woman. He did not know she was a lesbian. Bisexual youths may thus feel accepted by their father only if they act on the straight side of their bisexuality. As such, this "conditional" upswing in their dyadic interactions feels tentative, constricted, and false.

The Relationship Deteriorates

In relatively few circumstances does the father–son relationship become so severely impaired that it ceases to function. In these cases, relations prior to the disclosure were more than likely unhealthy. Ten percent of all youths report that the father–son relationship declines after coming out. One son struggled with his father for years over his grades, his friends, his clothes. They cohabited under conditions of a tightly monitored cease-fire by the youth's mother. The father's response to discovering his son's homosexuality was to assume he was trying to punish him—trying to even the score—and was a reflection of his son's immature rebelliousness. From the moment the son, in anger, told his father that he was "queer," they fought and yelled and then completely avoided each other.

From initial to subsequent reactions, relatively little appears to change in the majority of father–son relationships. Most of those that do undergo transition get better; only a few become worse. In anticipation of coming out to their father, sons may envision the best of all possible outcomes—that the two share a sexual identity. Then the son would be fully understood! Although such situations might afford the youth considerable support, it can also evoke a deterioration in communication and affection if the father is jealous or envious of the lifestyle his son is living. Being raised in a more repressive environment or time when his own same-sex attractions were stifled, the father may well have had to make the "supreme sacrifice"—to forgo his sexuality to live an "acceptable lifestyle." He may resent his son for being able to live a life prohibited to him.

WHEN FATHERS HAVE SAME-SEX ATTRACTIONS

Having a closeted gay father can present unique challenges. The presence of a "gay dad," a striking feature of family life for some gay sons, is seldom if ever discussed in the literature. Yet, of the nearly 100 young gay and bisexual men whom I have interviewed during the last several years, slightly over 10% know or strongly suspect that their father is gay or bisexual, has "homosexual tendencies," has engaged in sex with other men (usually in college), or is a "homosexual in denial."

Suggestions about the father's possible homoeroticism often comes, in confidence, from the boy's mother. One youth's parents never married, and since his birth his father has never had girlfriends or spoken about female friends. "He's very good-looking, and he's 42. Mom and I both think he's gay. He never dated after my mother, and he seems to really have a funny relationship with other males."

Sons also deduce their father's sexuality when numerous closely related kin are gay in the father's family. Many of these same youths note that their father has a number of characteristics they believe typify gay men and conclude that he must be the genetic bearer of their same-sex attractions.

∇   He tends to have very strong friendships with other males, and he really appreciates the beauty of the male body. His father is very effeminate and has feminine interests. He has a gay brother, and he has an uncle, or something like that, who I think is gay. His family forced him to marry, and shortly thereafter he committed suicide. And several of my cousins I've had sex with, so I suspect them as well.

This attribution of homosexuality to paternal influences occurs for both nature and nurture reasons. When asked why he thought he was gay, one youth concluded that his father was largely responsible.

∇   I wonder sometimes if he's gay, and my mother has actually told me that she suspects he might be. I do blame him. Maybe just that he wasn't a good father, and so I rejected masculinity because of the model he presented to me.
    I think it's probably both genetic and environmental. He comes from a long line of unmarried men and mysterious deaths, and he raised me as a distant father. I had a sense of my sexuality very early on, and so this makes it sort of nature. On the nurture part, it's my circumstances with my father that helped to make this natural thing develop. I had a physically absent father, sort of emotionally absent from me.

Other indicators that generate suspicions among sons are fathers who become overly upset with the son's homosexuality, have obsessions with masculinity, or are excessively focused on gay issues. One son has not disclosed to his "closeted gay dad" because of his virulent verbal attacks on gay people.

∇   I think my father must have tendencies. He's very homophobic. I don't know about his own sexual development; maybe he had some bad sexual experiences—or some good ones! Sometimes I wonder about him because he's so homophobic, macho. He always seems to assume people are gay, like me and my brother. He always seems to have gay on his mind, and he spends all his time at the health club.

Occasionally, a seemingly typical, decent father–son relationship is irrevocably breached, from the youth's perspective, because of the father's unexpectedly negative reactions to his son's same-sex attractions. One such relationship had always been rather formal, but because the father was educated at a liberal institution, the son felt that he would handle the news in an enlightened manner. The youth's only explanation for his father's subsequent emotional abandonment was the father's envy of his son's freedom to fully embrace his sexuality.

▽   I told him I was nervous telling him because I wasn't sure of his reaction. He took it very well, but then he still took it very hard. My father was very, very intellectual about it. He kept trying to say that it was a diagnosis [pathological disorder] and that I ought to reconsider it for my career's sake. Then that was it. We have not spoken since. When I come home he makes sure he's out of town or at the office.

Mom said she wondered if my father might be slightly bisexual. She thinks maybe in college he experimented around with gay sex and that he is just repressing his homosexual side. It was the '60s, and he had this friend in a commune, and they'd all sleep together in the same bed, a water bed no less. He grew very attached to this guy who was injured during the Chicago riots, or protest, or whatever it was, and then disappeared in San Francisco. I was named after him, actually.

No youth recounts a life with an openly gay or bisexual father. Many yearn for such models or circumstances but know it can occur only in their fantasies. For those with a "suspected" gay father, nothing in the narratives suggests that relations with him are better or that he is more accepting and understanding once they come out to him. Indeed, the limited evidence indicates the opposite—homoerotic-oriented fathers appear strikingly put off by their gay son. Perhaps the son's articulated homoeroticism reminds these fathers of that which they have suppressed, denied, or concealed for many years.

A FINAL WORD

Gay and bisexual youths report that their father is slightly more accepting of them after the initial disclosure than is their mother. This counterintuitive finding may well reflect a selection bias—those who are out to their father first made sure he would react well. That is, perhaps youths who have not come out have not done so because they realistically fear that their father will react in a disapproving fashion.

Many sexual-minority sons do not have as intimate or caring of a relationship with their father as they would like. In this regard they may be no different than many other youths reared in 20th-century North America. Regardless of sexual orientation, male youths often describe their father as a distant, authority figure who rarely provides emotional guidance or encouragement.[14] Indeed, the one characteristic about their father that most gay and bisexual sons want to change is this absence of physical and emotional closeness. In one empirical study, having a satisfying relationship with relatively little contact with their father predicted positive self-evaluation among gay and bisexual youths.[15]

Few youths report in their narratives a deeply felt, complex, and loving relationship with their father. By disclosing to him this most intimate, secret facet of themselves, they hope to initiate a process that will strengthen the father–son relationship. They want all previous misunderstandings and battles to become relics that pass, at worse, into subliminal awareness. They want to receive healing and empathy from this man; they believe they deserve a father in their life but are ambivalent whether they want *their* father to play this role. Others do not disclose because they fear that by coming out they will destroy any future chance of developing a positive, healthy relationship with their father.

Perhaps most surprising, fathers do not customarily react negatively to the disclosure—certainly not as horribly as imagined by many gay and bisexual youths. Not uncommonly, fathers react, to their child's horror, with indifference. For these fathers, the coming out hardly registers a blip. It is a benign event. Perhaps the father already suspects his son's sexuality to the point that he "knows," or their relationship is so impaired and of such minor connectedness that this one additional disappointment matters little. It is my impression that many gay and bisexual sons ache for a genuine relationship with a father (perhaps theirs); most have given up and have settled for what they had prior to the disclosure, whether that be nonemotional, distant, polite, guarded, or sentimental.

ENDNOTES

[1] Bell, A. P., Weinberg, M. S., & Hammersmith, S. K. (1981). *Sexual preference: Its development in men and women.* Bloomington: Indiana University Press.

[2] Chapter 2 in Savin-Williams, R. C. (1998). " . . . *and then I became gay": Young men's stories.* New York: Routledge.

[3] Lever, J. (1994, August 23). Sexual revelations. *The Advocate,* pp. 17–24.

[4] See review of this literature in Savin-Williams, R. C. (1998). The disclosure to their families of same-sex attractions by lesbian, gay, and bisexual youths. *Journal of Research on Adolescence, 8,* 49–68.

[5] This literature is reviewed in Savin-Williams, R. C. (1996). Ethnic- and sexual-minority youth. In R. C. Savin-Williams & K. M. Cohen (Eds.), *The lives*

of lesbians, gays, and bisexuals: Children to adults (pp. 152–165). Fort Worth, TX: Harcourt Brace College.

[6] D'Augelli, A. R., & Hershberger, S. L. (1993). Lesbian, gay, and bisexual youth in community settings: Personal challenges and mental health problems. *American Journal of Community Psychology, 21,* 421–448.

[7] D'Augelli, A. R., & Hershberger, S. L. (1993). Lesbian, gay, and bisexual youth in community settings: Personal challenges and mental health problems. *American Journal of Community Psychology, 21,* 421–448; D'Augelli, A. R. (1998, February). *Victimization history and mental health among lesbian, gay, and bisexual youths.* Paper presented at the Society for Research on Adolescence, San Diego, CA; Rotheram-Borus, M. J., Rosario, M., & Koopman, C. (1991). Minority youths at high risk: Gay males and runaways. In M. E. Colten & S. Gore (Eds.), *Adolescent stress: Causes and consequences* (pp. 181–200). New York: Aldine DeGruyter; Savin-Williams, R. C. (1990). *Gay and lesbian youth: Expressions of identity.* Washington, DC: Hemisphere; and Sears, J. T. (1991). *Growing up gay in the South: Race, gender, and journeys of the spirit.* Binghampton, NY: Harrington Park Press.

[8] Remafedi, G. (1987). Male homosexuality: The adolescent's perspective. *Pediatrics, 79,* 326–330.

[9] D'Augelli, A. R., & Hershberger, S. L. (1993). Lesbian, gay, and bisexual youth in community settings: Personal challenges and mental health problems. *American Journal of Community Psychology, 21,* 421–448. See also Bell, A. P., & Weinberg, M. S. (1978). *Homosexualities: A study of diversity among men and women.* New York: Simon & Schuster.

[10] See research by Cramer, D. W., & Roach, A. J. (1988). Coming out to mom and dad: A study of gay males and their relationships with their parents. *Journal of Homosexuality, 15,* 79–91; D'Augelli, A. R., & Hershberger, S. L. (1993). Lesbian, gay, and bisexual youth in community settings: Personal challenges and mental health problems. *American Journal of Community Psychology, 21,* 421–448; and Herdt, G., & Boxer, A. (1993). *Children of Horizons: How gay and lesbian teens are leading a new way out of the closet.* Boston: Beacon Press.

[11] Ben-Ari, A. (1995). The discovery that an offspring is gay: Parents', gay men's, and lesbians' perspectives. *Journal of Homosexuality, 30,* 89–112.

[12] Robinson, B. E., Walters, L. H., & Skeen, P. (1989). Response of parents to learning that their child is homosexual and concern over AIDS: A national study. *Journal of Homosexuality, 18,* 59–80.

[13] D'Augelli, A. R., & Hershberger, S. L. (1993). Lesbian, gay, and bisexual youth in community settings: Personal challenges and mental health problems. *American Journal of Community Psychology, 21,* 421–448; Herdt, G., & Boxer, A. (1993). *Children of Horizons: How gay and lesbian teens are leading a new way out of the closet.* Boston: Beacon Press; and Pilkington, N. W., & D'Augelli, A. R. (1995). Victimization of lesbian, gay, and bisexual youth in community settings. *Journal of Community Psychology, 23,* 34–56.

[14] Larson, R., & Richards, M. (1994). *Divergent realities: The emotional lives of mothers, fathers, and adolescents.* New York: Basic Books.

[15] Savin-Williams, R. C. (1990). *Gay and lesbian youth: Expressions of identity.* Washington, DC: Hemisphere.

8

NEGOTIATING HEALTHY
RELATIONSHIPS AMONG
FAMILY MEMBERS

From the perspective of a differential developmental trajectories approach discussed in chapter 2, coming out to parents occurs within the general context of adolescent development and the unique relationships that youths have with their parents. Many issues confronted by sexual-minority youths and their parents parallel ones that challenge heterosexual youths, consistent with the first tenet.

1. Sexual-minority youths are similar to all adolescents in their basic developmental processes and needs.

Regardless of sexual orientation, many adolescents struggle to renegotiate their childhood relations with parents. For some, it is a major undertaking; for others, the give-and-take is seamless and relatively uneventful. Whether the issue is when to do homework, whether to stay out with friends, or how to date, parents frequently feel compelled to offer advice or to establish what they feel is expectable and unacceptable behavior. Adolescents, however, seldom welcome such unsolicited guidance or strict regulation.

Sexual-minority youths desire and need the love of their parents. Some fear that the disclosure of same-sex attractions or identity will exacerbate tensions along preexisting fault lines. To what extent will they remain attached to parents? Must they now bargain for their assurance and support? As do all youths, sexual-minority teens seek autonomy and self-assertion, to find their personalized way in the world. Although I can think of no comparable socially stigmatized event that heterosexual youths typically undergo in their relations with parents that has such far-reaching personal consequences, if there were one I believe their parents would face it in a manner similar to the parents of sexual-minority youths.

Yet, differences exist, both between these two populations of youths and among sexual-minority youths. Whether because of their unique biological predispositions or cultural attitudes toward them, youths with same-sex attractions may act and think differently from heterosexual youths, consistent with the second tenet of a differential developmental trajectories perspective.

2. Sexual-minority youths are unique from heterosexual youths on some domains.

For example, few heterosexual youths are concerned with whether their parents will accept and support their sexual orientation. It is highly unlikely that they come out to their parents as heterosexual or even consider their orientation to be a matter worthy of discussion. It is a nonissue. Parents will not be shocked, disappointed, angry, or horrified with the heterosexual orientation of their child.

The third postulate asserts that variations occur among sexual-minority youths, both individually and as members of subgroups.

3. Sexual-minority youths vary among themselves, usually in predictable ways.

Although many potential origins for these dissimilarities were articulated by the youths during the interviews—personality characteristics, cognitive skills, social class, gender, ethnicity, and regional location—the discriminating category given priority in this study is gender. That is, it matters whether a youth is female or male and whether the youth is coming out to his or her mother or father. This has informed my interpretation of the meaning of the study's findings—both the empirical results and the youths' narratives.[1]

The individual narratives spotlight many of the essential dynamics between a particular sexual-minority youth and her or his parents and the fourth tenet.

4. Sexual-minority youths are unique individuals.

Each story is inimitable, sometimes suggesting specific strategies regarding how best to come out and ideas about how to prepare youths and parents for the postdisclosure life.

Although both child and parent characteristics should be considered when deciding how best to navigate the coming-out process, previous research has failed to demonstrate which predictors are most critical. Thus, it is often necessary to rely on empirically unverified terrain when mental health professionals make suggestions regarding how a teen should disclose and how parents should respond. Data from the current investigation, however, suggest that knowledge about these matters is greater than a mere crapshoot. The youths' responses on their questionnaires and interviews provide informed answers to these questions.

* * *

This chapter is intended to promote such understanding. Summaries of basic findings, as reported in chapters 4–7, are presented throughout the chapter in boxes. Two other types of information are presented in boxes: Suggestions for how youths and parents can best traverse the coming-out process. I offer not specific advice on how to do therapy, conduct educational programs, or write public policy with sexual-minority youths and their families; each necessitates a separate volume and a firmer and broader knowledge base than that provided in this book. My intent is to provide information to mental health professionals that will prove helpful for implementing these activities and for suggesting ways to help sexual-minority youths decide whether to come out to their parents and, if so, when and how. Recommendations are also proposed for helping parents better support themselves and their children with same-sex attractions. In the last chapter, I propose a modest agenda for researchers as they continue their quest for knowledge about sexual-minority youths and their families.

WHETHER TO COME OUT TO PARENTS

Whether a youth should come out to her or his parents and whether parents should inquire about their child's sexual orientation are not easy or simple considerations, largely because many factors, perhaps even seemingly small or insignificant ones, can have an enormous impact on the youth, the parents, and their relationship. Although the percentage of youths who disclose to parents varies from study to study, little is known about the critical factors that account for this variation—except, as might be expected, the younger the sample the smaller the proportion of youths who are out because they have had less time to disclose. When compared with previous generations of youths, the proportion who are out is clearly increasing, probably because of the staggering visibility that has been given to individuals with same-sex attractions. It is nearly impossible to open a newspaper or turn on the television without being exposed to the casualness and acceptability with which alternatives to heterosexuality are presented. Popular movies, television shows, recording artists, books, and the Internet have taken the shock out of same-sex attractions.

This is a remarkably different worldview for today's youths, an observable cohort effect. On some college campuses, primarily on the East and West Coasts or in very liberal college towns, coming out has become a nonevent, a "big yawn"—everybody is doing it! According to recent national polls, college students are more likely than other age groups to accept alternative lifestyles, to believe homosexuality is not morally wrong, to know someone who is gay, and to support same-sex marriage.[2] One hundred percent of college students I teach know someone who is not heterosexual; a somewhat smaller but still significant number has a friend or family member who is lesbian, bisexual, or gay. Half attended a high school that had a gay-oriented student group.

These developments have contributed to a climate in which coming out to parents feels manageable for many contemporary youths. For example, Caroline Hostetler, a self-confident 16-year-old bisexual teenager at Las Lomas High School in Walnut Creek, California, has not experienced the problems of earlier cohorts of young women because, "No one had ever told me that it [same-sex attraction] was wrong. I have a gay uncle, and we grew up calling his boyfriend Uncle Steve. It was never an issue."[3] Caroline attends the same high school as did Bobby Griffith (see chapter 3), who graduated in 1981, 2 years before jumping off an overpass to his death because he could not garner the support of his family. Caroline has the full, unconditional support of her family, which contributed to her decision to disclose to them.

Study Findings: Whether Youths Come Out

- Two of every 3 youths are out to their mother.
- Almost 1 of 2 youths is out to their father.
- Age of coming out to one parent predicts coming out to the other parent.
- Forty-two percent of youths are out to both parents, 20% to mother only, 2% to father only, and 35% to neither parent.
- Over 2 of 3 youths first told their mother; 1 of 10 first told their father; and 1 of 5 told both parents simultaneously.

One consistent finding across all studies, regardless of where or when samples are recruited, is that mothers are told earlier than fathers and, if only one parent knows, then it is usually the mother.[4] This is the result of the more intimate, caring relationship youths generally have with mother. This suggests the first rule of disclosure:

> 1. Sexual-minority youths are most likely to disclose to individuals they anticipate will be receptive and supportive.

Further evidence for this imperative is that best friends are told before casual friends, sisters (especially younger sisters) before brothers, and immediate family before extended family members.

This rule is not negated but confirmed by circumstances in which youths first disclose to their father or to both parents at the same time. Although unusual, the narratives clearly indicate that some youths have a better relationship with their father than with their mother, and thus come out to him first, and that some youths have a near-equal relationship with their parents. In the latter situation, both parents are told simultaneously or within a relatively brief period of time.

Regardless of which parent is told first, nearly all youths must ascertain whether they should come out to *any* parent. In part, this decision rests on their ability to predict how parents will react. The best advice from the youths' narratives in this book constitutes the second rule of coming out:

2. *Parents react in character.*

Parents who are generally understanding, respectful, and supportive when the youth is a child will likely respond well to the news when the youth discloses as a teenager. If parents love their child conditionally, then they might well reject the youth if she or he fails to conform to traditional notions of sexuality.

Advice to Youths: Whether to Come Out

One basic principle that should guide the decision of whether a youth should come out is to realistically assess if parents will be supportive. However, some parents will, without the youth's consent, tell their spouse. A youth should be prepared for this, especially if the other parent is likely to react poorly.

On the basis of the narratives in this book and the speculations of others,[5] the outcome of disclosure is likely to be particularly negative if parents

- Are intolerant of differences, whether in matters of status (e.g., gender, race, ethnicity, and social class) or conduct (e.g., non-traditional beliefs and attitudes).
- Display negative attitudes about homosexuality, make gay jokes, and have no gay friends.
- Are authoritarian and have few skills to cope with deviations from normal routines or beliefs.
- Work through difficulties by adult-centered displays of power and rigidity.
- Use drugs or alcohol and have a history of mental illness.
- Have a history of neglecting or abusing family members.
- Are struggling to hold together their marriage.

Consequences of coming out should be realistically assessed. Is a youth in jeopardy or at risk of being

- Kicked out of the house or physically harmed?
- Forced to support himself or herself financially?

(continues)

(*continued*)
  - Isolated from other sources of social and emotional support?
  - Placed in a psychiatric institution?

A second basic principle is to delay coming out if a youth's sense of self-worth rests on parental acceptance—a youth should accept himself or herself before and regardless of how parents react. Authors Bass and Kaufman noted, "We all want our parents' approval and support. But whether that is offered to you or not, you have the power to create a life rich with inner satisfaction, accomplishments, and respectful, loving relationships."[6]

If a youth truly has parents who are understanding and welcoming of diversity and who give unconditional love, and if a youth has the kind of relationship with them in which it feels safe to disclose, then coming out might lead to a greater sense of self-worth and appreciation and can help a youth work through self-acceptance issues.[7]

In the decision of whether to come out, the narratives suggest two overriding considerations:

  - This is uniquely the youth's decision. Others can be helpful and offer suggestions and support, but ultimately the youth should not be pressured to come out because no one knows his or her situation as he or she does.
  - It is not cowardly or less politically correct but wise to take good care of oneself and to be circumspect regarding whether to disclose. Unless reasonably certain of a positive reaction or a secure fallback option, a youth should delay coming out.

Several youths interviewed for this book provide graphic examples of families in which it was not safe to come out. In most circumstances, youths did not choose to disclose at a particular moment in time but were forced out by others. Other youths, because of the need to be accepted by their parents, made the unwise decision to disclose. These youths seriously risked their college education and emotional well-being. This leads to the third rule of coming out:

3. Youths should not come out if it places them in physical or emotional danger.

It is not always easy to ascertain or predict negative parental reactions; youths are occasionally truly shocked by their parent's horrified response. There are legitimate reasons why some youths should not come out to their parents.

REASONS WHY YOUTHS SHOULD OR SHOULD NOT DISCLOSE

In deciding whether they should or should not come out, youths confront a complex array of possible motives and consequences. Granted, it is not always an easy course in North American culture to be young and gay-identified. The facility with which they manage this status can, to a large degree, be dependent on how their parents cope with this sexual reality. Most youths want their parents' acceptance and yet acknowledge that they have no guarantee that they will receive it once they come out. Some know with near certainty that the response will be positive or negative, but the vast majority is in doubt about their parents' reception of the news.

Reasons to Withhold Coming Out

Good, valid reasons exist for not coming out to parents, and these must be seriously considered when youths contemplate disclosing to their parents. Disclosure can be a risky venture for those who have legitimate concerns about their physical and psychological safety if their sexual orientation were to be known. An adult who led a support group for youths wrote that an overwhelming majority who had not told their parents "feared that they would be rejected, punished, perhaps physically assaulted, or expelled from the family."[8]

Traditional coming-out narratives emphasize the fear motivation, warning about the dire concerns that should be considered by closeted youths. Will they be exploited? Criticized? Hurt? Betrayed? What will others do with this information? Will relationships be endangered? Are these changes in family dynamics reversible? Are they responsible for their parents' pain? When the possible answers to these questions are frightening and the danger of disclosing is real, not disclosing might be the best and only option. These youths strategically wait until they are less financially and emotionally dependent on their parents to fully come to terms with their sexual attractions.

However, only limited research supports the contention that the greatest deterrent to more openness between youths and their parents is the youths' fear of rejection and verbal or physical abuse. In addition, all studies reported thus far assert a greater fear of coming out to father than to mother.[9] Whether this fear is realized once they disclose has not been empirically supported; the present study suggests that it is not—the reactions of fathers were actually slightly more positive than were those of mothers (see discussion below).

What is clear from the narratives in this book is that if sexual-minority youths fear abuse, assault, and rejection once they come out, it is primarily boys—and a minority at that—and not girls who express these fears. Nevertheless, at least in one regard the stories are on the mark: Sex of parent is vital to understanding why youths choose to disclose or withhold information about their sexual attractions. Youths do not disclose to mother because they fear losing her love and support; to father, for fear of what he might physically do to them. However correct this observation, the popular narratives do not well represent the primary motivations for not coming out articulated by the interviewed youths: Only 1 in 4 young men and 1 in 10 young women noted fear of negative reactions as the primary deterrent to coming out to parents.

Study Findings: Reasons Not to Disclose

To Mother

- Nearly 1 of 2 young women and 3 of 10 young men believe it is not the right developmental time.
- One of 4 young men fears negative reactions.
- One of 5 youths has not gotten around to it.
- One of 5 young women does not want to hurt or disappoint her.

To Father

- Over 4 of 10 young women and 3 of 10 young men are not close, so disclosing does not feel important.
- One of 4 young men fears negative reactions.
- One of 4 young men believes it is not the right developmental time.
- One of 5 young women has not gotten around to it yet.

When youths do not come out to their mother, the primary reason is their sense that the present time is not the best time for the mother, the daughter or son, or their relationship. Perhaps their mother is going through a very difficult time in her marriage or career; how could they add more stress to her life? Perhaps youths still feel sufficiently insecure in their sexuality that they want to be certain it is their final answer before disclosing to her. Or, the two have recently gone through turbulent times (e.g., going away to college is hard for both), and youths are waiting until their lives and that of their mother stabilize.

Certainly some youths—more young men than women—withhold disclosing to their mother because of fear. However, the fear seldom emanates from any physical terror she might wreak in their lives, but from her emotional investment in their lives. That is, they fear that she will be so keenly hurt that she will withdraw support, will cause an emotional scene, or will make them feel guilty. Young women also do not want to disappoint their mother, but their feeling is less based on fear and more centered on sadness; the relationship with their mother has been so excellent that they will be saddened if the intensity of their emotional bond is lessened.

In her book describing the process of coming out within the context of a famous family, Chastity Bono did not disclose to her mother Cher because she did not want to disappoint her or risk destroying their relationship.

> My mom's idea of closeness was premised on the idea that we had to be similar. As we became more and more dissimilar, she found it more and more difficult to relate to me. . . . When my mother became distracted by other people or her career, I was convinced that she was withdrawing from me because I disappointed her. . . . I heard her comments or questions about how I dressed and how I acted as criticisms of my entire person. I didn't understand the distinction between my mother's love for me and her discomfort with how I was expressing myself.[10]

Motivations for not coming out to father are often quite different. Many, especially young women, do not disclose because they are not particularly close to him, now or while growing up. They thus feel no obligation to share this part of their life with him; communicating about important life events is not something they do. Most have discarded any hope that the father–child relationship would improve with disclosure. Of course, some youths report that they intend to disclose but just have not gotten around to it yet—which also reflects a lack of emotional intimacy with this parent.

Advice to Youths: Survival Tactics for Living in the Closet

Youths may need to develop defensive maneuvers that help them manage being in a family in which it is dangerous to be known as gay. The following are ones that youths in the present study sometimes used. They are not equally appropriate and depend on unique circumstances.

- Disclosing to the parent, sibling, or extended family member who is most likely to be supportive in the masquerade of heterosexuality. She or he becomes a lifeline and source of support.
- Evading indirect questions about sexuality by inquisitive parents and then gradually disclosing by eliminating various hiding maneuvers, testing the waters along the way to gauge likely reactions.

(continues)

(continued)

- Avoiding discussions of personal issues by establishing a "demilitarized zone" of off-limits topics. These boundaries are either implicitly or explicitly negotiated with parents, who often cooperate because they fear coming to know a truth they do not want to hear.
- Maintaining an emotional distance from parents, sharing little with them, protecting oneself as best as one can, and considering oneself essentially parentless. This may entail becoming independent or emancipated with little physical or verbal contact with parents.

Of course, parents may know about their child's sexual attractions without ever being explicitly told. They might become increasingly suspicious because of the child's friends, failure to engage in stereotypic gender activities, or willingness to be "different," but decide not to confront the child directly. Their understanding is that particular aspects of the child's "lifestyle" are not to be discussed. The two thus collude in a "I know you know, but we won't talk about it" stalemate. The unspoken agreement is that neither will discuss personal, sexual, or romantic involvements, becoming accomplices in a conspiracy that creates family dynamics that are dishonest and potentially explosive, but necessary to maintain civility.[11]

Assessing whether a youth's fears and anxieties about coming out are real or imagined is difficult to ascertain because no prospective study has been conducted that compares the expectations of how parents will respond before disclosure and how they actually react once told. This difference between perception and reality is an important one because, as documented among the interviewed youths, those who have not disclosed often expect a more negative reaction than that received by those who are out to their parents. This gap could be due to characteristics of the parents. For example, perhaps youths who disclose perceive that their parents will respond in an accepting manner because they are liberal, have gay friends, or are by nature tolerant of unconventionality. Nondisclosers might very well be accurate in their expectations that their parents will likely react in a harsh and abusive manner because they are socially and religiously conservative, have little contact with sexual minorities, and have high expectations that all family members will be heterosexual. These issues are not resolvable until longitudinal studies are conducted that trace the developmental history of sexual-minority youths from the onset of same-sex attractions through the disclosure process.

> **Study Findings: Expected Parental Reactions**
>
> - Youths who have not disclosed expect more negative reactions from both parents than those who have disclosed.
> - Young men expect more negative reactions from their mother and father than do young women.
> - No youth expects rejection from her or his mother; 10% expect it from her or his father.
> - No son expects his mother to react positively or neutrally.
> - Nearly 60% of daughters expect parents to respond negatively.

Although the actual reactive valence of parents is generally indistinguishable regardless of whether it is a son or a daughter who comes out to them, nondisclosing young men are far more likely than young women to expect a harsh reaction from parents. They believe that parents will be more negative toward them than disclosed youths' parents were to them. Perhaps a selection bias exists. These sons have not come out precisely because their fears of how negative their unknowing parent would react if she or he were to know are on the mark. That is, the disclosers and nondisclosers represent two very different populations among young men but not among young women. Young men might be in the closet specifically because they know they will receive a harsh reaction once out.

Why is this the case? Perhaps these youths are more gender *conforming* in their appearance and mannerisms than are out youths and thus more able to hide their same-sex attractions from parents. Being less "obviously gay," these boys recognize that their parents have had few suspicions about their sexual orientation and thus will be greatly surprised or perhaps shocked when they do find out. Not having had time to adjust to this possibility, parents might indeed react more stridently than if their child had been more "evidently gay" during their childhood. Because sex atypicality is less frequently associated with same-sex attractions among young women, parents are less likely to predict which daughter will have same-sex desires, and are thus less shocked when their "feminine" daughter declares her attractions to other women. If these speculations are accurate, it might be erroneous to assume that male youths who decide not to come out would have received the relatively mild response of those who have disclosed. We need to know far more about youths with same-sex attractions who do not "appear" to be gay.

Reflecting the relative value of masculinity and femininity in our society, another explanation for the sex difference is that a son's heterosexuality matters more to parents, on average, than does the heterosexuality of a daughter. Parents might believe that the reputation of the family and their future legacy are more tied to the lifestyle of a male than a female offspring. For some parents, a son not marrying is more difficult to explain or justify than an unwed daughter. In addition, lesbian daughters are more likely to have children than gay sons. Some young men feel this heterosexual obligation and thus become frighteningly obsessed with what their parents will do if they were to find out about their nonheterosexuality. Several of the interviewed young women noted that their parents were not *that* upset when they discovered that they have a lesbian or bisexual daughter; their parents would have been more outraged if it had been their brother who had come out.

Another facet of gender might account for a second striking sex difference in reasons not to disclose to parents. Nearly two thirds of sexual-minority young women who have not come out to their mother state that they do not want to hurt or disappoint her or to potentially harm their relationship. Considerably less than half of young men gave these same reasons for withholding the information. Most strikingly, youths of both sexes seldom refrain from coming out to their father for these altruistic motivations. Not coming out as an act of love—of desiring not to disappoint or hurt parents, of not placing parents in an awkward position with relatives and neighbors, and of wanting to avoid the long-term effects that such disclosure would have on relationships within the immediate and extended family—are serious considerations that have not been adequately discussed in the literature. We must recognize that youths decide not to disclose for both self-protective and unselfish reasons.

Regardless of motivation, lying and misrepresenting the truth as defensive avoidance is seldom a healthy alternative to open and honest communication within a family. Although youths might need to keep their true selves private and locked away if they want to avoid feeling responsible for disrupting family relationships, this very secretiveness amplifies their sense of unacceptability and further erects barriers between themselves and their family, resulting in alienation and loneliness. Perceptive parents might sense that their child, now an adolescent, has some unspecified, unshared secret but not know what it is. Why has their son or daughter become increasingly distant, irritable, and uncooperative— or, conversely, ever more good and obliging? Should they do something quickly? Their child is escaping them; a crisis is upon them and they cannot stem the tide. Consistent with everything we know about contemporary cohorts of sexual-minority youths, most who identify as lesbian, gay, or bisexual during adolescence are known to be gay by at least one parent.[12] If parents suspect homoeroticism is the core of the changes, should they ask "the question"?

Advice to Parents: Don't Ask? Don't Tell? Don't Pursue?

Should a parent who strongly suspects or even knows that a child has same-sex attractions ask about her or his sexual attractions? As a general rule, it is not wise for a parent to inquire directly unless there is good reason to ask, such as an emergency (e.g., a child who may be suicidal). In some families, a direct, open atmosphere prevails, and questions such as "Are you attracted to other girls/boys?" and "Do you think you might be lesbian/gay?" are appropriate and in keeping with the family spirit. Most effective is creating a climate of affirmation and acceptance in which members will *want* to disclose. According to Ellen Bass and Kate Kaufman,[13] P-FLAG,[14] and the interviewed youths, this can best be done by

- Apologizing for any past insensitivities, such as homophobic jokes or language.
- Ridding oneself of heterocentric assumptions regarding the youth's future.
- Speaking favorably about the contributions sexual minorities have made to our culture, especially current popular figures.
- Letting it be known that one is open to communicating about any subject.
- Initiating conversations about sexuality, including testaments about one's openness to sexual-minority individuals.
- Giving unconditional support and love to one's child.

It is never too early to begin these conversations in age-appropriate language. If any of these are problematic, a parent should seek support from other adults, not the child. A parent should respect a child's need to go through her or his own story at a comfortable pace and to emerge when ready. A parent might never fully understand where the child is in this process, and thus it is important to promote from the beginning an atmosphere of acceptance rather than rejection. Even seemingly insignificant statements or acts—for example, expressing disgust with a same-sex kiss on a television program—can have major, inhibiting effects.

One thing is clear: Not talking to the child about her or his sexuality will not change it, only how the youth feels about it or expresses it. Sexual attractions are rarely if ever under conscious control; they are present from an early age. The fact that a parent does not want these particular attractions to endure will do nothing to alter their existence.

Reasons to Come Out

According to conventional wisdom, the self-awareness associated with labeling one's same-sex attractions creates anxiety for a youth, leading to feelings of self-contempt, largely because of society's negative stereotypes of lesbians and gay men. Anxiety is supposedly at its apex just prior to the initial disclosure and increases rather dramatically when confronted with the decision of whether to disclose to parents. Will danger and uncertainty dominate my life? Can I maintain my sense of self? Will I be on my own? Given these issues, it is a wonder any youth comes out to parents.

Counter to this conventional wisdom, the youths I interviewed were seldom wracked by unbearable anxiety prior to disclosure or fearful of being rejected, disowned, or physically abused by their parents. Certainly it is seldom easy to discuss one's same-sex attractions and romantic relationships with parents and risks do exist, varying from enormous for a few, slight for the majority, and nil for a minority. So why come out? Many youths come out to share their life—at least with their mother—and to thus feel liberated and to make their life easier. Or, they come out because their mother asked, because it was about time that their father knew, or to elicit support from their father. Perhaps relations with parents have not been great, and coming out is an opportunity to connect, to make things better.

Study Findings: Reasons to Disclose

To Mother

- One of 3 youths has a mother who asked them.
- One of 3 young women and 1 of 5 young men want to share their life with her.

To Father

- Four of 10 young women and 3 of 10 young men are out to their father because someone else told him.
- Three of 10 young women report it is time to get it over with.
- Three of 10 young men want to elicit father's support.

Youths disclose to parents for reasons that vary, in part, on the sex of the youth and the parent. For both the young women and men I interviewed, coming out to mother was primarily motivated by the close relationship they share—how could they not tell the one person who knew everything about them? Had they not communicated so well in the past? Did they not have a tacit agreement that anything important was to be divulged?

The relationship was particularly intense between a daughter and her mother because of the close, share-all nature of their lives. Who has a choice? Mom is a "best friend"—a daughter cannot imagine withholding anything from her. As a result, most daughters do not expect a highly negative response. Indeed, their relationship is so intimate that one third of the time mothers ask their daughters if they are "dating a woman," "attracted to a best friend," or "not heterosexual." This knowledge is nearly equally characteristic of mothers and sons; the number one reason sons came out to their mother is that they did not—she asked! Sexual-minority youths might simply be reflecting the larger population of youths who overwhelming report having excellent or very good relations with their mother.[15]

With fathers, someone other than their child tells them much of the time. This "other" is usually their wife. Their child, especially a daughter, merely acknowledges the truthfulness of the information. If a young woman directly tells her father, then she does so because she "ought to" or "the time is right." If the father is told, then it was simply something that should be done. Sons, however, often use coming out to their father as an opportunity to garner support or to get closer to him. In many cases their relationship has been so impaired for so many years that this sharing is a last-ditch effort to connect with him, to gain an intimate father figure in their lives, and to establish some kind of a relationship with him before adulthood.

Advice to Youths: Coming Out as an Act of Self-Love

For youths who do not come out to their parents, the level of stress can become unbearable. Keeping secrets, becoming emotionally inhibited, and passing as something one is not are major stressors. Although coming out can invite reactions from parents that compromise physical safety and psychological integrity, there are many advantages to publicly proclaiming one's sexuality:

- Decreased feelings of loneliness and guilt.
- Greater comfort and wholeness with personal identity.
- Greater psychological adjustment and higher self-esteem.
- Better sense of personal freedom.
- Increased ability to merge one's sexual and romantic interests.
- Greater access to supportive communities.
- Increased feelings of authenticity—feeling loved and accepted for who one is, not living a lie, and being truthful in relationships.
- Stronger parental bonds and support.

Most parents would rather have a truthful relationship with their child than one based on deceit.

After establishing a reason to disclose, the next decisions are when and how to come out. No singular pattern emerges from the interviews, largely because sexual-minority youths are exceedingly creative in terms of the timing, manner, and even what they disclose.

WHEN AND HOW ADOLESCENTS COME OUT

When Adolescents Come Out

Coming out to parents is a late developmental milestone for most youths, occurring years after first awareness of same-sex attractions and years after the realization that the directionality of sexual libido means something. Eventually, an integrated identity and the establishment of intimate, fulfilling relationships signify self-acceptance and positive self-esteem. At some point in this process, same-sex attracted youths risk coming out to their parents.[16] Of course, considerable variability exists in the timing of this milestone, from early adolescence—in the present study these were usually teenage girls who, through the act of talking with their mother, become aware of their sexuality and its meaning—to young adulthood, including those who vow never to come out. They will wait until the grandparents are buried, the parents are in the grave, and hell freezes over before they disclose. Most youths, however, desire to first solidify their sexual identity, even to the extent of becoming involved in a same-sex romantic relationship.

Study Findings: When Youths Come Out

- Youths come out to parents, on average, between the ages of 18 and 19 years, with a wide range, from age 13 to "never."
- Age of first coming out to the first person predicts age of telling parents.
- The earlier a young woman develops a romantic relationship, the more likely she is to come out to parents.
- Age of disclosure is unrelated to internalized processes of self-disclosure.

Despite the late developmental age in a youth's life when she or he discloses to parents, youths are increasingly coming out to parents at an earlier absolute age, often while still in high school or, occasionally, while in junior high or middle school. Thus, parents have the opportunity to address disclosure while their child is dependent on the family for financing post–high school education. As such, parents have a greater chance than previous generations of parents to legislate how their child should respond to her or his same-sex attractions, including coming out to siblings, the extended family, and other communities.

Clinician Laura Brown suggests that parents are often told last because youths fear their rejection.[17] Little research supports this view, although it is likely to be true for some families and for previous cohorts of youths. The present study highlights alternative temporal cases in which parents are not the last to know. Occasionally, a parent is one of the first to know because youths are fairly certain that she or he will be supportive.

This diversity in timing of disclosure alludes to a long-standing debate: Should youths come out while living at home, under the rule of their parents, or should they wait until they are in a safe place, such as at college or among supportive friends? Although convincing arguments can be made for either side, the "correct" answer is appropriately, "It depends." Family context matters in these deliberations. Some clinicians might suggest delaying coming out until independence is achieved; however, it is not difficult to imagine a situation in which disclosure should occur during early adolescence, when a youth, struggling against heavy peer forces, needs family support to maintain her or his integrity.

Advice to Youths: When to Come Out to Parents

Some suggest that youths should not come out until they feel good about themselves and when self-worth does not depend on parental acceptance. Youths should take the time they need, come from a position of strength, and be realistic in considering whether their family system can cope with the information. No absolute rules exist about when is the best time. One should trust her or his own intuition.

The youths' narratives in this book suggest that one might want to consider the following:

- Determine what are the motives for coming out, and evaluate whether these are good reasons by assessing the pros and cons of disclosure. Good reasons include sharing one's life with parents and being authentic; bad reasons include desiring to hurt and "pay back" parents.
- Determine if the communication skills of parents, their respect for their child, and their ability to work out difficult issues are positive. If so, then the present might be a good time to come out.
- Know the likelihood is that coming out will be a lifelong process, with many small steps over an extended period of time.

(continues)

(*continued*)
An alternative perspective to waiting until one has a solid sense of self is one that maintains that parents can help their child feel better about having same-sex attractions. If parents are exceptionally understanding, open minded, and welcoming of diversity, then they can help a youth work through self-acceptance issues.[18]

From a research perspective, little is known about why some youths disclose while in middle or junior high school and others only once they are on their own after graduating from college. Do the former have stronger self-esteem that allows them to face a hostile world or a sexual libido that "motivates" them to recognize the sexual component of their life? Are they more sex atypical and thus more "obviously" gay to others, who then label them gay, facilitating self-awareness? Or, is it a matter of temperament— being more extroverted, they are more likely to share their homoeroticism with others because in general they are likely to talk about themselves or, being more sensitive, they are more likely to engage in self-analysis and hence become aware of their sexuality? Perhaps the critical factor resides in characteristics of the parents: Do more liberal and communicative parents encourage their child to disclose to them his or her same-sex attractions? Or, is it merely a matter of accident or happenstance that parents discover their child's sexuality, catching their child in a sexual act or extrapolating from their child's friends?

The only significant predictor assessed in the present study of when youths come out to their parents is the age of telling the first person. Thus, once the process of coming out begins with best friends and perhaps a close sibling, the process of telling parents is set in motion. The fact that age of same-sex awareness and age of self-labeling are unrelated indicates that the processes of coming out to self and to others are relatively independent trajectories, other than that the first is usually reached before the second is initiated. Many youths want to be absolutely certain of their sexuality and have alternative sources of support before telling parents; a few turn to their parents for assistance in coming out to self and others.

For some young women, a same-sex romantic relationship is so important that they *have* to tell their parents about this new person in their life. Perhaps they want to share their joy or they feel dishonest with their partner by being closeted. Or, they find it increasingly difficult to hide their sexuality with the increased number of telephone calls, letters, and visits from this particular woman. The fact that having a romantic relationship is not a predictor of coming out to parents among young men might indicate the lesser significance of same-sex romantic relationships for their sexual identity or their greater ability to hide the relationship from their parents.

How Adolescents Come Out

Disclosure can be initiated by a youth or by parents, and it can be an unplanned or planned event. Some youths come out by gradually letting down their pretense of heterosexuality, by refusing to play a heterosexual role, or by dropping "hints" such that parents eventually are left with little option but to conclude that they have a gay son or daughter. Wives more often than husbands tell the other spouse about this conclusion.

Youths may merely assume parents know, or ought to know, without offering a candid acknowledgment. Or, they are outed by school officials, newspapers, friends, or ex-lovers.[19] Although these indirect means are not unusual, most youths tell parents directly, face-to-face. Among the interviewed youths, this is especially true in mother–child dyads and less so in a father–daughter dyad.

Study Findings: How Youths Come Out

- Three of 4 youths disclose to their mother face-to-face.
- Three of 4 young men and 3 of 5 young women come out to their father face-to-face.
- One of 3 young women and 1 of 5 young men are out to their father because someone else told him.

A disclosure technique preferred by one youth is often inappropriate or unwanted by another. Teenagers generally favor a direct approach but differ among themselves regarding whether coming out should occur when one parent is present, both are in attendance, or the entire family is gathered for a family meeting. The most daunting challenge for those who want to help youths come out is to convince them to take control of the situation. Rather than permitting random events or "accidents," such as being outed by others, sexual-minority youths should take the initiative and control how they will disclose to their parents.

Advice to Youths: How to Come Out to Parents

Several writers and the youths' narratives in the present study suggest possible issues that should be considered when deciding how best to come out to parents.[20] Youths might want to

- Work through their own fears and concerns before talking to parents, perhaps with friends or a professional mental health provider.

(continues)

(*continued*)

- Plan ahead and put serious time and effort into preparing the coming-out event. It is probably best not to simply leave hints around the house.
- Ask others for their coming-out script or write their own, but have something clearly in mind; select a quiet, safe, and private location, unless they expect a dangerous reaction, in which case they should choose a public place; exude certainty and calmness in their voice; and talk only when they have the parents' full attention.
- Choose a nonhectic time when everyone is not tired. Holidays are usually a bad time because the congestion interferes with time needed for parents to process the information; consider whether they will need time to escape the family and whether parents will need time to "cool off."
- Test the waters by raising contemporary issues such as same-sex marriage, gays in the military, and antigay Boy Scout policies. If responses are generally positive, then this is a good sign. However, parents can react in a very different manner if it is *their* child who is gay.
- Have modest expectations, and give parents time to adjust.
- Avoid blaming, anger, and self-doubt.
- Use nonparental support networks if necessary. Expect the unexpected.
- Consider that coming out can be a very different experience depending on the unique characteristics of the parent. It may be necessary to develop different strategies for each parent.
- Remember that the manner in which they come out is uniquely their decision. Others can be helpful and offer suggestions and support, but ultimately it is not their decision. Do not be pressured.

Youths should be sensitive to their parents' feelings and needs. Youths have had years coming to terms with their sexuality and thus should not necessarily expect parents to accept them within minutes after learning about their sexuality. Youths should make this an act of faith in parents and should thus be respectful of them; this will improve chances for a positive outcome. This is an act of love—because youths want to be closer to their parents and share their life with them. It is not necessary to bring up disturbing topics during the first conversation (such as AIDS/HIV, sexual conduct, violence) or to tell other relatives without consulting parents.

PARENTS' INITIAL REACTIONS

Remarkably few investigators have examined the reactions of parents once they discover that their child has same-sex attractions. By so doing, researchers simply reflect the cultural silence about this coming-of-age marker for sexual-minority youths. Rituals, positive acknowledgments, or celebrations rarely commemorate the act of coming out, and sexual-minority youths are seldom thrown "coming-out parties." Fewer still receive appropriate Hallmark cards. If there is revelry, it is usually with close friends.

Popular mythology has far more strident narratives with vivid examples of parental travesties. The featured cover story of *Newsweek*, January 13, 1986, portrayed the reactions of one family to a son's homosexuality. "He's queer! He's queer!" Kelly's mother screamed as she ran "hysterically into the arms of her husband, who held her and tried to tell her it was going to be OK." Kelly's father's response was to get "the hell out of the house" because he "needed to be alone with his anger, sadness and confusion." He tried to blame his wife, felt anger toward his son, and wanted to send him to a psychiatrist. He cried, and then had a mild heart attack.[21] Chastity Bono dreaded coming out to her mother. "We avoided the subject by mutual consent: I didn't want to deal, and she didn't want to deal." Her mother, as expected, reacted harshly and demanded that Chastity "get out." Cher's previous exposure to gay people did little to assuage her anxieties or stereotypes. "Well, they were not my children," Cher said. "It's a different thing that happens with your child—it's not the same. None of those people had successful home lives or successful relationships."[22]

These two cases recount disclosures that caused major disruptions in familial relationships and initiated a process of parental mourning. Is this merely a cohort effect or is this typical of today's parent–youth relationships? Two books, one devoted to the care and counseling of gay and lesbian youths and the other to the academic study of sexual minorities, appear to argue the second—the crisis modality.

> Just as coming out precipitates an emotional crisis for individuals, disclosure of lesbian/gay identity to parents *generally* [italics added] promotes a family crisis. Like adolescents or adults who self-identify as lesbian or gay, parents undergo a kind of multistage "coming-out" process during which they grieve the loss of their child's heterosexual identity and ultimately reframe negative social sanctions and lost expectations into positive experiences of lesbian and gay lives.[23]

> Disclosure to parents and other significant relatives *often* [italics added] precipitates a period of turmoil for the family, frequently involving three initial reactions. First, parents feel guilt and personal responsi-

bility for their child's homosexuality and experience a sense of failure as parents. . . . Second, parents may ignore their child's individuality and personal experience by applying negative values and misconceptions about homosexuality to their son or daughter; likewise, they may fear others will similarly apply stereotypes to them, leading to isolation and ostracism from their social network. Third, the "new" identity may create feelings of alienation, and family members might react as if the person were unfamiliar and estranged; as a result family roles and relationships can be disrupted.[24]

Those who do not survive physically or are left with permanent physical, emotional, cognitive, or social scars often live in homes in which parents verbally or physically abuse them *prior to* knowing the youth's sexual orientation. These are the youths who run away from home, abuse drugs and alcohol, engage in criminal behavior, become sex workers, or attempt to kill themselves. One example is given below.

Parental Reactions: "Mom, Why Do You Hate Me?"

Dear Mom, I wonder sometimes if you miss me, even think about me?

Maybe I trusted you too much when I told you the biggest secret I had. I wish sometimes I could take it all back and never have told you that I'm gay. I wish I could go back to the way things used to be.

I miss all the fun we had together. . . . I wonder why you had to change. I grew up knowing you loved me, and now I live with the knowledge that you hate me. But I can't go back. I just have to accept the fact that my mama—who raised me and worked three part-time jobs to support me; who left a husband who hit her because she was afraid he might hurt me; who didn't get an abortion even though her boyfriend urged her to; who suffered so much for me—that mother hates me because I'm gay.

You looked so scared and shocked when you found out. But I never wanted to hurt you, Mom. I think about you when I wake up. I picture your face in my mind and trace it with my fingers in the air. Sometimes, though, I can't remember what you look like, and that scares me.

Do you think about me? I grew 3 inches, and my feet grew even more. I look a lot older. My hair grew out and it's not frizzy anymore, just wavy. Would you recognize me if you saw me?

No. If you walked by me all you'd see would be a dirty homeless girl with matted braids and smelly shoes and dirty clothes. If I asked you for spare change you'd just walk on by. Only if you stopped and looked in my eyes would you recognize me.

I hate you for hating me, but can't stop loving you. Why do you hate me for who I am? I'm not evil. . . . God, I hope you change your mind

(continues)

(continued)
some day. But I can't keep trying to call you. How many times can you try when nobody will ever accept the charges? Do you know how that makes me feel?

But I still miss you. And I wish that you missed me.[25]

Many early studies focused on these problematic youths, as does more recent research that samples from sources where "troubled" youths are most likely to frequent. For example, one study reported that over half of youths attending urban support groups had experienced some degree of verbal or physical harassment from a family member, ranging from verbal insults to physical assaults.[26] Because the investigators sampled from a source that attracts youths who feel they need support for their difficult life situations, it is not surprising that the research reported that these youths have difficult life situations.

Although parents might not be thrilled with the news or immediately embrace homosexuality as a central dimension of their daughter or son, empirical research documents that very few parents reject or harm their child. The sensationalism of the media, including the gay media, leads us to believe otherwise. The extreme cases sell newspapers and magazines and increase television ratings. For example, although a recent article in the gay and lesbian magazine *The Advocate* eventually presents a balanced view of the range of responses parents have to their child coming out to them, the author states that for every parent who accepts her or his gay child, "there is a mother who publishes a legal notice in the newspaper declaring her very alive gay son dead or a father who gives his daughter 15 minutes to get out of the house for good."[27] This is patently untrue and is meant to alarm rather than reflect reality.

Advice to Parents: Common Concerns With Disclosure

By the time adolescents share the truth about their sexuality, they have probably spent years struggling with their same-sex attractions. Parents, however, are often caught off guard by the suddenness of the revelation and yet are expected by their child to immediately understand, adapt, and support. One P-FLAG parent wrote,

> In our experience, gay youth often have unrealistic expectations of their families, failing to take into account the time needed after disclosure for the family to acquire information, assess this new reality, and reexamine the internal assumptions they have lived with for years.

(continues)

(*continued*)

Youth tend to overestimate the knowledge parents have about homosexuality. They frequently do not understand the nature or magnitude of the issues their families are dealing with. Even when they do, they are not in a position to offer assistance.[28]

This event might well disrupt parents' view of their child, her future, and themselves as parents. According to P-FLAG, common responses include

- "What did we do wrong?" Parents may believe that they were not "good enough," did not give sufficient attention or gave too much attention to their child, or favored another child too much.
- "What did his mother/father do wrong?" Parents may blame their spouse for not providing an adequate or suitable same-sex or opposite-sex role model.
- "We should never have divorced!" Parents who indict their broken marriage for setting a bad heterosexual example.
- "It was the gay teacher in school!" Parents may reproach someone else for their child's homosexuality, such as neighborhood playmates, a teacher, or "homosexuals" who put bad ideas into their child's head.
- "Our child is going to hell/is sick!" Parents may believe that their child has a disease or is committing a sin and that they must "save" their child.

Parents might fear, with some justification, that peers will harass their child or that she or he will be the target of discrimination. Or, parents might be anxious that they will be embarrassed in front of friends and relatives (especially their parents), will be perceived as failed parents, will have no grandchildren, or will have their myth of having the perfect family destroyed.

Rather than accepting that homosexuality is a healthy, natural fact of life, parents might rush their child to the local psychiatrist or therapist to correct the "psychological deviance." Although reparative and conversion therapies offer "redemptive" promises and can change a youth's sexual *behavior* (at least temporarily), they have no effect on her or his sexual *orientation*. Any attempt to convert a sexual-minority youth is made at a high cost—her or his possible alienation from parents.

Therapy, if deemed necessary, should focus on helping all family members feel better about the youth's sexuality, assist parents to place their child's sexuality in proper perspective, and teach youths and parents the necessary skills for living in a heterocentric society.[29]

Although in some cases families disintegrate after the disclosure because parents are unable to move beyond their initial shock and anger and erupt in verbal harassment or physical assault, the reality, of course, is that considerable diversity characterizes the reactions of parents to the disclosure.[30] Indeed, most parents recoup and adapt to the new reality. It can even be humorous, as was actor Nathan Lane's coming out story.

> I'd let my mother know I was seeing someone, but she assumed it was a girl. I never lied to her; we were always very honest with each other. . . . "I know you think it's a girl," I told her, "but it's a guy." The blood drained from her face, and she said (*very deeply*), "You mean you're a homosexual?"—why does she suddenly sound like Harvey Fierstein? She's an Irish Catholic woman. "Well, yes, I guess so." And she said, "I would rather you were dead." I said, "Well, I knew you'd understand." And once I got her head out of the oven, everything went fine.[31]

Although their child's same-sex attractions might be alien to them, parents might nevertheless cherish the disclosure because they finally have an answer to something they have long suspected or a reason as to why their child has become a foreigner to them. Here is an opportunity to "get their kid back." One mother, Marlene Fanta Shyer, worried about her "odd little fellow" since kindergarten. He was *too* tidy and obedient and was always ridiculed as too effeminate and not athletic. Once he spoke the magic words, "I'm gay," she flinched, then chilled. "This is what I had been dreading since he was 3, 4, 5. But almost immediately I had a new reaction— liberation. It was a done deal, and I accepted him and his sexual orientation wholeheartedly."[32]

Such constructive outcomes are seldom articulated in coming-out narratives or advice-giving tracts even though they are far more familiar scenarios than the visible and electrifying stories that seek to warn youths against disclosing to their parents. In reality, by not disclosing, sexual-minority youths could be forfeiting latent sources of support. This potential must be weighed against the very real circumstances faced by those who would not emotionally or physically survive a disclosure.

More common than either the traumatic or celebratory reactions are those of a knowing, relatively calm recognition. Playwright Jon Robin Baitz told his family over a West Hollywood brunch. "My mother started laughing . . . [and] my father looked at her and said, 'He's not kidding,' and my brother piped up triumphantly, 'I've always known!' It was a seamless event— over French toast—of no enormous melodrama."[33] When movie critic Gene Shalit discovered that his son is gay, his reply typified their relationship, "I thought you had something important to tell me." Shalit expressed concern for his son's safety and the effect that being gay would have on his son's career. His life's credo has always been, "Let children follow their own star."

If parents stay awake at night worrying about the role they played in their child's sexual orientation, Shalit's advice is simple, "Go back to sleep."[34]

Photographer David LaChapelle credits his parents with helping him through very difficult childhood and adolescent times. "My parents are really nurturing and supportive, and they cared about me a lot. They kept me from killing myself in more ways than one when I was a kid." He dreams of a day when families celebrate their kid's sexuality. "They should have a fucking parade down the middle of suburbia," he laughed, breaking into a mock celebratory pro-gay ditty: "Hooray! Hooray! My son is gay! I found him in a dress today!"[35]

Even factors that researchers report foretell very negative parental reactions can fail to predict bad outcomes. Betty and Raul Moreno had much to learn about homosexuality and considerable religious and ethnic stereotypes to overcome. However, "There's no way I could say I'm not going to love him because of this," said Betty, a fundamentalist Baptist. Raul, a Hispanic Texan realized, "All the gay community wants is the same thing all of us want—to be loved and accepted for who and what we are." Both have joined the Metropolitan Community Church (a gay-affirming denomination) and are "very proud" of their son.[36]

As these parents illustrate, predicting initial parental reactions has met with mixed results. Most commonly, researchers investigate the attributes and beliefs of parents, such as family culture, parenting style, religion, ethnicity, gender role orientation, and age, but no consistent patterns have emerged.[37] One reason may be that little if any attention has focused on particular attributes of the *pair*—such as the gender composition of the dyad. One clinician suggests that same-sex parent–child dyads elicit the most negative parental reactions. Because they are primarily responsible for the well-being of daughters, mothers might feel particularly rejected or hurt when their daughter is not heterosexual. How can their daughter feel fulfilled or secure without a man? Fathers can be so ashamed or repulsed by their son's abandonment of masculinity that they cannot stand the sight of him. In terms of cross-sex dynamics, fathers may feel less threatened by their lesbian daughter's female partner than they would if she were dating a potential male rival; mothers may take solace in knowing no woman will take her place in her son's life.[38]

The young women and men in the present study do not support these suppositions. First, the youths' narratives lucidly demonstrate the abundance not of extremely positive or extremely negative responses but of modest reactions. Second, earlier I indicated that the gender composition of the dyad matters in terms of reasons for disclosing or not disclosing to parents and in parental reactions. Third, the most problematic relationships are not same-sex but cross-sex dyads.

> **Study Findings: Parental Reactions**
>
> - Parents react worse than the first person or sibling told.
> - Mean positive or negative reactions are the same for mothers and fathers.
> - Most common mother responses to sons are "slightly negative," followed by "negative." One third of the responses are "slightly positive" or "positive."
> - Most common mother responses to daughters are "slightly positive." Nearly one half receive "positive" or "slightly positive" responses from mothers. One quarter of the responses are "slightly negative."
> - Over one third of fathers are "slightly positive" to the disclosure of sons and daughters.
> - Fathers are twice as likely to be more than "slightly negative" to sons than to daughters.
> - With the disclosure, 4% of parents reject or abuse their child.
> - Mothers told directly by their daughter react better than those who find out because someone else tells them.
> - Mothers react best when their daughter tells them because they share a close relationship.
> - Mothers react worse when they discover their son's same-sex attractions because someone else tells them or their son attempts to elicit support.
> - Fathers react worse when someone else tells them about their daughter's same-sex attractions.
> - No relationship exists between age of coming out and parental reactions.

Although young men report receiving more negative first reactions from their parents than do young women, this difference is only slight. More striking are the differences attributed to mothers versus fathers. It is clear that one cannot talk intelligently about parent–child interactions without reference to the gender of the participants. Mothers more so than fathers are perceived by their children, especially by sons, as having suspicions about their child's same-sex attractions before the actual disclosure. Why? Perhaps fathers are not sufficiently around their child to notice or are less sensitive to such issues. Or, fathers notice but are more inclined to dismiss them as insignificant or not their concern. Even after being told, many fathers appear somewhat distant from the discussion about their child's sexuality or are, as one young woman reported, "diffusely annoyed with my lifestyle."

Many of the interviewed young women appear to agree with a recent Yankelovich Partners Survey that found 94% of girls report that their mother is a friend (87% of mothers list their daughter as a friend). Nine out of 10 daughters report that their relationship with their mother is a very happy one, 9 of 10 believe their mother's approval is very important to them, and 2 of 3 say they would go to their mother before a friend if they had a personal problem. Mothers and daughters also tend to share similar values, somewhat less so regarding issues of sexuality and independence.[39] Many of the young women I interviewed agree, reporting an intimacy with their mother that is absent from any other parent–child dyad.

Several research design issues, however, should be kept in mind in considering these findings. Although youths were encouraged to recall the exact context of the disclosure and specific reactions, findings are the reports of youths and not their parents; these are also retrospective accounts collected moments to several years after the disclosure. Moreover, gender is just one of many potential discriminating variables that likely matter in predicting a parent's initial reactions. We know relatively little about most others, including ethnicity, social class, and regional differences.

Equally unknown are the consequences of disclosing to parents at one age rather than another. Although it is generally believed by clinicians that the timing of a youth's disclosure influences the response of parents, we do not know if this is actually true. Mental health professionals suggest that youths should only come out when they are comfortable being gay and can survive on their own without family support. Generally this is not during early adolescence. Although these speculations are not empirically documented with diverse populations of sexual-minority youths, they shape the advice given to youths about when and how to come out.

Advice to Youths: What to Expect From Parents

Although parental reactions vary immensely, youths should consider the following as generally true:

- Rarely does the initial response represent full support and understanding. Few parents begin by saying, "I'm so glad you know this about yourself and that you wanted to share it with us."
- The first response is seldom how things will conclude. Total approval is not necessary. It may take a few minutes or years, but things usually get better.
- A good reaction is one in which parents feel comfortable, are nonchalant, or wished that their child had shared it earlier.

(continues)

(*continued*)

- A bad response—withdrawal of love and rejection—can be weathered. Even loved ones sometimes have difficulty accepting, blame themselves or someone else, or say things that upset everyone.
- It is good for youths to surround themselves with caring and supportive nonfamily individuals.
- If in danger, youths should protect themselves and be prepared to remove themselves from parents. A cooling-off period may be necessary.
- Honesty is not always the best policy—it may be best to renege on the "I'm gay" statement if safety is at stake. Youths should then keep it as *their* preserved truth until they are in a more favorable environment. Remaining in the closet until a better time and place can be arranged might be best.
- Youths should stay clear in their heart about their sexuality.[40]

In sum, parents can be hurtful in their reactions, but seldom are they abusive or rejecting. Many have stereotypes and are concerned about safety and status—theirs and that of their child. However, most react with a mildly positive or slightly negative response. Their reactions are perhaps best predicted by the kind of relationship they have with their child before disclosure. The range of reactions initially and eventually spans the spectrum, and it is this possibility that confronts every youth who discloses to parents.

THE PARENT–CHILD RELATIONSHIP AFTER DISCLOSURE

Perhaps more important than a parent's initial response to disclosure is that which happens after disclosure. Is the topic discussed again or does everyone avoid it? Do all members of the family know, or are some left to wonder and speculate? Does one parent use the youth's sexuality as a weapon against the youth or the other parent? Is the youth rejected or mistreated by parents in the years following? We know little about what leads to healthy long-term family relations once the disclosure information is acknowledged.

The disclosure can bring out the best, or the nastiest, in parents. Most likely it will be predictable; parents will react the way they typically do to "crises." Only a few parent–child dyads in the present study deteriorated following the initial reaction. More often, they improved considerably thereafter, increasing in mutual communication and respect to a level sometimes more positive than before the disclosure. Most, however, stayed the same. That is, parents acquiesced to this new, or not so new, information and continued their predisclosure relationship with their child. The same issues present before disclosure were there afterward—curfew, discipline, taking out the garbage, dating, homework, politics. Many youths could visualize a time when matters would improve, perhaps not dramatically but gradually as new communication patterns and styles of interactions replaced maladaptive ones.

Study Findings: Parent–Youth Relationships Over Time

- Nearly 90% of father–daughter relationships and over 60% of mother–daughter relationships did not change.
- Four of 10 sons reported that relationships with a parent did not change.
- Over 5 of 10 sons reported improvement in their relationship with a parent.
- One of 3 daughters reported improvement in their relationship with mother.
- Fewer than 5% of parent–youth relationships deteriorated over time.

Reports of positive changes in the parent–child relationship are not uncommon. Although little is known about why or how this occurs, parents who accept their sexual-minority child have overcome whatever barriers they might have had—or perhaps never had—from their personal or cultural heritage that were preventing them from saying, "I love you regardless of your sexuality." Reaching this position can be relatively easy; perhaps the parents were raised in a family atmosphere that accepted diversity or was low in judgmentalness. Or, reaching this position can be extraordinarily difficult; perhaps the parents were affected by deeply rooted homophobia or social or religious conservatism. Although accepting one's child should require no special aptitude other than unconditional love, those who are flexible in religious and moral values, keep open intrafamilial communications, have a strong attachment and affection for the nonheterosexual family member, and have access to informational, emotional, and social support fare best.

This is not to say that parents who "get better" are now fully supportive of their child's sexuality. Most remain somewhat ambivalent. One young woman remarked that her parents accept her sexuality because, "They have no other choice. I will never quite be their daughter because I'm not the daughter they wanted."[41] Parents may love their child, desire that she have a good life, and want what is best for her. Yet, they also grieve for the pain and hardships she will now face and what "might have been" if their child had been heterosexual. Carla Hansen, an associate dean at Brown University, noted, "We have this pervasive notion that good parents will have successful children who get well-paying jobs, do exciting things, and marry someone we like, and anything else is a negative reflection of the parents."[42] Thus, parents lament not only for their child but also for themselves.

This ambivalence, according to writer and soccer coach Dan Woog, characterizes parents who had clear indications that their child is not heterosexual and yet are stunned when a child comes out as lesbian, gay, or bisexual.

> Even mothers and fathers who guessed the news for years or prided themselves on being open-minded display classic emotions: anger, worry, denial, shame. But if the immediate reactions are similar, the ensuing weeks, months, and years are not. Each person's journey to understanding, acceptance, and even celebration of a gay child is unique. Some parents spend a lifetime hobbling just a few steps; others race along, gaining momentum as they go.

Parents frequently need to be 100% sure. As one parent put it, "Looking back, I wonder why I didn't [ask], but I guess there was this doubt: *What if he isn't and he thinks I think.* . . . I was 97% sure, but with your child it has to be 100."[43] Although Woog argued that for every acceptance there is a parent who rejects their child, we have no evidence—and now with this study sufficient *counterevidence*—that this number approaches 50%. Despite the ambivalence, in most families, parents follow the initial acknowledgment with conversations, questions, interest, and connections. Family members can and do change and grow in their understanding.

Adjustments might be most difficult for parents who feel accountable for their child's sexual orientation. After all, have they not influenced every aspect of their child's life?! If homosexuality is a choice or the result of early parenting, as traditional psychoanalytic theories and religious doctrine assert, then they must be responsible. Parents focus on only one aspect of their child—her or his sexuality—neglecting the fact that the youth is more than a bundle of sexual attractions. Disappointment overwhelms these parents: Their child will not realize the normative transitions into prescribed adult roles, including marriage and parenthood. They focus exclusively on the stigma, misinformation, moral judgments, discrimination, and violence their child will now face. They would be more comfortable if the youth stayed in the closet.

Advice to Parents: How to Move Toward Acceptance

If parents desire to show their acceptance of their child, they should first listen, ask questions, and then

(continues)

- Give unconditional love and reassure their child that they love and support her or him regardless of the child's sexuality.
- Continue to meet their child's basic needs, such as safety, structure, and affection.
- Refrain from pathologizing their child because of his or her sexuality.
- Help their child enjoy childhood and adolescence. Let their child be a kid and provide her or him space to be herself or himself. Give the child tools to take back power the child might have lost because of her or his sexual orientation (e.g., connect physical and emotional intimacy).
- Realize that integrating a new identity as a parent of a sexual-minority child requires time and stamina. The child has had years to reflect on his or her sexual feelings before self-identifying; parents should give themselves some slack and time to adjust to this new status: the parent of a sexual-minority child.
- Seek educational information for parents (e.g., literature from P-FLAG, or Parents, Families and Friends of Lesbians and Gays) that will help in coping with the sexual status of their child. Without such resources, acceptance or even tolerance is an arduous task. In coming to terms with their son's or daughter's same-sex attractions, it is critical that parents modify previous beliefs regarding the consequences of a nonheterosexual identity.
- Talk with other parents in similar situations to gain information and support. Groups such as P-FLAG and We Are Family provide opportunities to openly discuss fears and concerns about having a gay, bisexual, or lesbian child. Also available are therapy and support groups that can answer questions and provide stories by other parents about their experiences.
- Be aware that extended family members can play an integral role assisting parents to adapt to their new status. It is likely that some of these family members also have same-sex attractions and can thus offer a unique perspective about what the child needs.
- Encourage the child to share his or her history of same-sex attractions, the ways in which sexual orientation has influenced the child's life, who else knows and how they have reacted, and future expectations the youth has about his or her life as a gay person. Despite discomfort parents may feel with the subject, this conversation should be the first of many. If not

(*continues*)

(*continued*)

initiated by the child, parents should encourage these discussions because they normalize the youth's sexuality and the parents' alliance with him or her.

Parents have been given an honor, a gift—the opportunity to know their child better, more completely than previously. Parents who adjust best give preeminence to the relationship they have with their child, preserve the child's integrity, and enhance family unity through unconditional love. In the XY *Survival Guide*, Benjie Nycum asks parents to "thank your child for trusting you with such personal information." His 20 point ideal parental response list is a "cut-out" that should be given to all parents.[44]

Three media examples of a positive transformation in a mother–child relationship illustrate the resolutions possible. First, from the 1986 *Newsweek* account we learn that Kelly's mother struggled, finally emerging when she was able to say for the first time to a gay crisis telephone counselor, "My son is gay." Seeking information and encouragement from a parents' support group and attending gay events moved her to a place where she could reconnect with her son. Once this hurdle had dissipated, she immersed herself in the trappings of her son's life.

> She listened and learned, quickly realizing that Kelly was not going to change and that no one was to blame. She started manning the hot line and joining excursions to Portland's gay bars. She talked with all kinds of people—from drag queens and lesbians to other parents of gays—and if she couldn't completely understand, at least she was beginning to accept.

Her final act was to march in a Gay Pride Day parade as the mother of a gay son.[45]

Second, Cher was initially far from ready to embrace her daughter Chastity Bono. She censored information from other people, felt that she had failed as a parent, struggled to accept homosexuality for *her* daughter, and feared for what Chastity's life would be like. She associated unstable relationships with gay people, who to her were promiscuous and conformed to butch/femme roles. "At first I thought I was a failure as a parent; then I felt that you were going to be the failure and that you wouldn't be able to succeed and have a normal life." She could not understand why Chastity "had" to wear a pink triangle.

> Why do you have to wear that shit? Why does it have to have a triangle on it? I just really didn't talk about your being gay. . . . It was still a secret, so it was still a negative thing. I wasn't comfortable and what I

did was choose to ignore, and no one chose to confront me with it. When anyone would ask me about you, I would try to walk around the subject and give other descriptions or statistics about you, staying away from one specific point, and hopefully people wouldn't talk about it.[46]

Slowly but surely Cher moved toward full acceptance, in her own time and in her own manner. Now, according to Chastity, Cher is "a really cool person. I think she appreciates all the good qualities I have as a person, and this one thing is not such a big deal. She's really been amazing. I can really talk to her."[47] Chastity offers advice to youths about how to enhance their parents' acceptance. "The turning point for parents, what really allows them to separate their experience of their child from negative images of homosexuality, is when they see their child happy, healthy, and strong." As Chastity came out of her own closet, accepted herself, and emerged with a strong sense of self, "My mom responded and became much more accepting of my being gay." Cher admitted, "It made me feel better about you as a person, and so therefore anything you got involved in, you would be choosing that thing from a position of strength and not weakness, not neediness. From that place, you wouldn't make the wrong decision." Cher began the path toward true acceptance and celebration of her daughter's life.[48]

The third media example is of Judy Shepard and her son Matthew, who came out to her when he was a student at the University of Wyoming. Although Mrs. Shepard was not thrilled with having a gay son, she tried to accept it in stride.

> I actually think I knew before Matt did. I don't know how, it's a mom thing, people tell me. . . . My first response was, "Why did you wait so long to tell me?"
>
> I don't want to make it sound like it was, "I'm gay, pass the potatoes," but we got through it. Children are a very precious gift from God. Voluntarily giving up your child for that reason is beyond my comprehension.[49]

Speaking before 1,200 hushed and tearful students at Cornell University, Mrs. Shepard described the events leading up to the October day in 1998 when her son was killed in a gay-related hate crime. Although there are days when she does not believe that she can go on, she knows that Matthew would be disappointed in her if she gave up. She turned her emptiness into activism, channeling her efforts to humanize gays, change cultural attitudes, and establish the Matthew Shepard Foundation, "dedicated to the principle of helping people move beyond tolerance to embrace and rejoice in diversity."[50] Mrs. Shepard is committed to eradicating what happened to her son; she has been transformed.

Advice to Youths: If Parents Remain Silent After Disclosure

If parents act as if the coming-out conversation never happened, ask no questions, never bring up the subject, and make comments that assume their child is heterosexual, then youths might well remember, "Each time you tell someone else in your extended family, each time you bring up a gay subject, when you bring a boyfriend or girlfriend home, when you meet new people and make introductions—all these are occasions when your parents will, once again, encounter the fact that you're gay."[51]

Although youths might feel abandoned, invisible, angry, and exasperated—and perhaps relieved that no one is talking about this embarrassing subject—it might be best to

- Be patient, compassionate, and persevere.
- Respect parents' feelings.
- Be compassionate when asserting the legitimacy of their sexuality.
- Strike a balance between the need to talk freely and openly and the parents' need to cope.
- Weave their sexuality into normal conversations, gently at first, so that parents adjust and learn how to talk about the subject. Youths may need to teach their parents this skill.
- Prepare them in advance of bringing home a girlfriend or boyfriend.

Although little is known about developments in the parent–youth relationship after disclosure because investigators have generally neglected the all-important issue of family life following disclosure, it is difficult to ascertain how common any particular pattern of response is—if indeed any patterns exist. In the aftermath it is probably rare that parents follow a sequence of predictable mourning stages, as noted in chapter 3. More likely, a diversity of sequences and processes permeates their reactions. Perhaps random events, the age of the participants, the context of the disclosure, personality characteristics of the parents, and other factors are critical. If developmental sequences of reactions exist, we have not yet discovered which parents fall into which categories for which reasons.

Advice to Parents: Mourning the Loss in Predictable Stages?

Heterosexual parents confronted by their child's same-sex attractions should be leery of accepting without question the Kübler-Ross developmental stage model of mourning. Although this model describes the

(continues)

(*continued*)

acceptance process of some parents, for many others it has limited, if any, applicability. Both research and personal stories indicate the following:

- Parents might not be shocked by the disclosure because of long-standing suspicions and thus move immediately to acceptance without denial, anger, or despair.
- Stages can be reversed. Parents can become depressed before becoming angry.
- Parents can skip stages. For example, parents may not bargain after denial and anger.
- Parents might never reach some stages. For example, parents may become fixated at denial by threatening the child with emotional isolation.

If parents expect their reactions to follow the grieving model, they may be imposing on themselves a false sense of what are "normal" responses, which may in turn cause further agony and confusion. Parents might ask such perplexing questions as

- What does it mean to be a parent who seldom feels anger toward one's child or to be told that one cannot move toward acceptance without venting rage?
- Should one feel "abnormal" if one never feels depressed, ashamed, guilty, or remorseful?
- What if one is so committed to unconditionally loving one's child that celebration follows disclosure?

Kübler-Ross's developmental model of expectable reactions has redeeming value if it gives a sense that one is not alone, that other parents share the trauma, and that current feelings are a necessary step toward peace and acceptance. More commonly, parents develop their own style of responding, in their own time.

The process of learning about their child and accepting him or her can also enhance parent development. Parents in one support group spoke of a pragmatic self-questioning that the discovery of their child's sexuality elicited: "Who is my child, and what do I want for her/him?" These queries often stimulated an inner process of self-examination:

This was an opportunity for growth and personal development, coincident with transitions in middle age. Some talked about feelings of guilt, not related to the question of causality, but rather because of their initially negative responses to the news of a gay or lesbian child. This introspective process frequently resulted in a more realistic assessment of parental expectations as well as delineated boundaries between parent and child.[52]

With this reorientation, parents alter their expectations of their child's future and hence themselves. In this self-transformation, a few parents become agents of social change, improving the life of their child, the children of other parents, and their own lives. In small, personal ways, they help other parents who are struggling to accept a child with same-sex attractions by providing accurate information and emotional support. On a larger scale, parents lobby or march in gay pride parades for fairer local, state, and national ordinances, laws, and policies. Some feel comfortable speaking publicly in the community and distributing accurate information on homosexuality. Mary Griffith, who lost her son to suicide because she failed to support him, turned her guilt into a crusade to help gay kids. On dozens of talk shows, school assemblies, and interviews and articles, she has helped to transform public attitudes and sympathies. Her mission has resulted in personal growth that she could not have imagined before her loss.[53]

A FINAL WORD

When sexual-minority youths disclose their sexual orientation to parents, all family members are affected. In a very real sense, everyone "comes out." The youth, individual family members, and the family system face subsequent developmental issues and clinical hurdles that may be unrivaled and considerably more formidable than anything previously encountered. It is not that parents matter so little but that they often matter so much. Or, it can be a relatively uneventful discovery that hardly registers in ongoing family relations. It is this diversity that counters any simplistic generalizations about parent–youth relationships before, during, and after disclosure.

One consistency that I found among the sexual-minority youths I interviewed is their need, similar to all adolescents, for a predictable, safe, and sustaining home—one that will honor and trust them, will let them lead an authentic life that is both fun and meaningful, and will nurture their growth toward adulthood.[54] In their book written specifically for sexual-minority youths, Ellen Bass and Kate Kaufman endorsed this view.

> If your family is working well, it is a supportive environment in which to be yourself. A healthy family is a safe place to explore your thoughts and feelings and to learn the skills you need in relationship to others. In healthy families, you experience yourself as lovable, precious, and valued. ... Whether your family is accepting and nurturing, critical, or abusive, there's no denying their influence on your life. For most people, family acceptance—or rejection—of their sexual orientation is very significant.[55]

Just because a youth has same-sex attractions does not lessen the historic centrality of the parents for her or his identity, sense of self-worth, and feelings of safety. Perhaps as a result, coming out to parents is often perceived by health care providers as an external measure of a youth's mental health and her or his commitment to a sexual identity. I am not so sure this equation is accurate. It might be smart or a measure of self-worth *not* to come out to parents, especially if by so doing a youth places herself or himself in danger. Or, coming out to parents might be such a *nonevent* that it is meaningless as an assessment of adolescent health. Whether one is out might simply reflect the nature of the parent–child relationship—whether it is close, distant, nonexistent, or in need of repair—and not necessarily the mental health status of the youth.

Of course the response a youth receives from parents can influence her or his acceptance of a sexual identity and thus be a measure of personal growth, but I doubt if it is a profound determinant. Many youths accept their sexuality *prior to* disclosing; indeed, it is this very affirmation that allows them to share the information with parents in the first place. For these youths, the reactions of parents matter less in terms of self-esteem and more in terms of how much they will continue to share their life on a daily basis with their parents. Perhaps they realize that the clearest and most accurate statement about coming out to parents is that the eventual outcome on the parent–youth relationship is best predicted by the nature of their prior relationship. This is not an insignificant point and yet it is often ignored in the popular and scientific literatures. However, it is *not* one that youths who are contemplating coming out can or should ignore.

Because the full range of positive and negative outcomes might ensue after an adolescent comes out to a parent, as friends, educators, health care professionals, and research scholars, we must be circumspect making recommendations to youths about whether, when, and how they ought to disclose. In particular, we should be sensitive to the changing image of what it means to be a sexual minority. Many stereotypes about the gay "lifestyle" have recently eroded, as well as the cultural representation of gay as a White, well-to-do identity. Wilson Cruz, who appeared on ABC's My *So-Called Life*, and Pedro Zamora, who appeared on MTV's *Real World*, were the early and visible exceptions. Clearly, deciding to come out to parents involves unique issues for ethnic-minority individuals who are also lesbian, bisexual, or gay.

As mental health professionals, we should also recognize our unique opportunities and obligations to assist youths and family members to shift from a possible trajectory of emotional turmoil to one of healthy development. If the youths' narratives are to be believed—as well as most research on sexual-minority adults—sexual-minority youths are fabulously successful navigating the terrain of their sexuality and becoming healthy, well-functioning adults. This resiliency—a necessary adaptation to living in heterocentric and homonegative environments—is generally not recognized in the popular media and clinical literature, which tend to emphasize the "doom and gloom" of gay youths. This clinicalization of sexual-minority youths does a great disservice to their accomplishments. The message is clear: To be young, happy, and gay is well nigh impossible, a contradiction, an oxymoron.[56] One young man I interviewed, still in high school, wondered during his interview whether he could really be gay because he had not yet attempted suicide. His sole source of information about gay youth has been gathered from news accounts, magazine articles, and television shows of the (supposedly) high suicide rates among homosexual adolescents.[57]

Whether resilient or troubled, sexual-minority youths have received increasing cultural visibility during the past decade. Most families today have a sexual-minority member or know someone who is. Nearly every junior high school student knows what homosexuality is. It is nearly impossible for a North American citizen not to see homosexuality portrayed on television or in the movies or written about in magazines or newspapers. Individuals might attempt to deny its existence, but this is becoming increasingly difficult to do with each gay pride march held or denied, each law passed or rejected, or each adoption granted or refused. The cultural zeitgeist has evolved such that even nominally or absolutely convinced heterosexual youths sometimes question their sexuality, wonder if they have or had same-sex attractions, or think about their sexual orientation or sexual identity.

I believe that these are positive developments, although cultural visibility can impose developmental handicaps for sexual-minority youths who do not want to "out" themselves. Today such youths have fewer options to hide, which takes away opportunities to pace coming out to fit individual developmental needs. Another option, discussed in the next chapter, has also become a reality for many youths: recognizing and acknowledging having same-sex attractions without declaring a sexual identity.

One of the most striking developments during the past few years has been a lowering of the disclosure age and the large number of sexual-minority youths who disclose to family members while still living at home. This contrasts markedly with earlier cohorts of youths, most of whom could remain safely hidden and tightly closeted until they moved into their own apartment, dorm room, or house. Thus, adolescents are coping with family reactions earlier, more immediately, and for longer periods of time than those who grew up during any previous generation. This fact has its developmental benefits—tackling developmentally appropriate issues of identity, intimacy, sexuality, attachment, independence, and authenticity—as well as its detractions—facing the loss of parental acceptance or support, peer harassment, emotional and physical abuse, and self-contempt during a particularly vulnerable time. Most youths I interviewed who are out to their parents successfully weather the majority of these developmental milestones; many others who have not disclosed are uncertain whether they should or whether the present is the best time.

Throughout this chapter, suggestions and advice for both youths and parents have been provided concerning how to approach the coming-out issue. Given the reality of cultural visibility and the difficulties of both hiding and not hiding, I offer one last suggestion. Perhaps what a sexual-minority youth needs most practically from parents is how to manage the disclosure process. Throughout one's life the issue of disclosure will be revisited—whether and what to tell, who to tell, when to tell, and how to tell. This process never ends, and one must learn to anticipate this. Although there is no correct answer to these questions, two incorrect answers exist: Tell no one anything, and tell everyone everything. If "it" is a secret, then it must be shared with someone at some time. If "it" is not a secret, then in today's world there are times when it is best not to disclose. This is unfortunate, but true—at least for now.

ENDNOTES

[1] Savin-Williams, R. C. (2000). *An exploratory study of sexual-minority youths' relations with their parents.* Manuscript submitted for publication.

[2] Varnell, P. (1998, March 6). A class act? How college freshmen stand on gay issues. *Frontiers*, pp. 34, 38.

[3] Ness, C. (1996, June 30). Out at an early age: High schools are the new frontier. *San Francisco Examiner.* Distributed via email list serve, July 1, 1996 by Channel Q News (qnews@channelq.com), Doug Case, manager (Doug.Case @sdsu.edu).

[4] For cross-cultural evidence, see Hillier, L., Dempsey, D., Harrison, L., Beale, L., Matthews, L., & Rosenthal, D. (1998). *Writing themselves in: A national report on the sexuality, health and well-being of same-sex attracted young people* (Monograph Series 7). Carlton, Australia: La Trobe University, Australian Research Centre in Sex, Health and Society, National Centre in HIV Social Research.

[5] See, for example, Bass, E., & Kaufman, K. (1996). *Free your mind.* New York: HarperPerennial; and Henderson, M. G. (1998). Disclosure of sexual orientation: Comments from a parental perspective. *American Journal of Orthopsychiatry, 68,* 372–375.

[6] Page 159 in Bass, E., & Kaufman, K. (1996). *Free your mind.* New York: HarperPerennial.

[7] Bono, C., with Fitzpatick, B. (1998). *Family outing.* Boston: Little, Brown; and Johnson, B. K. (1997). *Coming out every day: A gay, bisexual, or questioning man's guide.* Oakland, CA: New Harbinger.

[8] Page 165 in Anderson, D. (1987). Family and peer relations of gay adolescents. *Adolescent Psychiatry, 15,* 163–178.

[9] D'Augelli, A. R. (1991). Gay men in college: Identity processes and adaptations. *Journal of College Student Development, 32*, 140–146; D'Augelli, A. R., & Hershberger, S. L. (1993). Lesbian, gay, and bisexual youth in community settings: Personal challenges and mental health problems. *American Journal of Community Psychology, 21*, 421–448; and Cramer, D. W., & Roach, A. J. (1988). Coming out to mom and dad: A study of gay males and their relationships with their parents. *Journal of Homosexuality, 15*, 79–91.

[10] Pages 8–11 in Bono, C., with Fitzpatrick, B. (1998). *Family outing.* Boston: Little, Brown.

[11] Further discussion of these ideas can be found in Anderson, D. (1987). Family and peer relations of gay adolescents. *Adolescent Psychiatry, 15*, 163–178; Brown, L. S. (1988). Lesbians, gay men and their families: Common clinical issues. *Journal of Gay and Lesbian Psychotherapy, 1*, 65–77; and Herdt, G., & Boxer, A. (1993). *Children of Horizons: How gay and lesbian teens are leading a new way out of the closet.* Boston: Beacon Press.

[12] Reviewed in Savin-Williams, R. C. (1998). The disclosure to families of same-sex attractions by lesbian, gay, and bisexual youths. *Journal of Research on Adolescence, 8*, 49–68.

[13] See Bass, E., & Kaufman, K. (1996). *Free your mind.* New York: Harper-Perennial.

[14] *Our daughters and sons: Questions and answers for parents of gay, lesbian and bisexual people.* Washington, DC: P-FLAG.

[15] Phan, A. (1999, August 31). Drugs tied to trouble with dad. *USA Today,* p. 4D.

[16] Malyon, A. K. (1981). The homosexual adolescent: Developmental issues and social bias. *Child Welfare, 60*, 321–330.

[17] Brown, L. S. (1988). Lesbians, gay men and their families: Common clinical issues. *Journal of Gay and Lesbian Psychotherapy, 1*, 65–77.

[18] Bono, C., with Fitzpatrick, B. (1998). *Family outing.* Boston: Little, Brown; and Johnson, B. K. (1997). *Coming out every day: A gay, bisexual, or questioning man's guide.* Oakland, CA: New Harbinger.

[19] See example in Bils, J. (1996, February 22). Second gay teen drops out, joins suit against school—Riverside-Brookfield chief denies charges. *Chicago Tribune.* Distributed via e-mail list serve February 23, 1996 by Channel Q News (qnews @nsl.cyberspaces.com), Doug Case, manager (Doug.Case@sdsu.edu).

[20] Bass, E., & Kaufman, K. (1996). *Free your mind.* New York: HarperPerennial; Bono, C., with Fitzpatrick, B. (1998). *Family outing.* Boston: Little, Brown; and Johnson, B. K. (1997). *Coming out every day: A gay, bisexual, or questioning man's guide.* Oakland, CA: New Harbinger.

[21] Page 57, Reese, M., & Abramson, P. (1986, January 13). One family's struggle. *Newsweek,* pp. 55–58.

[22] Pages 84 and 206, Bono, C., with Fitzpatrick, B. (1998). *Family outing.* Boston: Little, Brown.

[23] Page 68 in Ryan, C., & Futterman, D. (1998). *Lesbian and gay youth: Care and counseling.* New York: Columbia University Press.

[24] Page 22 in Garnets, L. D., & Kimmel, D. C. (1993). Lesbian and gay male dimensions in the psychological study of human diversity. In L. D. Garnets & D. C. Kimmel (Eds.), *Psychological perspectives on lesbian and gay male experiences* (pp. 1–51). New York: Columbia University Press.

[25] Rachel B. (1997, May 9). Mom, why do you hate me? *Long Beach Press–Telegram*. Distributed via e-mail list serve May 11, 1997 by Channel Q news (qnews@channelq.com), Doug Case, manager (Doug.Case@sdsu.edu). Rachel B. lives on the streets of San Francisco and writes for YO! (*Youth Outlook*), a newspaper by and about young people produced by Pacific News Service.

[26] See research reported in the following reports: D'Augelli, A. R. (1991). Gay men in college: Identity processes and adaptations. *Journal of College Student Development, 32,* 140–146; D'Augelli, A. R., Hershberger, S. L., & Pilkington, N. W. (1998). Lesbian, gay, and bisexual youth and their families: Disclosure of sexual orientation and its consequences. *American Journal of Orthopsychiatry, 68,* 361–371; D'Augelli, A. R., & Hershberger, S. L. (1993). Lesbian, gay, and bisexual youth in community settings: Personal challenges and mental health problems. *American Journal of Community Psychology, 21,* 421–448; Pilkington, N. W., & D'Augelli, A. R. (1995). Victimization of lesbian, gay, and bisexual youth in community settings. *Journal of Community Psychology, 23,* 34–56; and Herdt, G., & Boxer, A. (1993). *Children of Horizons: How gay and lesbian teens are leading a new way out of the closet.* Boston: Beacon Press.

[27] Page 24 in Woog, D. (1997, October 28). Our parents. *The Advocate,* pp. 24–34.

[28] Page 373 in Henderson, M. G. (1998). Disclosure of sexual orientation: Comments from a parental perspective. *American Journal of Orthopsychiatry, 68,* 372–375.

[29] Parents, Families and Friends of Lesbians and Gays can be reached at their Web site: http://www.pflag.org; by email: pflagntl@aol.com; by phone: 202/638-4200; or by mail: 1101 14th St. NW, Suite 1030, Washington, DC 20005.

[30] For a recent example of youths' stories that present the true diversity of experiences, see Gray, M. L. (1999). *In your face: Stories from the lives of queer youths.* Binghamton, NY: Harrington Park Press.

[31] Page 32 in Vilanch, B. (1999, February 2). Nathan Lane. *The Advocate,* pp. 30–35.

[32] Shyer, M. F., & Shyer, C. (1996). *Not like other boys: Growing up gay: A mother and son look back.* Boston: Houghton-Mifflin.

[33] Page 81 in Scanlan, D. (1995, November 14). Hot property. *The Advocate,* pp. 80–83.

[34] Shalit, G. (1997, October 28). For the love of Pete. *The Advocate,* p. 9.

[35] P. 57 in Galvin, P. (1998, December 8). Shoot to thrill. *The Advocate,* pp. 51–60.

[36] Debenport, E. (1997, June 1). Young, gay and alone. *St. Petersburg Times.* Distributed via e-mail list serve June 2, 1997 by Channel Q News (qnews@ channel q.com), Doug Case, manager (Doug.Case@sdsu.edu).

[37] Bozett, F. W., & Sussman, M. B. (1989). Homosexuality and family relations: Views and research issues. *Marriage and Family Review, 14,* 1–7; Morales, E. S.

(1989). Ethnic minority families and minority gays and lesbians. *Marriage and Family Review, 14,* 217–239; Newman, B. S., & Muzzonigro, P. G. (1993). The effects of traditional family values on the coming out process of gay male adolescents. *Adolescence, 28,* 213–226; Savin-Williams, R. C. (1990). *Gay and lesbian youth: Expressions of identity.* Washington, DC: Hemisphere; and Tremble, B., Schneider, M., & Appathurai, C. (1989). Growing up gay or lesbian in a multicultural context. *Journal of Homosexuality, 17,* 253–267.

[38] Krestan, J. (1988). Lesbian daughters and lesbian mothers: The crisis of disclosure from a family systems perspective. *Journal of Psychotherapy and the Family, 3,* 113–130.

[39] Elias, M. (1998, December 14). Teen-age girls say Mom's become a pal. *USA Today,* D-1, D-8.

[40] Bass, E., & Kaufman, K. (1996). *Free your mind.* New York: HarperPerennial.

[41] Rimm, E., & Bailey, B. (1996, February 28). Teens are finding help coping with the challenge of being gay. *Fort Lauderdale Sun-Sentinel.* Distributed via e-mail list serve March 2, 1996 by Channel Q News (qnews@nsl.cyberspaces.com), Doug Case, manager (Doug.Case@sdsu.edu).

[42] Page 28 in Woog, D. (1997, October 28). Our parents. *The Advocate,* pp. 23–34.

[43] Both quotes are on page 24 in Woog, D. (1997, October 28). Our parents. *The Advocate,* pp. 23–34.

[44] Page 15 in Nycum, B. (2000). *The XY survival guide: Everything you need to know about being young and gay.* San Francisco, CA: XY Press.

[45] Pages 57–58, Reese, M., & Abramson, P. (1986, January 13). One family's struggle. *Newsweek,* pp. 55–58. Kelly's father approached the topic in an opposite direction, by largely ignoring his son's homosexuality. He did not reject Kelly but has since begun the process of coming to terms with his son's sexuality.

[46] Pages 227–229, Bono, C., with Fitzpatrick, B. (1998). *Family outing.* Boston: Little, Brown.

[47] Page D2 in Kelly, K. (1996, March 11). Chastity Bono comes out and into her own. *USA Today,* D1–D2.

[48] All quotes on pages 229–230, Bono, C., with Fitzpatrick, B. (1998). *Family outing.* Boston: Little, Brown.

[49] Neroulias, N. (2000, March 8). Shepard recounts son's "legacy." *Cornell Daily Sun,* p. 7.

[50] Cited from http://www.matthewsplace.com/foundframe.html.

[51] Page 150, Bass, E., & Kaufman, K. (1996). *Free your mind.* New York: HarperPerennial.

[52] Quotes on pages 83–84, Boxer, A. M., Cook, J. A., & Herdt, G. (1991). Double jeopardy: Identity transitions and parent–child relations among gay and lesbian youth. In K. Pillemer & K. McCartney (Eds.), *Parent–child relations throughout life* (pp. 59–92). Hillsdale, NJ: Erlbaum.

[53] Aarons, L. (1995). *Prayers for Bobby: A mother's coming to terms with the suicide of her gay son.* New York: HarperCollins.

[54] On young men, see my 1998 book, " . . . and then I became gay": Young men's stories (New York: Routledge); on young women, see the yet-to-be-written account tentatively titled, " . . . and then I kissed her": Young women's stories.

[55] Pages 123–124, in Bass, E., & Kaufman, K. (1996). Free you mind. New York: HarperPerennial.

[56] In particular, note the last chapters of my 1990 and 1998 books, Gay and lesbian youth: Expressions of identity (Washington, DC: Hemisphere) and " . . . and then I became gay": Young men's stories (New York: Routledge).

[57] Data supporting the lack of a suicide attempt rate differential between sexual-minority and heterosexual youths have been submitted for publication in R. C. Savin-Williams (2000). Suicide attempts among sexual-minority youths: An end to the controversy.

9

RESEARCH AGENDA

I can think of no issue concerning the relations sexual-minority youths have with their families that is not in need of basic ground-breaking behavioral science research. One intent of the present investigation is to provide descriptive and narrative accounts that will prove useful for creating hypotheses that will correct this paucity of research. Although it is difficult to recommend a specific research agenda because of the enormity of need—nearly any empirical data on the relations sexual-minority youths have with their parents would be welcomed at this point—in this chapter I highlight the most pressing needs in terms of research designs and content areas.[1]

DESIGN ISSUES

Defining Who Is a Sexual Minority

One major scientific obstacle to investigating sexual-minority youths is ascertaining who counts as a sexual minority. A related question is whether youths who *identify* as lesbian, gay, or bisexual are adequately representative of the larger population of youths who have same-sex attractions. That is, by recruiting gay, lesbian, and bisexual youths, have researchers sampled sufficiently to warrant generalizations to the much larger population of youths with same-sex attractions?

Nearly all investigators are silent about the topic of who is a sexual minority. Few question the postulate that self-identification as gay, bisexual, or lesbian is an adequate definition of a sexual minority. The obligatory, "cannot generalize to all gay youths," statement that adorns most Discussion sections not withstanding, most researchers appear to assume that their samples of convenience—usually attained from gay-identified organizations or individuals—are sufficiently inclusive, to speak about "gay youth."

Three surveys persuasively demonstrate that the number of individuals with same-sex attractions is certain to be considerably greater than the number of adolescents who identify as gay, lesbian, or bisexual. First, in a cross-sectional national study, just over 1% of adult women and about 3%

of adult men identified as lesbian, bisexual, or gay.[2] A much larger proportion, however, reported that they had thought about having sex with someone of their own gender (about 6%) or had experienced same-sex attractions (nearly 8%). Women and men did not differ significantly in these proportions. In a survey of Massachusetts' high schools, 2% of students identified themselves as gay, lesbian, or bisexual. However, an equal number engaged in same-sex behavior despite eschewing a lesbian, gay, or bisexual label.[3] A third study, the National Longitudinal Study of Adolescent Health, found that 8% of young men and about 7% of young women reported that they had same-sex romantic attractions or had been in a same-sex romantic relationship.[4] This proportion of individuals with same-sex *attractions* within a representative sample of adolescents is much greater than any previous report that inquired only about sexual identity labels.

These three investigations suggest that any study that defines a sexual-minority population as self-identified gay, lesbian, or bisexual individuals will, by design, underrepresent the overall population of individuals with same-sex attractions. This fact is rarely, if ever, considered when designing and interpreting research on sexual-minority youths. The net effect, I believe, is the entrenchment of a possibly distorted view of sexual-minority youths, offering information about *identity* rather than *behaviors*, *attractions*, *desires*, *fantasies*, and *affiliations*.

One example of the effects of broadening the population sample beyond identity labels is a surprising finding in the present study: Gender of child does not matter for whether parents are told. Previous research had found that young lesbian and bisexual women are more likely than gay men to come out to parents. The inclusion of a wider range of sexual-minority women than is customary could account for this disparate finding; questioning, curious, and other women who have not identified as lesbian or bisexual are unlikely to be out to a parent until they are more certain if a sexual identity label applies to them. Until they know the meaning of their sexuality, why would they complicate their lives by telling their parents?

Because only 1% to 3% of youths designate themselves gay, lesbian, or bisexual or report that they currently engage in or have had same-sex behavior in national or representative surveys, clearly many youths are not volunteering themselves as sexual minorities.[5] Reasons for their exclusion could include one or more of the following; this list should not be considered exhaustive.

- They are not "out" to themselves (i.e., not aware of their same-sex attractions) and are thus incapable of identifying as gay, lesbian, or bisexual. The average age of self-disclosure among contemporary cohorts of sexual-minority youths who are out by their early 20s is just before high school graduation.[6] Thus, high school surveys will underestimate the total number of sexual-minority youths because many individuals are not out to themselves until young adulthood or later. Based on the conservative assumption that 4% to 6% of the adult population is lesbian, gay, or bisexual, surveys directed toward sampling a population of sexual minorities will, by definition, miss at least half of those who will eventually identify as a sexual minority. These youths simply are not yet out to themselves. In addition, high school surveys can only identify sexual-minority youths as such if they are themselves in high school (i.e., have not been kicked out of the home, dropped out of school, or become homeless).

- Even among youths who self-label by college graduation, the average age for disclosing to others is just after high school graduation.[7] The first person is usually a best friend; coming out to "others"—which theoretically could, but probably will not, include researchers administering questionnaires in high school—may be years later. Thus, the vast majority of high school students with same-sex attractions are unlikely to out themselves on a stranger's questionnaire. I am not convinced that the anonymity of the questionnaire significantly alleviates a youth's anxiety about disclosing to a stranger, even for "research purposes."

- Many youths who are aware of their same-sex attractions and desires during adolescence are not willing to classify themselves as lesbian, bisexual, or gay because they do not fit their perception of the associated stereotypes of that label. Others detest the political or sexual associations of the label or feel that the terms are too simplistic or reductionistic to describe their sexuality. As illustrated in this book's narratives, young women are particularly likely to reject these terms.[8] In addition, not all youths with same-sex attractions engage in same-sex behavior during adolescence, and not all youths who have same-sex encounters are gay, lesbian, or bisexual. This raises doubts as to the validity of using same-sex behavior as an exclusive criterion variable for identifying sexual-minority youths—especially among young women.[9]

Thus, it is conceivable that researchers are missing at least half and maybe three quarters of youth with same-sex attractions, raising doubts about the generalizability of their findings. Although no study has directly compared these populations, same-sex attracted adolescents who report an awareness of their sexuality, identify as gay, engage in same-sex behavior, and disclose to others at an early age (during adolescence) might be a significantly different population than those who do not have these characteristics. Thus, many "potential" sexual-minority youths do not identify to self or to others during adolescence and therefore are not categorized as such in research investigations. They may well compose the vast majority of individuals with same-sex desires.

This conclusion is consistent with McConaghy's recent discussion of "unresolved issues in scientific sexology."[10] McConaghy asserted that too often researchers assume that sexual attractions are distributed categorically (gay or straight) rather than dimensionally. When forced in surveys to categorize themselves, most youths with same-sex attractions will identify as heterosexual, resulting in a "nongay majority" who have same-sex attractions. McConaghy concluded, "Such studies are investigating not homosexuality but *self-identification* as homosexual."[11]

Sample Differences

The question of whether these participants who volunteer for research adequately represent sexual-minority youths has largely been ignored. In research that purports to study youths who identify as gay, bisexual, or lesbian, youth samples are primarily culled from support groups or campus political and social organizations, creating the possibility of selection bias. Perhaps youths who join community or collegiate groups do so because they believe that their life is significantly difficult that they need the assistance of a support group, and youths who seek the allegiance of a political activist organization have emotional or social agendas they want to implement. The important question, however, is seldom addressed: Does this self-selection of youths into particular research studies have the potential to distort our view of their lives, including their family relationships? For example, would conservative Log Cabin Young Republicans participate in social sciences research and, if not, are their experiences coming out to their parents similar to those who join radical political groups on campus? Do closeted, by necessity, gay, lesbian, and bisexual ROTC cadets have the same reason for disclosing to their parents as do "queer" youths?

On the basis of my personal experiences advising and leading both community and collegiate groups, I believe that many of these youths have unique developmental histories that can create distinctive parent–child interactions. For example, when compared to their non-member, same-sex attracted peers, these youths may be more likely to adopt a radical political or social ideology that advocates breaking family ties and establishing "families of creation"; to feel rejected by their dysfunctional family of origin because one parent has a history of mental illness or abuse; to be harassed by peers because of their sex-atypical mannerisms, "pushing" them out of the closet earlier than is typical; and to have personal or emotional needs that can be addressed by these groups, such as developing personal boundaries, social skills, and support. Thus, youths in social and political groups might have exceptional reasons for deciding whether, how, and when to come out to their parents and have parents who react to the disclosure in an inimitable, albeit negative and distressing manner.

These two groups might, in turn, draw from significantly different populations. For example, those who attend college might be more reluctant than youths from urban support groups to disclose because they fear the power of parents to sever their financial support and to isolate them emotionally. Because they frequently live away from home most of the year, college students can lead a new, private life as a lesbian, gay, or bisexual person without disclosing to parents until a "safe" time arrives. Being out as a sexual minority on campus and closeted at home characterizes the lives of some young adults. In the case of urban support group youths, because they are more likely to live at home, they often have greater difficulty keeping their sexual identity a secret. They thus disclose or are discovered to be lesbian, gay, or bisexual, forcing everyone in the family to confront issues of having a sexual-minority member earlier and more directly.

The consequences of these biased sampling techniques and populations are unknown but likely distort the knowledge we have, the ways this knowledge is used to alter lives, and the construction of future research agendas. Investigators must make special efforts to assemble new strategies for recruiting more representative and seldom-studied populations. One resolution would be to eschew sexual identity labels and rely on descriptions of behaviors, desires, and attractions. And if we do conduct research using such labels, let us first recognize their limitations, be clear about this fact, and speculate as to how these labels might influence the results of the study. Rather than focusing on particular sexual identity labels, one method I use for sampling populations of sexual-minority youths is to recruit women who report physical or romantic attractions to other women.[12] Many of the young women I interview reject—and some abhor—the terms *lesbian* and *bisexual* because they sound "so sexual" or "so clinical" and carry connotations of a radical leftist political ideology. These young women have a mental picture of what a lesbian or bisexual looks like or is, and they do not like it or they feel that it does not fit them. One young woman told me, "Bisexual makes it seem that I have two sexes or split sexualities." If they must have a label, then many prefer *gay*. Their preference is to describe physical, affectional, and romantic behaviors and attractions and thus to offer a more accurate reflection of their sexuality.

Although young women are more likely to come out to their parents by describing their attractions or romantic involvements, young men more often use a sexual identity label. Sexual identity labels afford a greater degree of consensus among men in terms of their meanings and implications for development. No male I interviewed reported that he detests the terms *gay* or *bisexual*. Perhaps the problem is that researchers have simply not recruited a group of young men who are sufficiently diverse with respect to sexual identity to know if this unanimity is accurate. The degree to which the perspectives and experiences of this larger population of youths with same-sex attractions are distinct from self-identified youths needs exploration. It would help if more investigators, across a wide range of disciplines and research agendas, were asking questions about the existence, number, and proportion of sexual behaviors, attractions, and romantic relationships that an individual has with males *and* females. Let us not limit inquiries about sexual attractions to those who conduct research on gay and lesbian issues.

Another strategy for diversifying the research pool of sexual-minority youths involves using the Internet to recruit participants. On-line market researchers have discovered this technique by surveying a group of participants—young teenage girls—who seldom volunteer for their research. Trend consultant Marian Salzman noted, "In cyberspace, everyone is the same. If you don't have to look someone in the eye, you can ask them anything. And they'll tell you exactly what they think."[13] This strategy might also be particularly pertinent for youths who have attractions for other girls or boys but who would not designate themselves as such when traditional research methods are used. The Internet might also be particularly helpful with recruiting isolated youths who live away from research centers and support groups, shy youths, and adolescents who are just coming out. For example, researcher Lynne Hillier and her colleagues used the Internet to encourage rural and politically isolated youths to share their anecdotal responses to questions in the first national Australian study of same-sex attracted youths.[14]

Thus, the most challenging task for researchers is to adequately sample from the total pool of those with same-sex attractions. Because many youths do not identify as a sexual minority until young adulthood or later, attempts to recruit an adolescent population necessarily result in major methodological problems. Consequently, what is currently known about family relations among sexual-minority adolescents does not likely reflect the lives of the vast majority of youths who do not volunteer for research, many of whom are not prepared to acknowledge their same-sex orientation to researchers. A less desirable alternative is to depend on retrospective data collection techniques. Although psychologists Andrew Boxer and Bert Cohler articulated the pitfalls of using this methodology (e.g., accuracy of recall, biased memory),[15] recent research on autobiographical memory suggests that retrospective methodologies are often accurate for significant life transitions.[16] To improve recall accuracy, investigators must ground memories in concrete details and to assess participants soon after experiencing the recalled life transitions. However, until a diverse and large number of local samples of youths, who are fully described in terms of relevant characteristics, or representative samples of youths can be recruited—which will not happen until the stigma of being a sexual minority decreases rather dramatically— extreme caution must be observed when attempting to generalize or extrapolate from existing empirical studies.

Assessing Samples of Parents

Biases in sample selection are not limited to the discriminatory nature of youth populations. These problems may actually be magnified when assessing the attitudes, beliefs, and behaviors of parents, because most parent samples are solicited from social or political support groups, most notably P-FLAG, or from clinicians' caseloads. Research based on these populations might very well distort the reality of how typical parents react to having a sexual-minority child. For example, prior to joining these groups, these adults might vary from those who do not seek a support group in temperament, personality characteristics, cognitive styles, attitudes, ethnicity, and social class. Parents who attend a support group are more likely to be White, well educated, liberal, empathic, extroverted, and help-seeking than those who do not, and, perhaps, to have experienced an upsetting coming-out event that compelled them to seek assistance. Once in a support group, parents typically become more open, secure, and accepting than other parents and more likely to subscribe to the sequence of grieving stages propounded by their support group, thus creating a self-fulfilling prophecy in which all or most of the stages are experienced. Although these parent samples are not likely to be representative of parents with a sexual-minority child, the ways in which they vary are, at best, speculative.

Also not included are parents who do not participate in research because their child has not yet self-labeled as nonheterosexual or who do not know they have a sexual-minority child. Absent as well are those severely embarrassed by parenting a sexual-minority child and those who vow never to volunteer because of political or personal reasons (e.g., those who resent psychologists "studying us"). Other parents might feel comfortable with their new status but decide not to share this fact with researchers—either because, "Everything went so smoothly they wouldn't be interested in my story" or "We don't want to be public spectacles; we just want our privacy." The net effect of these recruitment difficulties is that little is known about how "typical" parents react to having a sexual-minority child.

Not all, however, is lost. One result of cultural shifts in the visibility and acceptance of sexual-minority individuals is the greater number and diversity of families that include youths who declare their same-sex attractions and are thus potentially available for inclusion in research samples. Although it is tempting to dismiss many of the early studies because they are based on a highly select, small subject pool, they provide an initial understanding of the important dynamics that need to be explored by investigators. I do not mean to imply that it is now feasible to draw representative or random samples of sexual-minority populations and their families, only that current samples can now be more representative of nonheterosexual populations than previous efforts allowed.

Given these realities, developmental researchers should not, without peril, generalize beyond the characteristics of a particular population of lesbians, gays, and bisexuals and their parents. To best advance developmental perspectives on sexual minorities, research designs should be elaborately described, especially the ways in which participants were recruited, and all relevant characteristics of the sample should be detailed. An honest appraisal regarding the limitations of the research sample (e.g., who is and is not represented) should be provided such that other investigators can compare findings among various populations. The ultimate goal is to have as many diverse samples as possible, each adequately described, that singularly characterizes some aspect of development and that, in combination with other studies, forms a mosaic of sexual-minority life.

Diversity of Samples

Recruiting diverse populations of lesbians, bisexuals, and gay youths is a difficult task; as a result, many "types" of sexual-minority youths are usually underrepresented in research studies. Few youths of color or those from diverse educational, socioeconomic, and geographical backgrounds have been adequately sampled. Youths with nonexclusive and changing sexual attractions, those who are unlabeled, those who are curious, and those who are questioning are nearly invisible in research. Given that participants must volunteer in order to be included in research, nonverbally oriented and shy youths probably seldom participate, regardless of how much anonymity is assured. Because more contemporary youths are attending college than in the past, it is not wrong to sample from college populations— as long as a diversity of colleges are brought into the research protocol, and noncollege youths are encouraged to participate. Sampling only private, state, or community colleges will distort findings because each excludes meaningful subpopulations of sexual-minority youths.

Perhaps the most neglected group is ethnic-minority youths. One deterrent to sorting through the effects of ethnicity is that relatively few studies on bisexual, gay, or lesbian youths have sufficient numbers of ethnic-minority individuals to conduct separate analyses. Those that include ample numbers have seldom included ethnicity as a discriminating independent variable, perhaps because investigators assume ethnic status does not or should not matter. A recent study I conducted with Eric Dubé challenges this notion in terms of developmental milestones.[17] However, even this study does not distinguish intragroup differences, treating, for example, Japanese, Chinese, and Korean youths as "Asian Americans." Targeted research studies comparing the coming out to parent experiences, directed at particular ethnic populations (e.g., Latino) and the various groups within this category (e.g., Cuban, Puerto Rican, and Mexican youths), would address this shortcoming.

Insufficient ethnic-minority representation can also result from such youths failing to disclose their sexual orientation to White researchers. The net effect has compounded the silence about ethnicity and sexual orientation and has perhaps precluded other ethnic-minority individuals from disclosing their sexual orientation and participating in research projects. Consequently, caution must be exercised when generalizing from studies conducted with White youths about the uniqueness or sameness of ethnic-minority gay, lesbian, and bisexual youths and their families. Although these youths face special circumstances attempting to blend their sexuality within the context of their ethnic identity and family, they may have distinct sources of community support that also need to be recognized.

Longitudinal Studies

Typical of fields of study without a long history of theory and research, many methodological issues plague investigations of sexual-minority youths and their families. Most needed from a developmental perspective are prospective, longitudinal studies that document and explain casual relations among variables. To date I know of only one such investigation with sexual-minority youths: Lisa Diamond's ongoing exploration of sexual identity development among young women with same-sex attractions.[18]

Longitudinal designs allow researchers to study relationship histories and family dynamics prior to disclosure, shortly after disclosure, and at regular intervals thereafter. For example, investigators could explore the casual relationship between motivations and methods of disclosure and prior parent–child interactions (do "good" and "bad" reasons and ways of disclosing really exist or are they merely a continuation of past patterns?), anticipated and actual parental reactions to disclosure (are the negative expectations of nondisclosing youths justified?), and coming out and psychological health (does disclosure lead to health, or are the healthy most likely to disclose their sexuality?). The processes and degree to which parents integrate into their self-conception their new status as parents of a sexual-minority child can thus be evaluated.

Several particularly vexing questions could be addressed by longitudinal designs. For example, does an agreeable prior relationship with parents encourage youths to disclose to them, or is their relationship now satisfying because youths have disclosed to them? This would be particularly useful information for youths contemplating whether to disclose—can they expect a rocky relationship to improve? Do they risk a positive, although perhaps not ideal, relationship with their parents if they come out? Another unanswered question that could be addressed is the process by which family members come to suspect or know the sexual orientation of a youth prior to an overt disclosure. What is the basis of these suspicions? Does this knowledge ameliorate their response to the disclosure? In addition, in combination with ongoing cross-sectional research, longitudinal studies would help distinguish findings due to historic, cultural changes (e.g., parents becoming increasingly comfortable with homosexuality because of cultural visibility) that affect different cohorts from those that occur within particular families (e.g., parent–youth dynamics improving over time independent of cultural changes).

Ideally these studies would begin early in the life of the family, perhaps even before a youth becomes aware of same-sex attractions—usually in early to middle childhood. An obstacle would be the lack of reliable early indicators, other than male sex atypicality, of same-sex attractions that would allow researchers to identify which children will not likely progress toward heterosexuality. Displaying characteristics typical of girls, failing to develop an interest in archetypal boy games and activities, and becoming erotically oriented toward boys predicts later same-sex attractions for some boys—but clearly not all. Reliable child precursors of later sexual-minority status do not exist for many young adult women.[19] Short of these data, researchers have relied on retrospective data from youths after they self-label, disclose, and volunteer to participate in research projects.

In addition to the problem of identifying appropriate participants, a prospective methodology has other logistic drawbacks. For example, few parents, human subject committees, social institutions, or funding agencies would approve a project purporting to follow a group of children for many years with sexual orientation as a primary variable—although they might be less adverse to the project if same-sex attractions or desires were proposed as one among many demographic or biological factors. The processes of self-labeling and disclosure can be so protracted, perhaps lasting a decade or two, that the required time for even identifying which participants are sexual minorities and which ones are not is dauntingly long. One alternative research design is to earmark particular children for study because of characteristics thought to correlate with a later sexual-minority status: early sex-atypical mannerisms, cross-gender role interests, large number of older brothers, or fingerprint ridge patterns. Historic or archival (e.g., home videos) data from presently defined sexual-minority individuals can also supplement retrospective questioning if the information needed is of childhood origins. A problem with both approaches is that not all sexual-minority youths have these sex-atypical or correlated characteristics and not all families have access to video equipment or film the intended behavior. Whether those who do are similar to those who do not is unknown.

Inclusion of Youths and Their Family Members

Much of what is known about families with a gay member has been largely derived from the perspectives of sexual-minority youths, seldom from their parents, and rarely, if at all, from siblings, grandparents, and other extended family members. The primary reason for this partiality to youth is that current cohorts of youths are more comfortable than their family members participating in research investigating same-sex attractions. Few family members are thrilled telling researchers that they have a gay relative. Thus, youths come forward volunteering their lives for inspection but not their families, who remain reticent about discussing these matters. The net effect is to limit the voices of nongay family members reflecting about the ramifications on their lives of having a gay member, which restricts our understanding of the complex dynamics between sexual-minority youths and their family.

Indeed, I have yet to find a single, substantial, scientific study that includes a sample of sexual-minority youths and their family members. The absence of this very simple research design is a major deficiency in the literature—one that the present study failed to address as well.[20] Knowing the youths' perspectives of the relations they have with their family is interesting in its own right—informing us about the perception of youths—but it yields a less than complete or objective understanding of what family members believe they are experiencing. It also handicaps an exploration of factors that determine how family members react to the disclosure, such as their attitudes, beliefs, prior experiences, friendships, temperament, and age. Needed is research that includes all parties to the disclosure, comparing information provided by sexual-minority youths and family members.

An example of how various sources provide different perspectives is vividly portrayed in a recent *Seventeen* magazine article. Mike, a gay son, reported that after he disclosed to his parents they argued with him and kicked him out of the house. His mother, however, maintained that it was not a fight and that she had asked Mike to leave because he was ignoring family rules regarding curfew.[21] Youths may accurately report parental behavior, including their initial reactions to finding out that they have a gay child, but may interpret these behaviors differently from the way in which they were intended. This perception may be at odds with how parents are actually experiencing the event.

Presentation of Results

Complicating an analysis of these issues is the variety of ways in which studies have addressed questions or presented results. For example, the gender of the parent to whom a youth has disclosed is not always distinguished, such as when data are reported as "at least one parent knows." In some studies, disclosure refers to a direct, open discussion; in others, youths simply report that they believe their parents "know" or should know. Often no clarification is given as to the certainty of this knowledge or the way in which parents found out. Parents might know through quite diverse methods, including being told directly by the youth or by someone else, such as another family member. Or, parents know because of their own suspicions or by accidentally discovering love letters or pornography while putting away clothes or cleaning under the youth's bed. Whether method of discovering the child's sexual orientation is important and for what reasons are open questions.

Another common problem is that results are usually presented as averages, which mask considerable variation. For example, although every study has shown that mothers are told before fathers, some youths explicitly discuss their same-sex orientation with their father years before telling their mother. Some youths tell parents before telling best friends, while the youth is in middle school or while the parent is on his or her deathbed. It can be a lag of minutes between coming out to one parent and then the other, or it can be years or even a lifetime. Parents and siblings can be shocked; others reply, "This is old news." Parents can reject their child; they can also celebrate the disclosure. Some youths tell both parents together; others tell their mother and ask that she tell the father or demand that she not tell, and the mother either does or does not honor the request.

Presenting mean scores is the norm in research reports describing the relations sexual-minority youths have with their family. Although this information is important, and I would not diminish its significance, averages by themselves are insufficient. Standard deviations, ranges, and qualitative presentations are critical to increasing our understanding of the diversity and complexity of parent–youth relationships.

CONTENT AREAS

Relatively little descriptive information has been systematically obtained about sexual-minority youths and their parents. The most basic information is often missing, such as the words used in the disclosure, the spirit in which parents are told, and the emotional state of either the youth or the parent during disclosure. Where did the conversation take place?

Who else was present? What role did each play? How long did the disclosure conversation take? What transpired immediately after disclosure? More complicated questions, such as how the parent–child relationship history affects initial and subsequent parental reactions or how the disclosure subsequently changes family dynamics, have been ignored.

Research on the reaction a parent has to discovering the same-sex attractions of a child has seldom distinguished the initial response from the current status of the relationship. Responses are usually superficially categorized as "accepting," "tolerant," "intolerant," or "rejecting." More options should be available and more questions should be asked. For example, were parental reactions predictable on the basis of their prior relationship? Did the reactions affect the youth's development? Following disclosure, how have parent–youth relationships changed over time? What factors are conducive to and what ones are destructive for development? Unclear from the empirical literature, what is the process by which parents take advantage of the opportunity to move toward acceptance of a sexual-minority child? Why have other parents failed to resolve this dilemma? One speculation is that a parent's response depends not only on the relationship the two have prior to disclosure but also on how the youth's same-sex attractions are discovered, such as whether one is told directly by the youth or indirectly by others. Indeed, it is difficult to ascertain from the empirical literature whether sexual-minority youths have better, worse, or the same relationships with parents compared with heterosexual youths. This is an astonishing admission given preconceived notions about the negative impact homosexuality has on parents.

Because little is known about how parents move from their initial response to the disclosure to their current position, the universal, inevitable grieving and loss stages described in chapter 3 are seldom documented. Are the stages characteristic of most transitions? Do these stages per se have a basis in reality, or, as suggested in this study, do they better represent the variety of ways in which parents initially respond to the disclosure? Empirical research with parents who do not belong to organizations that teach such models needs to be conducted. In general, too little attention has been paid to how parents respond over time—is it similar to the "coming-out" process of their sexual-minority child?

As evident in the present study, the gender of both the youth and the parent must be taken into account when describing any aspect of the coming-out-to-parents process. This is why I presented the parent–youth narratives separate by sex in chapters 4–7. The relations youths have with their parents are dependent on the gender of the parent—and youths differ in this regard depending in part on their gender. Generalizations about young women with same-sex attractions have been based on findings from young gay and bisexual men for far too long.[22] References to "parents," as if they were a single unit, a single sex, should also be reevaluated. Although we know that on average more mothers are told before fathers, little is known regarding whether mothers are told in a different manner than are fathers and whether ethnicity, social class, and regional differences contribute to these sex differences. The finding in this book that fathers do not react as horribly as the literature would lead one to expect needs explanation. Perhaps there is a new generation of fathers, some of whom are unwilling to throw away their connection with their son. Unfortunately, many fathers appear to have little or no significant relationship, either positively or negatively, with their daughter.

Another question seldom asked is, what is the basis for telling one family member and not another—such as mother and not father or one sister and not another? The easy answer is that it is related to how sexual-minority youths expect a particular family member to react. Yet factors that predict how family members react once a youth has disclosed to them are poorly understood. A starting point would be to understand both the family context (exposure to alternative lifestyles?) within which youths disclose and personality characteristics (novelty seeking or flexibility?) of family members. One mother, aware of many of these issues, added her own agenda questions.

> Is the youngster an only child? Do family members know gay, lesbian, or bisexual friends or colleagues? What are their political and religious attitudes? What are their styles of dealing with emotionally charged family issues? What geographic, social, economic, and ethnic milieus do they live in. . . . It would be helpful to know more definitely what influenced these families.[23]

Bertram Cohler and Jeff Beeler described difficulties parents experience attempting to maintain close emotional ties with their child while being forced to learn a new role as a parent of a sexual-minority offspring.[24] This "backward socialization" of parents into new roles creates role strain. Having nonheterosexual children often reminds parents about what their parents said to them—"You'll be a bad parent"—or reminds them of their own same-sex attractions that they forsook to lead a traditional life. Parents may resent the child who can now live the "queer life" they could not. Indeed, disclosure may have long-term effects on the self-conception of parents. Mitzi Henderson asserted that researchers must identify the "resources, internal and external, that supportive families draw on," such that whatever success they have can be available to families who encounter difficulties.[25]

Research must also converge on child variables that affect parental reactions, such as the child's age and status in the home, degree of sex atypicality, personality characteristics, history of relating to family members, method and style of disclosure, and involvement in a romantic relationship.

Although research has not tested the hypothesis that parental reactions are more severe if the child is not an adult—largely because too many other intervening variables, such as sample recruitment bias, are not controlled—it is an important consideration for youths pondering disclosure. Youths who disclose their same-sex attractions while concurrently disclosing that they are HIV-positive or that they are a victim of a hate crime might receive unique parental responses.

Obscured from a research point of view is whether parents know their child's sexual proclivities, not because the child disclosed to them but because they became suspicious of the child's sex-atypical behavior or mannerisms, friends she or he selected, or the absence of heterosexual activities. Worth distinguishing are the dynamics in families in which the youth's same-sex attractions have been openly disclosed, have not been discussed but everyone knows that everyone knows, are a source of parental suspicion, and are not known.

Disclosure beyond the immediate family is another fertile area for research. Neglected are studies that explore sexual-minority youths' relationships with siblings, grandparents, uncles, aunts, and cousins. Extended family members may be underused resources of acceptance and support. Although some individuals report that they will never be fully out until their grandparents are dead, they may be relinquishing potential sources of guidance from grandparents who could assume an intermediary role in salvaging the integrity and coherency of the family.

All areas of sexual-minority youths and their families are in need of empirical inquiry. Even the most basic information, such as average age at which youths disclose to parents or siblings, is seldom asked. Of all possible times, why did they come out then? Why not earlier or later? What provoked the disclosure at that particular time? Reasons for disclosing or not disclosing have never, to my knowledge, been systematically studied among sexual-minority youths. These fundamental questions—and many more—must be addressed before a full account of the disclosure process is possible.

A FINAL WORD

It is extremely difficult to conclude with confidence the exact percentages of sexual-minority youths who have told parents, siblings, and other family members about their same-sex attractions; when and how they disclosed this information to them; or the reasons they shared this secret, if indeed it was ever a secret. This uncertainty about disclosure information is compounded because of the selective nature of youths and their parents who have the opportunity to participate in research and decide to do so. Thus, previously recorded percentages, time frames, and processes in research studies might not reflect the lives of the vast majority of youths with same-sex attractions who do not volunteer for research, perhaps because they are not developmentally ready to acknowledge their same-sex identity to themselves or to others, or they are not in a support group or a college where gay research is being conducted.

Although much of the popular and clinical literature assumes that disruptions and chaos follow initial disclosure, their widespread prevalence is suspect. The crisis mentality of many of these writings has been considerably overdrawn, largely because they make good press. Given the remarkably few empirical studies that have examined the relations that normative lesbian, gay, and bisexual youths have with their parents, one must question the validity of the most disruptive, pathological scenarios caricatured by personal chronicles. I am not convinced by any evidence produced to date that the relations sexual-minority youths have with their parents are at significant variance from those experienced by heterosexual youths who also have important and at times disturbing news to tell their parents. Perhaps what differs most is the content of their discussions.

Personal narratives from both sexual-minority youths and their parents highlight the significance of each for the other. Parents are often figures of authority and respect—and increasingly friendship—and sexual-minority youths desire their parents' support and approval. For their part, regardless of the sexual desires and identity of their child, most parents recognize the sexual-minority youth as the child whom they love and accept. How different is this from heterosexual youths and their parents?

As should be apparent by now, what most impresses me about sexual-minority youths, their families, and the relations they have with each other are their commonalities with heterosexual families and the diversity among themselves. These realities have not been sufficiently appreciated in either the scientific or popular literature. Instead, stage theories that ignore or depreciate variations are our customary crutch. By their simplicity, they normalize a process of interpersonal relations that is perhaps nonnormative and fail to account for complex variations as a function of factors that do not lend themselves to the construction of the norm, such as social position, cohort, ethnicity, gender, and the "vicissitudes of life experiences."[26] Many have questioned the appropriateness and accuracy of coming-out models— for youths as well as their parents—that assume a linear progression of events, an epigenetic unfolding that minimizes the chance and contingency of life. Yet they appear to have a life of their own, pervading research and popular understanding of the coming-out process. They won't die! Do parents attempt to conform their reactions to the news of having a gay child to the cultural accounts previously heard, read, or seen? What happens if their circumstances do not follow this trajectory? Have they succeeded or failed?

With regard to stage theories of sexual-minority identity development, we must move beyond the cliché of "one glove fits all." Even if we rely solely on personal narratives, those who survive and flourish must counterbalance the lives of distraught families. As researchers we have been far too intent on examining common characteristics of sexual-minority youths, pretending each disclosure is homogeneous, and too lax in examining the ways in which relations with parents among same-sex attracted youths are diverse. Research that treats all sexual-minority individuals and their parents as a class, as if they were following an identical developmental pathway, is obscuring important developmental processes.[27] It is a lie.

Diversity cannot and should not be ignored. Any description or portrayal of the lives of sexual-minority youths and their parents and of their developmental histories is a daunting but fascinating undertaking. We need to begin, in earnest.

ENDNOTES

[1] Previous discussions of these issues appeared in Savin-Williams, R. C. (1998). The disclosure to families of same-sex attractions by lesbian, gay, and bisexual youths. *Journal of Research on Adolescence, 8,* 49–68; Savin-Williams, R. C., & Diamond, L. M. (1999). Sexual orientation. In W. K. Silverman & T. H. Ollendick (Eds.), *Developmental issues in the clinical teatment of children* (pp. 241–258). Boston: Allyn & Bacon; and Savin-Williams, R. C., & Dubé, E. M. (1998). Parental reactions to their child's disclosure of a gay/lesbian identity. *Family Relations, 47,* 1–7.

[2] Laumann, E. O., Gagnon, J. H., Michael, R. T., & Michaels, S. (1994). *The social organization of sexuality: Sexual practices in the United States.* Chicago: University of Chicago Press.

[3] Goodenow, C., & Hack, T. (1998, August). *Risks facing gay, lesbian, and bisexual high school adolescents: The Massachusetts Youth Risk Behavior Survey.* Paper presented at the 106th Annual Convention of the American Psychological Association, San Francisco.

[4] Russell, S. T., & Joyner, K. (1998, August). *Adolescent sexual orientation and suicide risk: Evidence from a national study.* Paper presented at the annual meeting of the American Sociological Association, San Francisco.

[5] DuRant, R. H., Krowchuk, D. P., & Sinal, S. H. (1998). Victimization, use of violence, and drug use at school among male adolescents who engage in same-sex sexual behavior. *Journal of Pediatrics, 132,* 113–118; and Garofalo, R., Wolf, R. C., Kessel, S., Palfrey, J., & DuRant, R. H. (1998). The association between health risk behaviors and sexual orientation among a school-based sample of adolescents. *Pediatrics, 101,* 895–902.

[6] Savin-Williams, R. C., & Diamond, L. M. (2000). Sexual identity trajectories among sexual-minority youths: Gender comparisons. *Archives of Sexual Behavior, 29,* 419–440.

[7] Savin-Williams, R. C., & Diamond, L. M. (2000). Sexual identity trajectories among sexual-minority youths: Gender comparisons. *Archives of Sexual Behavior, 29,* 419–440.

[8] Diamond, L. M. (1998). Development of sexual orientation among adolescent and young adult women. *Developmental Psychology, 34,* 1085–1095; Diamond, L. M. (2000). Sexual identity, attractions, and behavior among young sexual-minority women over a two-year period. *Developmental Psychology, 36,* 241–250; and Diamond, L. M., & Savin-Williams, R. C. (in press). Growing up female with same-sex attractions. *Journal of Social Issues.*

[9] Savin-Williams, R. C. (1998). " . . . *and then I became gay": Young men's stories.* New York: Routledge; Savin-Williams, R. C., & Diamond, L. M. (1999). Sexual orientation. In W. K. Silverman & T. H. Ollendick (Eds.), *Developmental issues in the clinical teatment of children* (pp. 241–258). Boston: Allyn & Bacon; and Savin-Williams, R. C., & Diamond, L. M. (2000). Sexual identity trajectories among sexual-minority youths: Gender comparisons. *Archives of Sexual Behavior, 29,* 419–440.

[10] Page 285 in McConaghy, N. (1999). Unresolved issues in scientific sexology. *Archives of Sexual Behavior, 28,* 285–318.

[11] Page 302 in McConaghy, N. (1999). Unresolved issues in scientific sexology. *Archives of Sexual Behavior, 28,* 285–318.

[12] This is not always possible, even when it is the explicit desire of the researcher. I have been a consultant on several projects in the midwestern United States in which university institutional review boards would not allow such a broadcasting of research subjects; only *explicitly* self-defined gays, lesbians, and bisexuals could be surveyed. The review board members were concerned that researchers not be perceived as recruiting the "undecideds"—or those not absolutely certain of their sexual identities. By participating in "gay research," these individuals might become gay.

[13] Page 2A in Horovitz, B. (1999, May 17). High level of comfort leads to truthful research worth a mint. *USA Today,* pp. 1A–2A.

[14] Hillier, L., Dempsey, D., Harrison, L., Beale, L. Matthews, L., & Rosenthal, D. (1998). *Writing themselves in: A national report on the sexuality, health and well-being of same-sex attracted young people* (Monograph Series 7). Carlton, Australia: La Trobe University, Australian Research Centre in Sex, Health and Society, National Centre in HIV Social Research.

[15] Boxer, A. M., & Cohler, B. (1989). The life course of gay and lesbian youth: An immodest proposal for the study of lives. *Journal of Homosexuality, 17,* 315–355.

[16] Rubin, D. C. (Ed.). (1996). *Remembering our past: Studies in autobiographical memory.* New York: Cambridge University Press.

[17] Dubé, E., & Savin-Williams, R. C. (1999). Sexual identity development among ethnic sexual-minority male youths. *Developmental Psychology, 35,* 1389–1399.

[18] Diamond, L. M. (1998). Development of sexual orientation among adolescent and young adult women. *Developmental Psychology, 34,* 1085–1095; Diamond,

L. M. (2000). Sexual identity, attractions, and behavior among young sexual-minority women over a two-year period. *Developmental Psychology*, 36, 241–250.

[19] Savin-Williams, R. C., & Diamond, L. M. (2000). Sexual identity trajectories among sexual-minority youths: Gender comparisons. *Archives of Sexual Behavior*, 29, 419–440.

[20] This shortcoming is being addressed by Cornell graduate student, Douglas Elliott, whose research explores perceptions of support among sexual-minority youths and their parents.

[21] Rorke, R., with Mannarino, M. (1999, April). Coming out in America: Gay teens tell the world, "Here I am, deal with me." Retrieved March 27, 1999 from the World Wide Web: http://www.seventeen.com.

[22] These differences are the basis of my next book, tentatively titled, " . . . and then I kissed her": Young women's stories. For additional discussion, see Diamond, L. M., & Savin-Williams, R. C. (in press). Multiple transitions and trajectories in the development of sexual-minority women. *Journal of Social Issues*; and Savin-Williams, R. C., & Diamond, L. M. (2000). Sexual identity trajectories among sexual-minority youths: Gender comparisons. *Archives of Sexual Behavior*, 29, 419–440.

[23] Page 374 in Henderson, M. G. (1998). Disclosure of sexual orientation: Comments from a parental perspective. *American Journal of Orthopsychiatry*, 68, 372–375.

[24] Cohler, B. J., & Beeler, J. (1998, December). *Management of ambivalence within the family: Adult offspring "coming out" gay or lesbian and their parents*. Paper presented at the German-American Transcoop-Program: Ambivalence in Intergenerational Relations Workshop, Cornell University, Ithaca, NY.

[25] Henderson, M. G. (1998). Disclosure of sexual orientation: Comments from a parental perspective. *American Journal of Orthopsychiatry*, 68, 372–375.

[26] Page 33 in Cohler, B. J., & Beeler, J. (1998, December). *Management of ambivalence within the family: Adult offspring "coming out" gay or lesbian and their parents*. Paper presented at the German-American Transcoop-Program: Ambivalence in Intergenerational Relations Workshop, Cornell University, Ithaca, NY.

[27] For a more complete discussion, see related publications: Savin-Williams, R. C. (1998). " . . . and then I became gay": Young men's stories. New York: Routledge; and Savin-Williams, R. C., & Diamond, L. M. (1999). Sexual orientation. In W. K. Silverman & T. H. Ollendick (Eds.), *Developmental issues in the clinical treatment of children* (pp. 241–258). Boston: Allyn & Bacon.

APPENDIX:
RESEARCH METHODS

THE STUDIES

After my initial exploratory study of over 300 sexual-minority youths in the mid-1980s,[1] I conducted a series of studies exploring various developmental milestones among gay and bisexual male adolescents and young adults. This culminated in the book, "... *And Then I Became Gay": Young Men's Stories*.[2] For the narratives and data on family relations reported in this volume, I drew on the interviews of 86 young men who constituted Sample 2 in this earlier work. A comparable sample of young women with same-sex attractions was interviewed regarding similar developmental transitions. For purposes here, I use the data provided by these 78 young women on the relations they have with family members.

Participating youths were between the ages of 17 and 25 years and met the inclusion criterion of claiming some degree of physical or romantic interest in same-sex others. They were diverse in social class, religious affiliation, and size of hometown community. Less diversity is apparent in the youths' educational level and ethnic or racial identification. Most were well-educated, articulate college youths (see Table A.1). Young women were more likely than young men to claim a bisexual or an unlabeled identity and to have been raised in urban and suburban environments.

Youths were recruited through announcements in college classes on gender and sexuality, flyers sent to campus social and political organizations, advertisements in a community newsletter and public places (bar, bookstore,

TABLE A.1
Sample Characteristics by Gender

Variable	Female			Male		
	M	n	%	M	n	%
Age (years)	20.8 (1.7)			21.6 (2.2)		
Sexual identification						
Lesbian/gay		27	38		70	81
Bisexual		34	42		7	8
Unlabeled		17	20		9	10
Ethic/racial identification						
White		61	78		62	72
African American		2	3		5	6
Asian/Pacific Islanders		10	13		6	7
Latina/Latino		2	3		10	12
Mixed race and other		3	4		3	3
Social class						
Upper middle		30	38		39	45
Middle		31	40		27	31
Lower middle		17	22		20	23
Community size						
Farm/rural		8	10		13	15
Small town		7	9		17	20
Small city/suburbs		48	62		31	36
Urban		15	19		25	29
Region where grew up						
Northeast		36	46		43	50
South Central		12	15		6	7
West		8	10		9	10
Midwest		6	8		9	10
South		7	9		5	6
North Central		7	9		5	6
International		2	3		9	10

Note. Numbers in parentheses represent standard deviation.

café) for sexual minorities, postings on Internet listservs for sexual-minority students on several college campuses, and referrals from other participants. This multiple recruitment strategy was undertaken to draw participants along the spectrum of same-sex attractions. For example, campus political organizations tend to include very "out" individuals who openly identify their sexuality; college Women Studies courses often draw students who are just beginning to acknowledge their same-sex attractions.

The research project was advertised as an interview focusing on growing up in the 1990s with physical or romantic attractions for someone of the same sex. To volunteer, youths contacted the principal investigator in person, by telephone, or by e-mail. Special efforts were made to include individuals who were not comfortable openly identifying as lesbian, gay, or bisexual by assuring them that such identifications were not necessary for participation and that the interviews were confidential and would neither be tape recorded nor videotaped.

Owing to the nature of the recruitment strategy, response rates cannot be calculated because it is unknown how many potential participants who met selection criteria did not volunteer for the study. However, somewhat fewer than 10% of youths who originally contacted the investigator either did not return efforts to contact them or did not show up for the interview or telephone appointment. Because of human subject considerations, no attempt was made to discover reasons for refusals to participate.

RESEARCH PROCEDURES

Participants were interviewed in person or by telephone. A male research assistant interviewed one third of the male participants, and I interviewed all other youths. Interviews were conducted in my faculty office or a place chosen by youths that afforded privacy and confidentiality. The nature and aims of the research project were explained, questions were answered, and consent was secured in accordance with the Cornell University Committee on Human Subjects' stipulations. Over 90% of interviews with male participants lasted from 45 to 90 minutes, with a median of 60 minutes. The same format and content were followed for interviews with young women, but several domains were omitted (community activities, current harassment, attitudes toward AIDS) so that interviews could be completed in less than 1 hour (median = 45 minutes). To increase diversity in the female sample, I posted announcements on several Southern and Eastern college campus listservs. Forty-one percent of the women participants took advantage of this opportunity, completing the same interview format by telephone (median time = 45 minutes). There were no demographic differences between women recruited in this manner and the other female participants, but women interviewed by telephone were more likely to identify as lesbian rather than bisexual or some other label.

Initial questions ascertained participants' age, ethnicity, hometown community size, and family social class (based on occupational status of parents). The remainder of the interview focused on milestones of sexual identity development, from earliest memories of same-sex attractions to current feelings about one's sexual identity.[3] For purposes of this book, only data concerning family relations are reported.

After basic developmental milestones were assessed, the interview focused on disclosure to parents. Basic information was first asked about the family constellation. Are your parents married to each other? If not, when was the separation, divorce, or death, and who did you live with? Have adults other than your biological parents served the role of parent? What were the occupations of each parent during your adolescence? What were the religious and ethnic affiliations of each parent? The following questions with prompts were asked regarding disclosure to each parent.

1. Have you told him/her about your same-sex attractions?
2. If so, when and why did you tell him/her?
3. If not, why haven't you told him/her? Do you have plans to tell him/her?
4. If you have told him/her, how did he/she initially respond?
5. If not, how would you expect him/her to respond if you were to tell him/her today?
6. Have there been changes over time in how he/she has responded to your same-sex attractions?
7. What is the nature of your relationship with him/her?

ENDNOTES

[1] Summarized in Savin-Williams, R. C. (1990). *Gay and lesbian youth: Expressions of identity*. Washington, DC: Hemisphere.

[2] Published in 1998 by Routledge (New York).

[3] For a review of this material, see Savin-Williams, R. C. (1998). " . . . and then I became gay": *Young men's stories*. New York: Routledge.

INDEX

Cohler, B. J., 248, 256, 260n15, 261n24, n26
Cohort effect, disclosure frequency, 201–202, 237
Coleman, E., 20n15, 21n21, 54n6
Collins, W. A., 105n12
Colten, M. E., 169n9, 198n7
Colucci, P. L., 57n27, n30, 59n57, n63
Coming-out. See Disclosure
Conley, T. D., 20n19
Conversion therapy, 222
Cook, J. A., 21n21, 57n24, 60n78, 241n52
Cornell study
    interview procedure, 265–266
    methods, 263–266
    recruitment strategy, 263–265
    sample characteristics, 264
Cox, S., 19n14
Cramer, D. W., 60n71, n72, n76, 168n8, n9, 198n10, 239n9
Crockett, L. J., 18n3
Cross-sex parent-child dyads, 224–225
Crouter, A. C., 18n3
Cruz, W., 236
Cultural proscriptions, 38. See also Ethnic minorities
Curtis, W., 5n2

D'Augelli, A. R., xn2, 19n9, n13, 54n2, n5, 55n12, n13, n15, n16, n17, n18, 56n18, n20, n21, 60n70, 104n3, n5, n6, n7, 111, 133n2, n3, n4, n5, 143, 157, 168n3, n6, n7, n8, 169n9, 198n6, n7, n9, n10, n13, 239n9, 240n26
Daughter-to-father disclosure, 107–133
    case vignettes, 107–109
    direct form of, 119–120
    effects over time, 126–129
    fathers' initial reactions, 121–125, 224–225
    and gay fathers, 130–131
    indirect form of, 120–121
    method of, 119–121
    negative reactions, 124–125
    neutral reactions, 123–124
    nondisclosure reasons, 112–116
    positive reactions, 122–123
    relationship prior to, 109–111

survey studies, 111–112
    timing of, 119
Daughter-to-mother disclosure, 66–105
    age norms, 80
    case vignettes, 64–66
    direct form of, 80–81
    effects over time, 91–101, 228
    fears, 73–75
    and lesbian mothers, 101–102
    method of, 80–84
    mothers' initial reactions, 84–91, 224–225
    negative responses, 87–91, 93–94, 100–101
    positive responses, 85–87
    and relationship improvement, 95–100
    relationship prior to, 66–68
    temporal rank of, 103
    timing of, 80
Debenport, E., 240n36
Deisher, R. W., 56n18
Demo, D. H., 56n21
Dempsey, D., 238n4, 260n14
Denial
    in mothers, 89–91
    in parents, 37–39, 52, 85, 89–91
    stage model limitations, 52
Depression, in parents, 42–45
Developmental course, 7–21
    biological perspective, 8
    cultural interpretation, 8
    differential trajectories approach, 7–21
DeVine, J. L., 21n20, 56n23
Diamond, L. M., 18n1, 19n9, n11, n13, 20n17, 251, 259n1, n6, 260n7, n8, n9, n18, 261n19, n22, n27
Direct disclosure
    daughter-to-father, 119–120
    daughter-to-mother, 80–81
    guidance for, 217–218
    son-to-father, 185–186
    son-to-mother, 152–153
    study findings, 217
Disclosure. See also Age of disclosure; Nondisclosure
    as act of self-love, 213
    basic principles guiding decision, 203–204
    cohort effect, 201–202

daughters-to-fathers, 107–133
daughters-to-mothers, 66–105
developmental stage models, 16–17,
    33–34, 51–52, 233–234,
    258–259
direct method of, 217–218
effects over time, 227–235
expected reactions, 209
and media sensationalism, 221
and mental health, 30–32
parental reactions, 33–51
popular literature on, 24–26
research agenda, 254–257
same-sex versus cross-sex parent-
    child dyads, 224–225
sons-to-fathers, 171–198
sons-to-mothers, 135–169
stress of, 29
and suicidality, 31
timing of, 214–216
Disclosure age. *See* Age of disclosure
Dubé, E. N., 19*n*9, *n*10, *n*11, 20*n*18,
    56*n*20, 250, 251, 259*n*1, 260*n*17
Due, L., 5*n*2
DuRant, R. H., ix*n*2, 259*n*5

Ego development, 11
Elias, M., 104*n*1, 241*n*39
Eliason, M. J., 19*n*4, 20*n*16, *n*19
Elliott, D., 261*n*20
Ellis, L., 18*n*7
Empirical research approach, 4
Enmeshment
    mother and daughter, 67
    mother and son, 139, 141
Envy, in parents, 94
Espín, O., 95, 105*n*11
Esterberg, K. G., 56*n*21
Ethnic minorities
    daughter-to-mother nondisclosure
        reasons, 72–73
    disclosure reactions, 51, 94–95
    family importance, 94–95
    and mother-son conflict, 142–143
    in research samples, 250–251
    son-to-father nondisclosure reasons,
        180–181
Extended family members, 257

Face-to-face disclosure. *See* Direct dis-
    closure

Fairchild, B., 5*n*1, 54*n*6
Familia, 95
Farrow, J. A., 55*n*18
Fassinger, R. E., 19*n*4
Fathers. *See also* Daughter-to-father disclo-
        sure; Son-to-father disclosure
    emotional unexpressiveness in,
        109–110, 112–113, 131–132
    order of disclosure, 202
    psychoanalytic theories, 42–43
    relationship with daughter, 109–111
    relationship with son, 173–178
    same-sex attractions in, 130–131,
        194–195
Fear, nondisclosure reason, 181–182, 189,
        205–206
Femininity values, and nondisclosure,
        209–210
Fine, M. A., 56*n*21
First disclosures, 32–33
Fitzpatick, B., 238*n*7, 239*n*10, *n*18, *n*20,
        *n*22, 241*n*46, *n*48
Fricke, A., 58*n*41, *n*47, 59*n*55, *n*64
Fricke, W., 38, 39, 42, 46, 58*n*41, *n*47,
        59*n*55, *n*64
Friedman, H., 18*n*7
Friends, first disclosure to, 32–33
Futterman, D., 239*n*23

Gagnon, J. H., 259*n*2
Gallois, C., 19*n*14
Galvin, P., 240*n*35
Garnets, L. D., 20*n*19, 240*n*24
Garofalo, R., ix*n*2, 259*n*5
Gay fathers, disclosure to, 130–131,
        194–195
Gay label
    interviewee reactions, 247–248
    as research obstacle, 243–246
Gender differences
    intimacy level, 12
    nondisclosure reasons, 209–210
Golden, C., 19*n*13, 20*n*17
Goodenow, C., ix*n*2, 259*n*3
Gore, S., 169*n*9, 198*n*7
Grandchildren, grieving source, 44
Grandparents
    disclosure acceptance importance,
        97–98
    supportive role, 257
Gray, M. L., 240*n*30

Green, R., 57n27, n30, n31
Grief/mourning
    popular literature on, 25–26
    stage models, 17, 33–34, 51–53,
        233–234, 258–259
        limitations, 52–53, 233–234
Griffin, C. W., 5n1, 27, 29, 32, 43, 44,
    55n10, 57n28, n29, n33, 58n34,
    n37, n39, n44, n48, n50, 59n54,
    n60, n65, n68
Griffith, B., 36, 37
Griffith, M., 28, 35, 36, 38, 41, 47, 48,
    55n11, 235, 241n53
Guilt
    mothers of gay sons, 157
    mothers' overcoming of, 97–98
    in parents, 40, 45, 52
    stage model limitations, 52

Hack, T., ixn2, 259n3
Hammersmith, S. K., 66, 104n2, 133n1,
    139, 167n1, 197n1
Hancock, K. A., 54n2
Hansen, C., 228, 241n42
Harrison, L., 238n4, 260n14
Hayward, N., 5n1, 54n6
Henderson, M. G., 238n5, 240n28, 256,
    261n23, n25
Herdt, G., 21n21, 56n19, 57n23, 58n51,
    59n66, 60n78, 104n4, 111,
    133n2, 168n3, n8, 198n10, n13,
    239n11, 240n26, 241n52
Heron, A., 5n2, 54n6
Hershberger, S. L., xn2, 18n7, 55n12,
    n15, n16, n17, n18, 56n19, n20,
    n21, 60n70, 104n3, n5, n6, n7,
    133n2, n4, 168n6, n7, n8, 169n9,
    198n6, n7, n9, n10, n13, 239n9,
    240n26
Heterocentrism, 15
Heterosexism, 15, 193
Hetrick, E. S., 26, 55n9
Hetrick-Martin Institute, 26–27
Hillier, L., 238n4, 248, 260n14
Holmes, S., 5n2
Hom, A. Y., 61n80
Homonegativity, 15
Homophobia, 15–16
Horovitz, B., 260n13
Hunter, J., 55n16

Iasenza, S., 57n27, n30, 59n57, n63
Identity-centric adolescents, 13
Indirect disclosure, 217
    daughter-to-father, 120–121
    daughter-to-mother, 81–82
    son-to-father, 186–188
    son-to-mother, 153–155
    study findings, 217
Individual differences, in development,
    7–21
Internalized homophobia, 189
Internet recruitment, 248
Interview procedure, Cornell study,
    265–266
Intimacy level, gender differences, 12
Isolation, in parents, 37–39

Jealousy, in parents, 94
Johnson, B. K., 238n7, 239n18, n20
Joyner, K., 259n4

Kaufman, K., 204, 211, 235, 238n5, n6,
    239n13, n20, 240n40, n51,
    242n55
Kelly, K., 241n47
Kessel, S., ixn2, 259n5
Ketterlinus, L., 133n9
Kimmel, D. C., 240n24
Kitzinger, C., 19n3
Koopman, C., 169n9, 198n7
Krestan, J., 241n38
Krowchuk, D. P., ixn2, 259n5
Kübler-Ross, E., 17, 21n20, n22, 33, 52,
    56n22, 233, 234

LaChapelle, D., 224, 240n35
Laird, J., 57n27, n30, n31
Lane, Nathan, 223, 240n31
Larson, R., 133n8, 198n14
"Latent homosexuality," 44
Latinos, mother-son bond, 150
Laumann, E. O., 259n2
Lesbian label
    interviewees' rejection of, 84, 102,
        247
    and survey statistics bias, 243–247
Lesbian mothers, disclosure to, 101–102,
    166–167
Lever, J., 104n3, 168n4, 197n3
Levine, H., 19n14

Life histories approach, 4
Liu, P., 57n31
Longitudinal studies, 251–253
Love, disclosure acceptance factor, 96

MacDonald, G. B., 55n7
Mahoney, D., 33, 53, 57n25, 61n82
Malyon, A. K., 239n16
Mannarino, M., 261n21
Martin, A. D., 21n20, 26, 55n9
Masculinity values, and nondisclosure,
    207–210
Matthews, L., 238n4, 260n14
McCartney, K., 21n21, 57n24, 60n78,
    241n52
McConaghy, N., 246, 260n10, n11
McConnell, J. H., 20n15, n16
Media "outings," 79, 117
Mental health, and disclosure, 30–32
Michael, R. T., 259n2
Michaels, S., 259n2
Miller, B. A., 19n4
Minorities. See Ethnic minorities
Morales, E. S., 60n74, 240n37
Moreno, B., 224, 240n36
Moreno, R., 224, 240n36
Morris, J., 20n19
Morris, J. F., 19n4, 20n16
Mothers. See also Daughter-to-mother dis-
    closure; Son-to-mother disclosure
    initial disclosure reactions, 219–227
    order of disclosure, 202
    psychoanalytic theories, 42–43, 139,
        141
    relationship with daughter, 66–68,
        226
    relationship with son, 139–143
        psychoanalytic theory, 139, 141
    same-sex attractions in, 101–102,
        166–167
Mourning. See Grief/mourning
Muller, A., 60n78
Muzzonigro, P. G., 60n74, n75, 241n37
Myers, M. F., 21n20, 57n23

National Longitudinal Study of Adoles-
    cent Health, 244, 259n4
Neroulias, N., 241n49
Ness, C., 238n3
Newman, B. S., 60n74, n75, 241n37

Newsweek, 219, 231, 239n21, 241n45
Nondisclosure
    daughter-to-father, 112–116
    daughter-to-mother, 69–75, 206–207
    gender differences, 209–210
    reasons for, 205–212
    son-to-father, 178–182
    son-to-mother, 144–148, 206
    survival tactics, 207–208
Nycum, B., 231, 241n44

Oasis, ix
Ollendick, T. H., 18n1, 259n1, 260n9,
    261n27
"Outed" by another, 78, 116–117, 151,
    184
!OutProud!, 56n18

P-FLAG, 45, 98, 100, 211, 230, 239n14,
    240n29, 249
Palfrey, J., ixn2, 259n5
Parental acceptance, 45–49, 229–231
    and disclosure motivation, 211
    levels of, 48
    mother-daughter relationship,
        95–100
    mother-son relationship, 162–164
    stage model, 46, 49, 52
Parents. See also Fathers; Mothers
    common disclosure concerns,
        221–222
    depression in, 42–45
    disclosure effects over time, 227–235
    disclosure reactions, 33–51, 219–227
    inclusion in research studies, 253
Parents, Families and Friends of Lesbians
    and Gays. See P-FLAG
Patterson, C. J., 19n9, n13, 54n2
Pearlman, S., 21n20, 57n23, 60n77
Penelope, J., 5n2
Peplau, L. A., 20n19
Phan, A., 239n15
Physical abuse, 110
Physical attack
    daughter-to-mother disclosure reac-
        tion, 85
    fathers, 182, 189, 191, 204–205
Pilkington, N. W., xn2, 55n17, 60n70,
    104n7, 133n2, n4, 168n6, n8,
    169n9, 198n13, 240n26

Woog, D., 55*n*7, 229, 240*n*27, 241*n*42, *n*43

XY Survival Guide, 231, 241*n*44

ABOUT THE AUTHOR

Ritch C. Savin-Williams, PhD, is professor of clinical and developmental psychology and director of graduate studies in the Department of Human Development at Cornell University. He received a master's degree in religious studies and a PhD in human development from the University of Chicago, where he studied the development of dominance hierarchies in adolescent groups at summer camp. Later research projects included examining behavioral and experienced domains of self-esteem and adolescent friendships.

Dr. Savin-Williams has written five books on adolescent development. The latest, " . . . *And Then I Became Gay": Young Men's Stories* (1998) is the first book in a trilogy exploring the lives of sexual-minority youths. This follows a work coedited with Kenneth M. Cohen, *The Lives of Lesbians, Gays, and Bisexuals: Children to Adults* (1996), and *Gay and Lesbian Youth: Expressions of Identity* (1990), a report of the earliest large-scale investigation of sexual-minority youths. Dr. Savin-Williams is currently writing about the experiences of growing up female with same-sex attractions, suicide attempts among sexual-minority youths, and the homoerotic attractions of heterosexual youths. His research on differential developmental trajectories attempts to supplant our generic stage models of identity development with a perspective that explores the similarities of sexual-minority youths with all youths and the ways in which sexual-minority adolescents vary among themselves and from heterosexual youths.

Dr. Savin-Williams is also a licensed clinical psychologist with a private practice specializing in identity, relationship, and family issues among young adults. He has served as an expert witness on same-sex marriage, adoption, and Boy Scout court cases and is on numerous professional review boards, including cochair of the American Psychological Foundation's Roy Scrivner Small Grant Awards. He has also written junior high school curriculum for the Unitarian Universalist Association, *Beyond Pink and Blue: Exploring Our Stereotypes of Sexuality and Gender.*